Walling In and
Walling Out

School for Advanced Research
Advanced Seminar Series
Michael F. Brown
General Editor

Since 1970 the School for Advanced Research (formerly the School of American Research) and SAR Press have published over one hundred volumes in the Advanced Seminar series. These volumes arise from seminars held on SAR's Santa Fe campus that bring together small groups of experts to explore a single issue. Participants assess recent innovations in theory and methods, appraise ongoing research, and share data relevant to problems of significance in anthropology and related disciplines. The resulting volumes reflect SAR's commitment to the development of new ideas and to scholarship of the highest caliber. The complete Advanced Seminar series can be found at www.sarweb.org.

Also available in the School for Advanced Research Advanced Seminar series:

For additional titles in the School for Advanced Research Advanced Seminar series, please visit unmpress.com.

Walling In and Walling Out

WHY ARE WE BUILDING
NEW BARRIERS TO DIVIDE US?

Edited by Laura McAtackney and Randall H. McGuire

SCHOOL FOR ADVANCED RESEARCH PRESS • SANTA FE

UNIVERSITY OF NEW MEXICO PRESS • ALBUQUERQUE

ISBN 978-0-8263-6123-3 (paperback)
ISBN 978-0-8263-6124-0 (electronic)

Library of Congress Control Number:
2019955078

Cover illustration: Young boy on the southern
side of the US-México border wall at Nogales,
2011. Photo by Randall H. McGuire.

Composed in Minion Pro and Gill Sans

The seminar from which this book resulted was
made possible by the generous support of the
Annenberg Conversations Endowment.

FIGURES

TABLES

**Walling In and
Walling Out**

CHAPTER ONE

Introduction
Walling In and Walling Out

RANDALL H. MCGUIRE AND LAURA MCATACKNEY

> *Before I built a wall I'd ask to know*
> *What I was walling in or walling out,*
> *And to whom I was like to give offense.*
> —Robert Frost, "Mending Wall"

In a twenty-first-century global phenomenon, walls are being built at a dizzying pace (Brown 2010; Rice-Oxley 2013; Vallet 2014; Jones, this volume; Saddiki 2017). At the macro-level, nations have raised barricades of barbed wire, steel, brick, and concrete as the focal points of militarized landscapes that often include inertias (deliberately empty spaces that impede movement) and watchtowers to patrol their borders (Jones, this volume). These walls purport to provide security, control movement, and fortify against the ill-defined dangers of terrorists, smugglers, and undocumented migrants. At the micro-level, barriers partition modern cities; they are often hidden in plain sight, facilitating social segregation that frequently has ethnic and religious as well as economic dimensions (Bishara and McAtackney, both this volume). Town planners, usually at the behest of communities, wall off preexisting streets and curtail access and freedom of movement. Developers design new neighborhoods based on the form of the defensive cul-de-sac or gated community to allay fears of violence and of contact with undesirables. At the individual level, people of means build walled enclaves as part of their homes to protect themselves from "crime" and "the poor." While the proliferation of walls as a multiscalar phenomenon has many negative connotations, they are associated with the fundamental longing for security in an insecure world and therefore include the positive, if insular, desire to protect. Their use to demarcate space can engender a sense of community and belonging in an otherwise dispersed society—but how you feel about them is often determined by which side of the wall you happen to find yourself on.

The chapters in this volume are arranged in three parts in order to engage with the forms and experiences of walls across various scales and temporalities. After a timely overview of historical walls (McGuire), the first part explores three forms of local manifestation of walls: walls built to differentiate on the basis of economics and race (Dinzey-Flores) and those constructed to maintain political and ethnic divisions (McAtackney, Bishara). Moving onto national walls in part II, we begin with an enduring case study of the famous Cold War remnant, the Berlin Wall. The author considers how the material remains of supposedly defunct walls can make a difficult and long transition from active barrier to heritage (McWilliams). The two other national walls—to the north and east of Greece and between the United States and México—reveal two very different approaches to border hot spots between the Global North and Global South in contemporary Europe (Papadopoulos) and in North America (Dear). The last part of the book examines how surveillance technology and software compromise our civil rights and add to the potential roles of walls (Dorsey and Díaz-Barriga), and what meanings, roles, and symbols we associate with walls at a global scale (Jones).

This range of case studies is intended to reveal the particularities of a variety of wall-building projects across the globe. In doing so, the contributors point out an array of commonalities, such as the idea of using walls to keep undesirables out, as well as differences, such as the form and use of the material that walls put in place. This diversity is to be celebrated, but throughout this volume we emphasize two questions: How do contemporary walls succeed or fail at resolving the problems they are built to address? What are the unforeseen repercussions of an increasingly materially segregated world?

This volume developed from an Advanced Seminar held at the School for Advanced Research, Santa Fe, New Mexico, April 17–21, 2016, a time that could not have been more apt for studying this subject. Only two days before the workshop began, Human Rights Watch publicly condemned Turkey for closing its border crossing with Syria, stopping 30,000 recently displaced people from fleeing the war-torn country, and for shooting at the prospective refugees as they approached the newly erected wall marking Turkish sovereignty (Human

Rights Watch 2016). Such material divisions provoking violent interactions are becoming increasingly commonplace at the outer reaches of Fortress Europe.

The proliferation of walls to solve local, national, and transnational social problems has become a global reaction to a variety of issues and not only has provoked critique from scholars across many disciplines, including geography, anthropology, sociology, and archaeology, but has garnered mass media, political, and public attention. The seminar included a cross-disciplinary group of open-minded scholars working in various locations, across a multitude of scales, with varying time depths, and with different disciplinary insights to discuss the phenomenon of walls. We met to bring a different perspective and insight on the scale, form, and impact of this phenomenon of walling in and walling out. The aim of the seminar was to bring together diverse perspectives, mind-sets, and problematizations fundamentally based in real case studies. Ultimately, we aimed to locate some common ground regarding what we are doing, how we are doing it, and why. We think we were at least partially successful in achieving our aim, and we discuss new insights and our agreements (as well as disagreements) more fully in the conclusion.

Which Walls?

The barriers going up all around the world are of many types and are built from many materials for a variety of purposes. In this context of a vast proliferation of walls, what can we say about wall building and the types of walls that are most meaningful to this investigation? Most commonly, builders, government officials, the press, and those who reside within the barriers refer to them as "walls" or "fences." The choice of terms in this context is neither technical nor innocent; instead, the words' sheer mundanity hides deeply partisan intentions. The everyday and normal terminology used to describe these material barriers belies the scale, level of technology, facilitation of wider surveillance (Dorsey and Díaz-Barriga, this volume; Nieto-Gomez 2014), and role of brutality (Bishara, this volume) in maintaining their form. Therefore, the use of "wall" or "fence" naturalizes and diminishes the real purpose of these material barriers and intrusions. The walls and fences proliferating in the twenty-first century that we examine in this volume do not share a common form or type, but they do share a common political purpose: they define, defend, and determine social belonging. In this respect we consider these barriers to be political or ideological walls.

In English, the term "wall" has two simple meanings in reference to structures. Walls are the vertical constructions that form the sides of a room or building, and they are solid vertical structures built to divide, enclose, or shut off an external space. Many other languages use different words that distinguish between the wall of a building and an outdoor wall. For example, in German, some of this distinction can be seen between *Wand* and *Mauer*, in Spanish between *pared* and *muro*, in Arabic between *aljidar* and *jadar*, and in Hebrew between *qir* and *chomah*. Our research engages with these linguistic distinctions and ambiguities and argues that while the English "wall" is a deliberately flattening term, not all walls are the same. In this volume we focus on the outdoor wall (*Mauer*, *muro*, *jadar*, or *chomah*) that was constructed with ideological or political intent.

A fence is a vertical structure that encloses an area, typically outdoors, that builders usually construct from posts connected with boards, wire, rails, or netting. Builders intend fences to be less complete in their creation and maintenance of division; they make them out of less permanent materials (frequently wood or metal wire rather than concrete or stone); and fences often allow visual transgression in the inertias between posts. Furthermore, a fence differs from a wall in not having a solid foundation along its whole length. A wall implies a more substantial, complete, and massive structure than a fence, thus there is a need for a solid foundation along the length of a wall. However, the term "fence" can be used when the material structure also includes a solid concrete base, or when there are planes of fencing placed in a way to prevent any visual interactions, or when the structure is an amalgam with a solid base and fencing elements only at the higher reaches (McAtackney, this volume). In this context, the material distinctions between a "wall" and a "fence" are blurred and can be difficult to discern; this ambiguity allows those who create the structure to use one label while those who live with the edifice to experience another.

Beyond the technical differences reflected in definitions, fences and walls carry very different semiotic significances. As the much-quoted proverb "good fences make good neighbors" shows, the word "fence" implies a tension between maintaining boundaries and hospitality (Mieder 2003, 155–56). People around the globe and through time have recognized the pros and cons of a fence marking property lines and preventing people from (intentionally or otherwise) trespassing on each other's space. The word "wall," however, has a stronger, clearer sense of permanence, circumscription, and hostility. In English, the word originally denoted defensive barriers and ramparts, and the term "wall" still carries that martial air. Walls do not simply define boundaries to avoid quarrels between neighbors; they monumentalize and implant division. They prevent the free movement of people, inflame antagonisms, evoke violence, provide security, and legitimate difference.

This distinction in meaning is not lost on the people who build twenty-first-century walls nor on the people who live with them. In the United States, the Department of Homeland Security consistently refers to the barriers along the US-México boundary line as a "border fence" (Dear and Jones, both this volume). The Israeli government insists that the barriers it has put up to divide Palestinians from Israelis be called a "separation fence" and not a wall (Bishara, this volume; Parry 2003). The residents of the US-México border community of Ambos Nogales (Nogales, Arizona, and Nogales, Sonora) remember the chain link fence that defined the boundary for most of the twentieth century as a "picket fence between neighbors" in contrast to the massive steel wall that now divides the community (McGuire 2013). In a similar semantic sleight of hand, at the local level US developers refer to exclusive, walled neighborhoods as "gated communities," with an implication of movement, to avoid the use of the word "wall" (Low 2003). Similarly, in Belfast, Northern Ireland, where massive snaking walls have been in place for generations as a means of preventing violent intercommunity clashes, the range of terminology employed is as extensive as it is deliberate. A list of slippery and interchangeable terminology—from "peace lines" to "environmental barriers" and "interface barriers" to "security fences" (McAtackney 2011, 82)—is employed to distance those who do not have to live beside them from the harsh realities of constructing monumental walls as a blunt solution to a variety of deep-rooted social problems.

Walls in Context

Wall building is not a recent phenomenon (McGuire, this volume; Frye 2018). From the walls of Jericho to the walls of China to the medieval walled cities of Europe to the French Maginot Line, people have built fortifications to defend homes, cities, kingdoms, and nations against perceived and real threats. Modern military technology, aircraft, artillery, tanks, and missiles have made such military fortifications largely obsolete, but still they are built because of their symbolic importance.

The chapters in this volume examine walls through both their spatial and temporal dimensions, exploring how walls have been built to provide security and protection but often have changed in meaning and form over time. Walls are temporally and spatially significant as they materialize at points of contact—and even conflict—and once constructed they can become naturalized and their presence unquestioned. They can also change. Walls can start as one form and then be added to, replaced, extended, and connected to other forms of natural and constructed barriers (Papadopoulos, this volume). Their mutable and multiple meanings and uses indicate that while walls may no longer function as defenses as originally intended, still they are retained and even elaborated. Modern walls play a primarily psychological and symbolic role.

Throughout time and across the globe, people have built walls and fences for many reasons, to serve different purposes, and to theoretically solve sundry problems. At a micro-level, walls and fences have always been used to mark property lines. They denote the border between private and public spaces and ensure that people do not accidentally or unintentionally transgress the private. They keep pets and livestock in, and they keep pets and livestock out. Garden walls provide privacy and create intimate spaces. Walls can be decorative (Dinzey-Flores, this volume) and provide backdrops for vines and climbing plants. In arid climes, patio or compound walls break the wind and provide sheltered places to create mini oases. The walls and fences of prisons and jails incarcerate criminals: in all institutions they wall some members of society in and others out. Walls and fences also provide security in the face of perceived threats from the "other," and in doing so they materialize social belonging.

Social belonging refers to how individuals assume roles that include them in social collectivities, such as nations, races, genders, ethnicities, and classes. Social belonging explicitly references inclusion and implies exclusion because people define their membership in one social collective always in opposition to the members of other social collectives. Places and lines define social collectives on landscapes, which is why those places and lines are increasingly located on national borders. However, the geometry of social belonging extends beyond national borders and includes state boundaries, city limits, the streets surrounding neighborhoods, residential compounds, and the perimeters of playgrounds. Orthodox Jewish communities use preexisting structures (walls, wires, poles) to construct an *eruv hazerot* that allows observant Jews to carry needed things in public on Shabbat. Navajos use four sacred mountain peaks to define their sacred land, the Dinétah. The most clearly demarcated "imagined community"

(Anderson 2006) of constructed social belonging has long been the nation-state. As nation-states have increasingly materialized their borders through monumental walls, so too smaller collectives of social belonging have built local walls to more closely define those who belong and exclude those who do not. The national border wall is mirrored in urban contexts to distinguish between inclusion and exclusion, which often equals the haves and have-nots at a more local scale.

When social collectives perceive a threat, they build walls and fences on the lines that define them, although the materializing process of wall construction allows for transgression and the deliberate acquisition of lands that had previously been conceived as belonging on the other side of the barrier (Bishara, this volume). These new barriers follow the example of other social collectives in how to materialize the collective's belonging and its members' feelings of threat. In this attempt to feel more cohesive and more secure, the recourse to walls and fences transforms social belonging and social collectives both positively and negatively. Walls concentrate and intensify social belonging and magnify social difference. They also maintain and solidify difference at the time and place they materialize divisions, and this materialization restricts or makes impossible returning to previous situations or moving forward to allow new forms of social belonging to emerge. The hard edge that walls give to social belonging integrates social collectivities but at the same time forces the segregation of those excluded based on the temporally situated identities. Lines on the landscape and psychic barriers that had been blurry, soft, and mutable become distinct, rigid, and situated. The walls also become symbols of belonging and not belonging that may endure and divide long after any real or even perceived threats have passed.

Even as walls have been built to keep threats out, they have simultaneously been used to confine and control those residing within (McGuire, this volume). Medieval European municipalities built walled Jewish ghettos that the inhabitants could not leave at night. Early modern colonialists constructed walled towns during the plantation of Ulster in the north of Ireland as citadels to control bilateral social and economic interactions, survey the outsider, and proclaim their intention to remain (Horning 2013). The East German state built the Berlin Wall to keep its citizens from fleeing to the West, and the fall of this wall both physically and symbolically signaled the end of the Cold War (McWilliams 2013).

Contemporary wall building cannot simply be defined as creating social cohesion. Walls have taken on a distinctive character that serves different purposes and have been implemented to resolve emerging problems of the neoliberal world. Often, they act as a smokescreen to focus attention on curtailing a perceived problem when the real issues are more difficult to target. In a world of tightening borders and building barriers, walls act as a materialization of wider attempts to control mobility. At a national level this is particularly the case where walls are placed to prevent illegal entry, such as at the US-México border, when in fact those who legitimately enter the United States and then overstay their visas are a substantially bigger problem (McGuire and Van Dyke 2017).

National border walls target nonstate, transnational actors rather than international enemies, reacting to a world where nation-states no longer exclusively define global political relations and conflicts (Brown 2010; Jones 2012; Vallet 2014). Israel materializes its fear of the enemy within by building hundreds of miles of walls and highways to separate Palestinians from Jews and to appropriate land for the Jewish state (Weizman 2007). Sari Hanafi (2009) has identified the destructive power of these walls as material barriers being used not simply to separate but with the intention to disrupt the traditional lifeways of those who are forced to live beside them. The United States has fortified its border with México to stop drug smuggling and the entry of undocumented migrants (Dorsey and Díaz-Barriga 2010; Dear 2015; McGuire 2013). Spain, Greece, South Africa, Morocco, India, Uzbekistan, and Saudi Arabia have put up border walls to likewise prevent the mass movement of people from nearby troubled lands (Rice-Oxley 2013; Saddiki 2017; Jones, this volume). The use of walls to control these issues is most evident in national border walls, but a similar use is also manifest in local walls.

The intention to exclude based on identity, socioeconomic status, and being designated undesirable has led to the proliferation of walls in modern cities. In this context, walls create enclaves or materially defined micro-communities to communicate security and to exclude criminals, the poor, and the culturally different. In the *condomínos fechados* of São Paulo, Brazil (Caldeira 2000), in the gated communities of the United States (Low 2004), and throughout the neoliberal world, the privileged have built walled enclaves and privatized public spaces to separate themselves from fellow citizens they fear. Walls separate Protestant and Catholic in Belfast, Northern Ireland (McAtackney 2011 and this volume), Sunni and Shia in Baghdad, Iraq (Jones 2012), and other antagonistic religious/ethnic neighborhoods in cities around the globe.

In all these cases, the word "wall" signifies much more than the physical barrier itself. Walls embody violence, but they are easily breached if not supported by armed agents, dogs, ground vehicles, drones, airplanes, and surveillance devices (Dorsey and Díaz-Barriga, this volume; Nieto-Gomez 2014). The need for the range and scale of these material and technological backups reveals that walls cannot fulfill their promise alone. Eventually, all walls crumble and fall, but faith in their efficacy ensures that some are patched up or replaced, and new walls continue to be built often right up until they come down (McGuire and McWilliams, both this volume).

Like all social constructions, material or not, walls produce unanticipated consequences and are usually unreliable in fulfilling the roles they are built to complete. Theresa Singleton (2015) writes about the nineteenth-century Cuban coffee plantation of Santa Ana de Biajacas. The owner built a wall three and a half meters high and almost a meter thick to enclose the homes of enslaved people on the plantation. He did so with the intention that the wall would give him greater control over the activities of his slaves and assert the hierarchical order of the plantation. Contrary to his intentions, the wall he built to enclose the enslaved people created a private space where they could develop their own community and culture. It also became a space that harbored people fleeing enslavement on other plantations. At the national level, border walls built by one side can become canvases on which people from the other side register protest at their construction, maintenance, and meaning. The US-México border wall is a particularly revealing example. The side that faces México exhibits a range of commentary from graffiti to large-scale, formal, and funded artistic interventions condemning the spatial divisions and violence engendered by the wall. In contrast, on the US side, government agents strictly control access and quickly cover or erase any marks that appear on the wall (McGuire 2013; Dear, this volume).

Who Do We Fear?

We agree with the philosopher Hannah Arendt (2005, 129) that the freedom of movement is "the substance and meaning of all things political." Walls materialize the political by restricting the movement of some people (those who do not belong) but not others (those who do belong). Often, belonging is determined by access to social, political, and economic capital that links to nationality, religion, race, and class. The key question is what is being enclosed and whose movements or actions do the walls attempt to prevent or control. Walls enclose space, and the walls that concern us almost uniformly enclose domestic and social places on a variety of scales: from the nation to the mansion. Existing political walls and those being constructed in the twenty-first century are ideological walls because they demarcate and define social belonging and home. Their very placement and monumental materialization provide the boundary for social belonging, and in doing so walls exclude those who have no right of access and do not belong there. But how is social belonging defined?

Sari Hanafi (2009, 2012) uses the concept of "spacio-cide" (also "spatio-cide") to explore the power dynamics of the Israeli-Palestinian conflict in ways that are useful in the context of using material barriers as sophisticated exclusion devices. He argues that Israel deploys three approaches in its relationship with Palestinian territories: colonization, separation, and exception. These aims combine to limit use of, control of, and access to place through material borders as a focal point within other strategies. Hanafi identifies the practical implementation of these intertwined strategies, which ensure access to land, control of it, and surveillance of actors on it, as the focus of government policy. In such a system, movement, particularly across material boundaries, is linked to perceptions of privilege that are freely given to the selected few and inaccessible to those whom the state wishes to exclude.

Hagar Kotef (2015) discusses how equating privilege with freedom of movement gives rise to regimes to control movement. In other words, liberty becomes a physical experience based on rights of access. The contrast here is between "self-governing" movement and "unruly" movement. Privileged people in motion have the resources, legal status, and cultural identity that allow them to self-govern. They carry documents, have property, follow the rules, pay for things, fit in, and have homes to return to. Stigmatized or undesirable people are "unruly" in motion because they lack the resources, legal status, and/or cultural identity to self-govern. In such a context, the privileged view themselves as international citizens of the world whereas they characterize the colonized subject as a nomad, the poor person as a vagabond, the homeless as a bum, the refugee as an intruder, the "gypsy" as a thief, and the migrant worker as a drifter. Undocumented migrants who "illegally" cross national borders therefore demonstrate their inability to self-govern and give up their right to freedom of movement.

Thus, we have a schism between people who can govern their own movement and therefore rule and the people whose unruly motions are consider threatening by the privileged and therefore are violently resisted. The unruly must be surveyed, curtailed, evicted, captured, enclosed, deported, or imprisoned.

This schism contrasts the movement of the white, affluent, propertied people with the threat of the "other," who are the desperate, the enterprising, the colonized, the poor, the refugee, or the migrant. But why around the world have people increasingly turned to walls as means to manage the fear this schism has created? We find the answer for this question in the global neoliberal transformation that occurred at the end of the twentieth century and continues to the present day.

Walls and Neoliberalism

Paradoxically, wall building is expanding in a twenty-first-century world in which neoliberalism purports to tear down barriers, facilitate global reach, increase freedom of access, and break down differences (Ganti 2014; Jones 2016). The neoliberal D-L-P formula of deregulating the economy, liberalizing trade, and privatizing state-owned industries promised that privatizing economic activities and removing restrictions on free trade would globally increase economic competition and lead to universal economic growth (Steger and Roy 2010, 14). These economic policies, new technology (such as computers, the internet, and container ships), and global media have led to a surge in the international flows of goods, capital, culture, ideas, and people. Even while these flows have risen to unprecedented levels, the same processes have produced a new enclosure movement through the privatization of public lands and public accesses. Thus, movement in one sense has increased while at the same time walled exclusivity of access and ownership has also increased.

Despite the claim of a faster, glossier, more accessible future, these promises are not open to the "unruly"; not everyone in the world has benefited from neoliberalism and globalization. These processes have created a more unequal world locally, nationally, and globally (Steger and Roy 2010; Ganti 2014, 93). The D-L-P formula increases inequalities due to the built-in inconsistencies and stark differences as to who wins and who loses in this more "open" and "free" world (see González-Ruibal 2017 on postindustrial Brazil and Penrose 2017 on contemporary Britain). Rather than neoliberal forces facilitating greater freedom, security, and prosperity, we live today in a geopolitical crisis that includes greater economic insecurity, environmental degradation, religious tensions, and increasing violence.

Economic inequalities have always existed in the world economy, but neoliberalism has amplified them and intensified economic insecurities (Jones 2016).

In the Global North, increased competition and declines in manufacturing have lowered real wages, reduced unionization, eroded job security, diminished social welfare programs, and increased social inequality (McDonough, Reich, and Kotz 2010). Despite these declines, wage rates in the Global North remain significantly higher than in the Global South, and higher wages remain a pull for migrants. There are also massive pushes. At the end of the twentieth century, the Global North and the programs of international organizations (such as the structural adjustment policies mandated by the International Monetary Fund and the World Trade Organization) pushed, cajoled, and forced developing nations to eliminate social support programs and to open their markets to foreign goods. Nations have also entered into agreements, such as the North American Free Trade Agreement, that remove tariffs and trade barriers. These changes have resulted in a modern global enclosure movement as farmers can no longer support themselves without national subsidies and conglomerates buy up their lands for corporate agriculture (McMichael 2006). The lowering of protections for local businesses has diminished or destroyed such industries in the Global South. Many workers displaced from agriculture or local industries have found work in export manufacturing, but such manufacturing tends to be volatile, with contracts from major corporations jumping around the world in search of the lowest cost and short-term tax incentives (McDonough, Reich, and Kotz 2010). Export manufacturing also tends to be environmentally destructive because ignoring environmental impacts and minimally engaging with community interests (e.g., the mining industries in the Global South) raises competitiveness (Parr 2012; Bavinck, Pellegrini, and Mostert 2014). Environmental degradation strips the land, displaces people, and increases the push to leave.

Violence and conflict have also been globalized. Economic instability has contributed to sectarian conflicts in the Near East and in Africa. More important, the United States–led and the Global North–supported invasions of Iraq and Afghanistan and the ongoing and increasingly broadly conceived "war on terror" have destabilized political relations in the Middle East. The conflict and violence continue to permeate much of the region today (Chomsky and Achcar 2015). In the Americas, US deportation of Honduran and Guatemalan gang members from Los Angeles has led to the establishment of gangs in Central America (Vogt 2013). Finally, US and European demand for illegal substances has fueled the drug trade in South America, México, and Afghanistan, leading to the rise of criminal organizations. As borders solidify, these and other globalized criminal organizations and networks have also participated in people smuggling, often at great expense and danger to those who wish to migrate to the increasingly walled more-developed countries (Andreas 2015).

All of these processes have changed social and cultural relations within Global North states and launched the movement of massive numbers of people around the globe who want to be included in those states. These changes have raised a longing for entry to Global North countries among those who are excluded and have raised fear in the citizens of the Global North who wish to retain their privilege and continue accumulating. This escalating process of structuring and situating inequality has made belonging and not belonging more important, more sharply defined, and more materially controlled (Andersson 2014).

However, the accumulation within Global North countries is not dispersed equally throughout the populace. In recent years, in real terms, working people in the Global North have seen their standard of living decline and their economic security threatened. At the same time, they have observed rising standards of living for professional and administrative classes alongside immense increases in the wealth of the 1 percent. In their neighborhoods and on the mass media, which are increasingly controlled by opinion-shaping pundits, they see migrants from other countries who do not look like them but desperately want to be in their position. Politicians present these mediatized faces as the "problem," and they have become the scapegoats for these changes. At all levels of society, people criminalize and demonize the poor and the migrants because their unruly movements illuminate the structural inequalities that require they violate the law. Thus, those who have benefited from neoliberalism come to fear the unruly who are attracted by the promises of it. The self-governing identify those who do not belong as the threat to the perceived advantages of belonging (D'Appollonia 2012; Jones 2016).

Crosscutting all of this are globalized and increasingly acceptable levels of racism—a characteristic of European colonialism. The migrant "others" have changed over time, but they are usually defined by their difference. This takes the form of distinct characteristics that can be identified easily through sight or sound. The development of chattel slavery in the seventeenth-century Atlantic slave trade equated race with skin color and resulted in the forced movement of millions of people from Africa to the Americas (Eltis 2000). The expansion of European colonialism until the end of the nineteenth century brought millions of darker-skinned people under European domination. The Europeans justified the subjection of colonized peoples in terms of their racial inferiority, and today despite claims of color blindness (Dinzey-Flores, this volume), color remains an excluding factor.

A sinister recent development is the rise of fake news stories intended to deny the realities and legacies of the historical racism connected to colonialism. This phenomenon is associated with the rise of the white-supremacist "alt-right" movement in the United States and is becoming increasingly mainstream. As an example, it attempts to deny the history of slavery and colonialism by distorting nineteenth-century discrimination against (implicitly white) Irish migrants in the United States. Ahistorical and frankly untrue assertions that "Irish slaves" not only existed but were treated worse than enslaved Africans are propagated through poorly researched books, unprincipled newspaper articles, and pictorial social media memes. These are shared by tens of millions of people who unwittingly or not wish to have their prejudices confirmed. Some of those who accept the validity of these self-serving fake histories are self-proclaimed white supremacists, but many are victims of the "post-fact" avalanche of dubious "news" and simply do not question the legitimacy, origins, and racist intentions of such claims (Hogan, McAtackney, and Reilly 2016).

These widespread fake news stories are so dangerous because they extrapolate from a kernel of truth that they twist with sinister intent. It is widely accepted that there were hierarchies of whiteness in the European colonies, with historic discrimination against some groups of white European migrants widespread and enduring. From the mid-nineteenth century onward, global movements of migrant populations seeking work resulted in booming but segregated industrial cities in Europe and North America. In the Global North, this was one of the first periods that saw mass migration of the newly created working classes. Young, single women were included in significant numbers, adding a gendered aspect with sex and the control of sexual reproduction and practices becoming increasingly public concerns. New migrant groups commonly settled in ghettos and then integrated slowly into the preexisting city structures (Boal 2002, 690). In the nineteenth century feared migrants were always from the working class and often from a suspect religion, such as Catholicism, but over a century their character changed. In the United States this migrant "other" moved from the German to the Irish, then the Italian, Slavic, or Greek before these older, established migrant groups respectably assimilated (Bonnet 1998; Roediger 1999, 2006)—to be replaced by people of color.

The ability of new migrants to integrate has depended on several factors, including their ability and desire to assimilate into the norms of the predominant middle-class culture, including adopting dress and language and downplaying non-Christian religions. They also benefited from waves of migration ensuring the creation of a new migrant class to supplant them and to make them acceptable and respectable. As Mary Hickman (2012) has discussed for the United Kingdom, when a migrant class retains a strong distinguishing character—either through race, religion, language, ghettoization, or the maintenance of strong diasporic ties—and this manifests in resistance to assimilation, it can become threatening to the society. Such classes can be transformed into "suspect communities."

Starting in the middle of the twentieth century, colonialism bit back with migrants increasingly coming from the former European colonies of Asia, Latin America, the Middle East, and Africa. So today, whether the context is the neighborhood, the city, or the nation, the feared unruly, non-self-governing people in the Global North tend to be foreign, darker-skinned, and linguistically distinct with different cultural and religious codes. In contrast, today's migrants from the European working classes are the preferred and acceptable face of migration. On a national or a local scale, these distinctions flow from histories of exploitation and racism. On a global scale, the contemporary sending countries of migrants are largely in regions such as the Near East, Africa, and Latin America, long considered racially inferior by the West.

In this context of increasing neoliberal inequality, walls appear as solutions to the threats to social belonging. The perceived threat lies in stigmatized, undesirable people who do not belong, who do not look or sound the same as the majority, and who originate from outside—outside the neighborhood, outside the city, or outside the nation. The obvious solution is to keep them out, to wall them out. Developers, governments, and politicians easily pick up on this fear of the "other" and present walls as understandable, tangible solutions to preserving social belonging and keeping the threat at a materially defended distance.

The Contemporary Relevance of Walls

Walls have become a preferred solution to many of the security problems of the neoliberal world. This leads us to ask: how do twenty-first-century walls succeed or fail at resolving these problems, and what are the repercussions of an increasingly materially segregated world? To answer these queries on a global scale, the contributors in this book raise specific questions at their local level about the common characteristics, intentions, and repercussions of walls, whether they surround nations or neighborhoods:

1. How does the materiality and physicality of a wall enable or restrict its efficacy, its experiential qualities, its symbolic meanings, and its being in the world? McGuire (2013) discusses how in Ambos Nogales rematerializing the US-México border from chain link, to steel plate, to steel bars transformed people's sense of community, increased violence, and affected struggles, both material and symbolic, on that frontier.

2. How does a wall mutate in form and meaning over time and space? The deterrence value of walls is a key factor in their construction, but it is always temporary and incomplete. Archaeology and history reveal that every wall changes and eventually crumbles and fails. Walls check the ability of people to move freely, but they also provoke willful responses that generate agency to resist this constraint (Bishara 2015). Transgressors rematerialize and deconstruct walls in ways that the builders never anticipated. In Israel, Palestinians defy the meaning of walls by projecting and painting defiant images on them, whereas militants transgress them through tunneling under their foundations (Weizman 2007).

3. How does a wall materially change cities or frontiers? A wall alters the flow, bodily experience, quotidian life, and cultural/human content of social spaces. It manages access, controls movement, and creates hierarchies of entry that are often linked to social and economic privilege. Walls can continue to have effect even after they come down. In Berlin, most of the physical wall has fallen, but it survives as a memory and a ruined presence. The empty space where it stood and its fragments still shape development, and social differences continue between East and West (McWilliams 2013).

4. How does a wall demarcate and accentuate difference and reinforce fear of difference? A wall may vilify the opposite side, making the people invisible, unlikable, and blameworthy. In this context fear begets and justifies loathing. In Belfast, walls prevent visual contact with the other side, enabling one-sided interpretations of a divisive past; they act as a

backdrop to memorialization based on partial memories of the recent conflict (McAtackney, this volume).

5. What unforeseen consequences does a wall produce? At a time when the Israeli state asserts the Jewish identity of Jerusalem, more than 60,000 Palestinians have moved back into the city to avoid the inconveniences of the security wall (Rice-Oxley 2013). In Northern Ireland, some "peace walls" are decorated and painted with bright swaths of color and are marked as tourist attractions; the US-México border has been the canvas for many artistic interventions protesting the violence of its existence. The painters and graffiti artists challenge and destabilize the gray monumental barriers while local governments promote their work as "dark tourism" (Ballí 2018; Lennon and Foley 2000). In Belfast, the walls direct tourists to spend time—and sometimes their money— in areas suffering from long-term economic decline (McDowell 2008); the US-México border wall acts as a form of protest while memorializing those who have died at the wall (Dear 2015; McGuire 2013).

6. Does a wall exaggerate the preexisting problem? The fortification of sections of the border with México by the US government makes the drug corridors in these areas harder to use, leading to drug cartels attacking rivals controlling passages at less fortified points of the frontier (McGuire 2013). The creation of walls and material borders along the southeastern boundaries of Europe have driven desperate refugees to the seas, often with the tragic consequence of overburdened ships sinking, or simply relocated the issue to increasingly unprepared and ill-equipped islands, such as Lesvos in Greece (Papadopoulos, this volume; Hamilakis 2016). In these circumstances, the creation of walls has increased violence, fear, and insecurity along the entire border, thereby exacerbating the problem the wall was built to solve.

7. What meaning and symbolic significance does a wall embody? Walls, because of their mass and public visibility, are symbolically powerful even if they are materially ineffectual. Their size and seeming impenetrability convey a variety of ideas, including where power resides, demarcating community but also divisions, security, and resistance. They communicate "keep out" externally and "feel safe" internally in a way that transcends language and law by appealing directly to

our engagement with our surroundings. In Nogales, Berlin, Northern Ireland, and other places, artists and graffiti writers use walls as canvases to contradict negative messages and even to protest the walls themselves. Conversely, in Palestine some communities have decided not to paint murals on the separation wall because "beautifying" them enhances their presence. They believe artistic protests do not challenge the meaning of the wall (Bishara, this volume).

8. What insights does a wall provide into public and governmental policy? Bureaucrats, police, and soldiers embrace walls as making boundaries "legible." They use walls tactically to control and confront transgressors and to claim states of being. Following Marcuse (1994, 43), we argue that walls have decipherable ideological meanings. They reveal official acquiescence with the concept of demarcating and controlling space that ultimately leads to segregation based on exclusion: "they represent power, but they also represent insecurity, domination but at the same time fear, protection but at the same time isolation."

Organization of the Volume

As material objects, walls exist in time and space and on various scales. We conceive of the proliferation of walls as a global phenomenon that has distinctly local expressions and often fits into an overarching national context. However, these scales are not deterministic, and these processes are not simplistic. We do not argue that the walls placed around gated communities in Puerto Rico are directly related to and intentionally derived from the increasing materialization of the border between the United States and México. However, both walls belong to a continuum of increasing acceptance that more walls answer a variety of questions and to widespread feelings of increased fear of the "other" in an ever more unequal world. In this volume we do not discuss garden walls or house walls that we almost do not notice due to their ubiquity and neutral presence. Our contributors analyze political and ideological walls that people intentionally create to define belonging and exclusion by controlling access and movement in and around public space. These walls derive their power from being made material in monumental and militarized forms and by proliferating at many scales across the globe. The case studies included in this volume address a number of contexts and move across a variety of scales, but they can be placed into one of two categories: (1) local walls, including walls that aim to separate the economic haves and have-nots (Dinzey-Flores) and walls that are intended to keep politically opposed communities apart (McAtackney, Bishara); and (2) national border walls that aim to control and curtail the flow of migrants and refugees from the Global South to the promised lands of the Global North (McWilliams, Papadopoulos, Dear). The category of supporting walls is explored as a means of engaging with the role of technology and surveillance (Dorsey and Díaz-Barriga) and the framing logic of wall building (Jones). Race and/or class crosscut the creation of belonging in practically all these cases.

The authors focus on the contemporary, but in doing so we understand that both the unique and universalizing aspects of modern wall construction require knowledge of the temporality and the spatiality of walls. Randall McGuire in chapter 2 reviews this history to provide a base for discussing what is both unique and universal about contemporary wall building. People have always built walls as solutions to social problems, but as with today, there is a long history of questioning the efficacy of walls to solve these problems. McGuire shows that walls have been widely used to define, fossilize, and intensify belonging and not-belonging. Contemporary walls, however, stand out because they are militarily obsolete, and people build them most often to control the movement of undesirable, nonstate, often transnational actors rather than international enemies.

Walls occupy space, and they may be studied, experienced, and understood at various scales. Belonging, not-belonging, and the social collectives so created also may be studied, experienced, and understood at various scales from the global to the national to the city to the neighborhood to the individual. For example, the perceptions and experiences of the walls, fences, and fortifications that materialized the Iron Curtain differed at the scale of Eastern Europe, Berlin, or the individual sprinting across the killing ground to scale a wall (McWilliams 2013).

In this volume we consider walls at all spatial scales, but our starting point for understanding and studying walls is the micro-scale. Whether walls are built to enclose nations, cities, or neighborhoods, people experience walls in their everyday lives at a local level. To someone not living in Ambos Nogales, the whole of the US-México border wall is an abstraction that exists on television or on the internet. But the steel bollard wall that cuts the community of Nogales, Sonora, and Nogales, Arizona, in two is a reality that the citizens of Ambos Nogales must confront every day (McGuire 2013; Coronado 2014; Jusionyte 2018).

Zaire Dinzey-Flores notes that pronouncements of postraciality and the steady flow of Latin American migrants have suggested a weakening of race divisions and a "Latin Americanization" of race relations in the United States. These pronouncements not only assume a broader and blurrier gradient of racial categories and a "liberalization" of race relations, but also reveal the continuing movement toward new types of racisms that are harder to pinpoint and decipher. Latin American racial discourse constructs the ideology of *mestizaje*, which results in a discursive and political displacement of race in favor of class explanations for inequality. Dinzey-Flores examines walls as built elements of (old and new) forms of racism. She argues that they codify specific racial formulations and inequalities that depend on the built environment as both euphemism and garment for their reproduction. Focusing on the neighborhood scale and the walls that surround racialized concentrations of poverty and wealth, she considers how the built environment cements racial inequality and enforces racial segregation while tolerating a myth of racial democracy that favors a class explanation. Her chapter suggests that the walls effectively "hide in plain sight," materially disguising the work of racism, displacing intent, and sustaining racial hierarchies.

Laura McAtackney notes that peace walls are famously one of the few manifestations of the Northern Irish Troubles (1968–1998) that have continued to grow through the course of the peace process. Despite extensive academic study, the impacts and experiences of these walls have seldom been considered through the vector of class and gender. McAtackney does not focus on the materiality of peace walls per se but instead moves from the material form of the barriers to the manifestations they facilitate and propagate. In particular, she analyzes materializations of memory making and shaping that lie in the shadows of these walls—in unofficial memorializations and official public art. She considers how these forms of material memory making are implicitly shaped by and reference the peace walls they reside alongside. Ultimately, they reveal a differential engagement with and treatment of gender in their associated communities. By engaging with materializations of public memory and how they intersect with gender, McAtackney aims to understand how the continued presence of walls impacts how we remember the experiences and roles of women from times of conflict and peace.

Amahl Bishara discusses resistance to the Israeli separation wall in Palestine. She builds her analysis from her long-term ethnographic fieldwork in the Aida

Refugee Camp on the outskirts of Bethlehem. She began her participant observation in the camp in 2003, and in 2006 the Israeli government circumscribed
the camp with the construction of a separation wall. This wall did not follow
preexisting boundaries but instead snaked through residents' agricultural land
and encroached on dwellings. She details how the camp's residents mounted
a sustained campaign of resistance against the wall starting in 2012. Bishara
concludes that many factors—tradition, the possibilities for repression and
retribution, global inspirations, or forms of global repression or devaluing of
struggle—condition resistance. All these factors came into play in Aida Refugee
Camp, and the material conditions of living in the shadow of a military base and
surrounded by the separation wall have had the strongest impact. She argues
that we must look to people's experiences of projects like the construction of
the wall and analyze their reactions to them to fully understand these policies.

Anna McWilliams discusses the Berlin Wall as a manifestation of the Cold
War and especially the Iron Curtain. She presents it as a physical, military barrier
that controlled movement around the city and between its two sections, the East
and the West. She describes it as a complex system with walls, no-man's-lands,
guarded train tracks, and tunnels. Its physicality made it almost impregnable,
and the East Germans constantly updated and reinforced it. She notes that it
began suddenly, but as time went on it became increasingly solid, secured, and
guarded. However, the Berlin Wall was not just a physical boundary; it also
materialized the powerful metaphor of the Iron Curtain—the idea of a world
divided between the communist East and the capitalist West. The Berlin Wall
became a strong symbol of the Cold War, and many directly linked its fall with
the end of this conflict. McWilliams examines how the physical divider and the
metaphor became so intertwined and how the two influenced each other. Even
after the Cold War, the Berlin Wall remains one of the strongest monuments of
this period. She asks: why are the remains and the memorials of this border still
important today for the people around it as well as for the remembrance of the
Cold War in more general terms?

Dimitris Papadopoulos discusses the European proliferation of walls and
the amplification of borders in terms of two moments in recent Greek history.
In the twenty-first century, European nations have raised new, heavily guarded
walls from Greece and North Macedonia to Serbia and Hungary. The humanitarian disaster in Syria and the conflicts in Iraq and Afghanistan have fueled
European discourses of exclusion, division, and separation. The political vision

of an integrated, borderless Europe has given way to building a Fortress Europe with the explicit objective of blocking immigration and constraining refugee flows. He argues that Europe wrongly perceives humanitarian crises as a border security issue and has responded by raising new physical and invisible walls. In doing so he compares the treatment of the Greece-Turkey border with the materializations of the northern border at the end of the Greek Civil War (1946–1949). In these two cases, Papadopoulos states we need to interrogate the effectiveness of walls and to capture a sense of urgency while also maintaining an awareness of historical depth.

Michael Dear discusses the enormous complexities that present apparently insurmountable challenges to assessing large-scale infrastructure projects, especially in zones of geopolitical sensitivity. In the case of the US-México international boundary line, the available measures of border security lack precision and breadth, but still provide important guidelines for at least some aspects of future policy making. However, too many other pertinent dimensions of evaluation are routinely ignored, including the negative effects in border-adjacent communities of the occupation by security apparatuses, overreach and abuse by agencies engaged by the border-industrial complex, and a lack of consideration for the needs and aspirations of border residents. He argues that by incorporating an understanding of such dimensions, binational planning in the US-México borderlands could be better targeted and prioritized to ensure more appropriate accountability and action to mitigate negative outcomes.

Margaret Dorsey and Miguel Díaz-Barriga advocate for an anthropology of the state that considers how the crossing of fortifications and other security apparatuses (walls, blimps, checkpoints, guards, dogs) with technology (algorithms, data aggregators, software suites) surveils and curtails the rights of citizens. They peer into the interface of walls and their technological backup, drawing attention to their meanings for politics, citizenship, and state reformulation. The US border wall marks the southern boundary of a security grid that extends up to a hundred miles north with internal Border Patrol checkpoints that include camera arrays and automated license plate readers. This material and technological backup thus renders the border wall not simply a tool for maintaining international boundaries but part of a wider security grid that subordinates the rights of US citizens to a digital security state.

Reece Jones analyzes the material and symbolic effects of building a wall on a national border. He begins his chapter by considering the ephemeral nature of borders that are imagined lines drawn on maps. He argues that building a wall on a border materializes the line on the map but has uneven security effects. Border walls, when supported by human patrols, block easier routes across borders and funnel migrants to ever more dangerous locations. However, most border walls fail because they do not cover the entire length of the border; they are too long to guard effectively; and they are susceptible to tunnels that go under them. Walls also have zero impact on people who pass through crossing points either with fake documents or with bribes to border officials. Jones concludes that the power of a border wall is primarily symbolic. Its role is to provide visual evidence that a government is acting against perceived external threats, and it reinforces the idea that the state has control over its territory.

Conclusions

The twenty-first century has witnessed a frenzy of wall building. Nations, cities, and neighborhoods have engaged in this frantic construction because politicians, citizens, and neighbors see walls as the solution to problems that they face. In this volume we confront walls around the world in various contexts from neighborhoods to national borders. The authors wrestle with the fact that more and more walls are being built even though they are now militarily obsolete and a paradox in a neoliberal world that claims to advocate freedom of movement and the breaking down of boundaries.

Walls have an enormous impact on the people who live near them and on those who seek to cross the boundaries that they exaggerate. They disrupt the daily lives of the privileged they are built to protect. They also increase levels of violence and suffering by endangering the lives of the stigmatized unruly whom they exclude. In all our cases, walls require a massive investment and supporting infrastructure to build, to maintain, and to support. This borrows from advances in technology and has facilitated the rise of the border-industrial complex (Dorsey and Díaz-Barriga 2010; Dear, this volume) that profits from the walls and that has become a powerful special-interest group devoted to maintaining, remodeling, and building walls. Also, once walls have reorganized the topography of social relations, they tend to have a life beyond the problems that they confronted (McWilliams, this volume). For example, in Berlin the wall came down, but distinctions between East and West survive. In Belfast the conflict known as the Troubles ended, but the peace walls stayed up and silently continued to proliferate and even increase divisions (McAtackney, this volume). People confront walls, and for this reason walls often have unintended consequences. Walls invite artists and protesters to use the fabric of the barrier as canvases or props to challenge the walls' existence.

In the twenty-first century, walls appear to be straightforward solutions to major global problems of violence, human movement, and crime. The simplicity of building walls makes them powerful tools for politicians, who invoke them to resolve complex and intractable issues that they are not able to answer in other ways. But in almost all contemporary cases, walls accentuate divisions between peoples, they endanger lives, they heighten privilege, and they enrich the few. This volume shows that walls may reveal and amplify, but they do not solve problems. Ultimately, we argue that walls do—and must—come down. Instead of focusing on walls as intractable, permanent solutions to insecurity and fear, all the authors in this volume accept that regardless of the question, walls are too blunt an instrument to provide an effective answer. Instead, this volume provokes the necessary question: if walls do not work, then what do we replace them with?

CHAPTER TWO

Barbarians at the Gate

A History of Walls

RANDALL H. MCGUIRE

> *It is a testament to the complex and often brutal dynamics*
> *of power relations for nothing makes insiders and outsiders*
> *quite like a wall. Building one means choosing sides, a model*
> *and a microcosm of the process whereby radical, ethnic,*
> *religious and national identities are defined, asserted,*
> *protected, and ultimately polarized.*
> —Hendrik Dey (2011)

We live in a world of walls. Since the beginning of the twenty-first century, nation-states have constructed almost 10,000 kilometers of linear barriers along their borders (Rice-Oxley 2013). They have backed up these walls with aircraft, lights, sensors, drones, armed guards, dogs, and watchtowers (Dorsey and Díaz-Barriga, this volume). Nations build these barriers to create a sense of security among their citizens who call on politicians to regain control of their borders. Increasingly and on a global scale, people have built thousands of miles of walls, fortified gated communities (Dinzey-Flores, this volume), and enclosed neighborhoods. These barriers divide modern cities, expediting social segregation that usually has racial, ethnic, and religious as well as economic and security dimensions. People have built walls for thousands of years, huddling behind them and harboring fears of the "other." The modern frenzy of wall building reflects this long history, but the modern barricading—across scales— of cities and national borders diverges from it in important ways. The contemporary "barbarians" at the gates are not Alaric's Visigoths prepared to sack Rome or German Panzer divisions poised to sweep around the Maginot Line.

Governments instruct their citizens to fear terrorists, criminals, and purveyors of drugs (Jones 2016). The modern "barbarians" they wall out, however, are mostly impoverished workers in quest of employment, refugees fleeing perdition, and families seeking reunification. The popular fear of the new "barbarians" has inspired modern wall building that both reflects and differs from centuries of earlier wall construction.

Examining the history of wall building reveals how walls have both participated in and been altered by cultural and technological change. Hendrik Dey (2011, 1–2) argues that long-standing monumental walls act as enduring markers, materializing where identities clash (McAtackney, this volume) and nations meet. They symbolize the political and ideological conflicts that they participate in, and they embody the fears, pathos, and suffering of the peoples that they divide. They speak to us with a degree of power and immediacy that few other human constructions can equal.

Walls in all epochs share certain social and cultural characteristics. Any proliferation of walls reflects the fundamental human longing for security in an insecure world and includes the positive desire to protect family and friends. Throughout history, walls have also been caught up in a dialectic of fortification and transgression. Building walls can have unexpected consequences that constructors do not always foresee and that their transgressors seek to exploit. Changes in the technology and tactics of transgressors constantly make the secure fortifications of the past obsolete even as wall constructors build new designs with new unexpected consequences. Constructing walls has always been expensive, and they create great inconveniences every day for those living on either side. In the end, all walls become obsolete before they crumble to dust or survive as tourist attractions. For these reasons, controversy about efficacy and benefit always accompanies wall construction, maintenance, and dismantling.

Every new wall built today references the history of walls, but they are not the same. To appreciate the modern phenomenon of wall building, we need to understand how they both resemble and differ from the centuries of wall construction that preceded them. Walls always rise up from perceptions of threat and a desire for security. The nature of these threats, however, differs in the modern context. This difference affects the physicality of the barriers and the complex social relations that they embody. Facile assumptions about the purposes and successes of earlier walls feed the gut reaction that a modern wall equals security. For example, there never was a Great Wall of China, and the walls that did exist failed to repel the Mongol horde (Lovell 2006).

As villages and towns transformed into cities, walls appeared (Frye 2018). Classical Chinese uses the same word, *cheng*, for both city and wall (Farmer 2000, 463; Lovell 2006, 25). Within cities, walls appeared to separate one population group from another or to segregate an undesirable group from other citizens of the city. Rulers also built linear barriers using ditches, walls, and ramparts of earth to create inertias to protect them. Together these series of barriers crossed the countryside, defending the frontier in response to the perceived threat of rival polities and "barbarians." In the fifteenth and sixteenth centuries, European cities ceased surrounding themselves with high, straight-sided, medieval-style walls that artillery can rapidly flatten. By the nineteenth century, cities all over the world began to tear down their walls, and those that survive today act only as symbols of a touristic heritage. In contrast, modern walls appeared in the chaos of the Second World War and the Cold War that followed not as successful defensive military works but rather primarily as means to keep people in. At the end of the twentieth century, new walls built on the US-Mexican border used detritus from wars (e.g., Vietnam War landing mats) as building materials (Dear, this volume). Nation-states are building twenty-first-century walls by asserting the ancient function of keeping perceived "barbarians" out (Nails 2015; Jones 2016) even as they use border control infrastructure to stealthily survey their own citizens (Dorsey and Díaz-Barriga, this volume).

Fortifying the City

Until 1500 CE, urban defenses around the world generally consisted of a high, flat-faced curtain wall with towers that was fronted by a wide ditch (De La Croix 1972, 8). Such city walls represented a substantial investment of wealth and labor that could bankrupt a community (Tracy 2000b, 73). Usually the city government expected all citizens to contribute land, labor, and wealth to build and maintain the walls. The greatest of such walls (for example, at Ur, Constantinople, Rome, and Beijing) were major projects that took decades to build. For these reasons, cities did not build walls when a polity could mount an effective defense in depth at its outer frontier. They only built walls in the face of severe threats to their security for which the only answer seemed to be fortification.

When these threats abated, citizens quickly built homes, workplaces, and shops that infringed on and compromised the city's defenses. They allowed walls to fall into disrepair, to become incorporated into the fabric of the expanding city, or to be torn down (Reyerson 2000).

Walls did facilitate aspects of the governance of cities in addition to their obvious defensive function (De La Croix 1972, 9; Dey 2011, 110–16). Walls controlled urban sprawl and made observation of populations by rulers easier. They also facilitated tax collection, especially on trade goods brought through a city's gates. They framed and monumentalized the urban fabric of the city. In this way, a well-constructed wall became an object of local pride, an indicator of a city's power, and a symbol of the greatness of a city's sovereign ruler.

Despite these symbolic uses, city walls greatly inconvenienced inhabitants' lives, had other unintended consequences, and invited transgression (De La Croix 1972, 9–10; Reyerson 2000; Dey 2011, 110–16). They retarded the development of the city and made difficult any increases or decreases in population. Inevitably a fortification was too big or too small for the number of people who lived within the walls. Security often dictated a defendable location on high points, hills, or islands that greatly inconvenienced the population's access to water, fields, fuel, and other resources. Walls required constant repair and often seemed to succumb more to subsidence and earthquakes than to attack. Changes in siege equipment and tactics also required the frequent redesign and rebuilding of city walls. Inexorably, conflicts existed between civilians' convenience and military uses of city spaces. For example, fewer gates made walls more secure, but more gates facilitated movement, trade, and the everyday lives of inhabitants.

The Bible tells the story of Jericho. Joshua's forces marched around the city six times, and on the seventh time they sounded their trumpets and the walls of Jericho fell down. Archaeologists have found little evidence to support the biblical account of the fall of Jericho, but they have established Jericho as one of the oldest walled towns in the world (De La Croix 1972, 13). Initially built around 8000 BCE, the population grew to 2,000 by 7500 BCE, when the inhabitants added a substantial wall four meters high with eight-meter-tall towers.

The earliest walls appear in the Near East. Eleven thousand years ago, a wall surrounded the structure at Gobekli Tepe in Urfa, southeastern Turkey (Mark 2009). In Mesopotamia, city walls were common by 2900 BCE (De La Croix 1972, 15–18; Tracy 2000a, 8). The walls surrounding these cities were more imposing than any built later in the Near East or Europe. For example, nine and a half kilometers of wall with 900 towers surrounded Uruk, and the walls of Ur spanned twenty-five meters in width with towers more than twenty-five meters in height. Many cities had multiple curtain walls (up to seven) with a fortified citadel in their center.

In the same time period, Egypt took a layered approach to defense (De La Croix 1972, 18–19). Deserts surround the Nile River on both sides, and outsiders could only enter the Egyptian domain by coming down the Nile from Nubia or coming up the Nile from the delta. The Egyptians walled their cities and developed a defense in depth by building fortresses on the upper Nile. The contrast between walling individual cities and a defense in depth along frontiers is evident in the history of walls through the twentieth century. In many epochs, the walling of cities reflected the failure of a defense in depth to protect the frontiers.

China also has an ancient heritage of building city walls. As early as 7000 BCE, Chinese people built protective walls and ditches around their towns (Sawyer 2011). The occupants of Shang dynasty (ca. 1766–ca. 1122 BCE) cities built rammed-earth walls. At Erh-li-kang in Honan, they built a seven-kilometer-long wall surrounding the community (Waldron 1990, 13; Lovell 2006, 31). From this time forward, virtually every Chinese city was behind walls. Walls developed in tandem with a coherent Chinese culture (Lovell 2006, 31). Walls came to symbolize sovereign power and the essence of China defining cities and regions (Steinhardt 2000). Chinese wall building peaked during the Ming dynasty (1368–1644 CE) and ceased with the introduction of European cannon in the eighteenth century (Farmer 2000). This rejection of walls was terminal even though during the Second Opium War (1856–1860), the most massive walls, such as those at Beijing, absorbed European cannonballs without collapsing (Parker 2000, 409).

When the Romans' defense in depth of their frontiers began to fail in the late third century CE, their cities rapidly threw up defensive walls (Tracy 2000b, 73; Dey 2011, 118). The two most renowned were the Aurelian Wall around Rome (Dey 2011) and the Theodosian Wall protecting Constantinople (Tsangadas 1980). The Romans built the Aurelian Wall in 270–275 CE, and it defended the city for almost a thousand years until the pontificate of Leo IV (847–855 CE). At its peak, the Aurelian Wall stretched for more than nineteen kilometers, stood sixteen meters high, had square towers almost every thirty meters, and was pierced by sixteen gates. The Theodosian Wall protected Constantinople for more than a thousand years beginning in the early fifth century. In its final form, the wall consisted of three curtain walls, each higher than the one before, creating a sixty-six-meter-deep defensive zone fronted by a twenty-meter-wide, six-and-a-half-meter-deep moat. The highest wall ran for six kilometers and stood twenty meters tall with ninety towers and thirteen gates.

In medieval Europe, many cities that had been established during the Roman Empire used and modified existing Roman walls. A second great wave of wall building occurred when Crusaders brought back innovations from the Byzantine Empire. For example, armies routinely used battering rams to breach medieval walls. The Byzantines had developed machicoulis galleries that projected out on the front face of a wall, allowing sheltered defenders to rain missiles, stones, and boiling oil on attackers at the base of the wall (De La Croix 1972, 35).

Cannons made several millennia of wall building obsolete. Artillery firing iron balls on a flat trajectory undermined walls, causing them to collapse. In 1453 CE, the Ottomans laid siege to Constantinople. They had two massive cannons firing iron balls, and these weapons blew a breach in the Theodosian Wall. Charles VIII of France invaded Italy in 1494 with artillery in his siege train. In a matter of hours, his cannon transgressed walls that had previously withstood sieges for months. The fall of Constantinople and Charles VIII's artillery signaled the beginning of the end for cities defended by a high curtain wall with towers and fronted by a wide ditch.

In response to Charles's success, Italian military engineers redesigned fortifications to create pointed bastion and rampart systems (De La Croix 1972, 42–44; Parker 2000; Pepper 2000, 284; Tracy 2000a, 12). They built low, triangular-shaped bastions with sloping walls constructed of rammed earth to absorb cannonballs. They fronted these bastions with deep ditches and positioned them so that defenders could provide covering fire and enfilading fire to support each other. These artillery fortresses (also called star forts) were the standard system of fortification used by Europeans for the next three centuries.

The new technologies of warfare posed a dilemma for early modern cities. In theory, a city could surround itself with bastions with no blind spots (De La Croix 1972, 45–46; Pollack 2010). In a few cases, cities, such as the new plantation city of Londonderry in Ireland (walls built in 1613–1619), did just that. Most municipalities, however, found it exorbitantly expensive to tear down a medieval wall and build an artillery fortress around the city. A pointed bastion system required a reconstruction of the city on a massive scale. Often, a fully built pointed bastion fortification could cover as much ground as the city itself (Tracy

2000a, 14). The quick fix was to pile up cannonball-absorbing earth against the medieval curtain wall. Such an expedient solution, however, would only last a handful of years and did not provide enfilading lanes of fire (Parker 2000, 389).

During the mid- to late 1600s, the French built a series of fortress towns along their eastern boundary. Planners laid these towns out with a radial street plan within a circle defined by a pointed bastion and rampart fortification (De La Croix 1972, 49). These towns provided a defense in depth for the national border. As a result of this defense, seventeenth-century French cities began to open their communities by tearing down medieval curtain walls (Wolfe 2009, 135–46).

Cannon and the artillery fortress gave European armies immense advantages on the global stage (Parker 2000). Eastern European polities built artillery fortresses to provide a defense in depth that repulsed the Ottoman Empire (Parker 2000, 415). The Ottomans adopted a non-Italian approach to gun fortification by building tall round towers with multitiered gun platforms (Pepper 2000). In the Americas, European powers, especially France and Great Britain, built star forts in the wilderness to attract indigenous support and to contest each other. In Asia, European armies quickly reduced Indian and Chinese cities that had not adopted the pointed bastion system (Asher 2000; Parker 2000, 409). In contrast, Japan rapidly adopted the artillery fortress after the 1590s and did not submit to European imperialism (Parker 2000, 412–13). Africa had an ancient history of walled cities, but few if any had been built to withstand artillery attack (Bloom 2000; Connah 2000). Perhaps the greatest of these was Sungbo's Eredo in Nigeria. This massive complex of earth walls and ramparts protected the city of Benin and covered 6,500 square kilometers (Pearce 1999). British artillery breached these colossal fortifications in 1897.

Just as changes in military technology and tactics brought down the medieval curtain wall, so too they transgressed the artillery fortress. In the seventeenth century, European siege engineers devised an entrenching system to attack pointed bastion fortifications (Tracy 2000a, 14). The development of rifled artillery in the nineteenth century signaled the end of the pointed bastion fortification. Instead, defenders surrounded cities with independent strong points and threw up trenches in direct anticipation of attack. The twentieth-century introduction of airplanes and tanks increased the extent and widened the spacing of this defense in depth. The great twentieth-century siege of Stalingrad involved fluid defense lines and house-to-house fighting that used the rubble of the city as fortification.

Dividing the City

As James Tracy (2000a, 3) discusses, citizens of cities have often built interior walls in reaction to internal hostilities, to separate one population group from another. The Chinese Ming dynasty created thirty-four twin cities to house ethnically distinct populations. During the Tang dynasty (618–907 CE), walled residential wards existed in many cities. After 1949, the communist regime built walled work unit compounds (Choon-Piew 2009, 5). In 1222 CE, the Spanish city of Pamplona built dividing walls to separate feuding neighborhoods. In many parts of the world, wealthy families have lived in walled compounds. Such internal divisions manifest as peace walls, defensive cul-de-sacs, and gated communities in the contemporary world (Dinzey-Flores and McAtackney, both this volume).

Perhaps the most well-known internal divisions within a city were the Jewish ghettos in many older cities of Europe. Cities forced Jewish people to occupy specific neighborhoods beginning in Roman times. In 1516 Venice, Italy, was the first city to wall off the Jewish neighborhood and coined the term "ghetto." The city of Rome created a Jewish ghetto in 1555, and other European cities soon followed Rome's example. The ghetto wall and gate served both to keep Jews in during Christian holidays and at other times and to protect the occupants from pogroms. Cities began abolishing ghettos in the Napoleonic era. In 1882, the Rome ghetto was abolished, and the city tore down the ghetto wall in 1888. During World War II, the Nazis established more than a thousand walled ghettos, the largest and most famous being the Warsaw Ghetto in Poland.

The history of modern gated communities began in the late nineteenth century (Gusterson and Besteman 2009). Early examples included the establishment of private places in St. Louis, Missouri, in the mid-1800s and the gated suburb of Tuxedo Park, New York, opened in 1886 (Blakely and Snyder 1997, 4). Primarily the superrich occupied these gated communities. During the country club/suburb period from the turn of the twentieth century until about 1929, US gated communities only numbered in the hundreds. In the 1940s and 1950s, gated and walled country clubs and resorts for wealthy clientele proliferated. Sea Pines Resort on Hilton Head Island in South Carolina (founded in 1957) is a good example of this trend. In the 1960s and 1970s, walled and gated retirement communities began sprouting up in Florida, southern California, and Arizona (Low 2003, 14). At the end of the twentieth century and into the twenty-first, there was a logarithmic takeoff in the number of US households (11 million) living in gated communities (Mohn 2012).

The growth of gated communities has become a worldwide phenomenon (Glasze, Webster, and Franz 2006; Choon-Piew 2009; Gusterson and Besteman 2009; Dinzey-Flores, this volume). Although gated communities remain rare in continental Europe and Japan, they have multiplied throughout the rest of the world, including formally communist countries, such as China and Russia. People live in these communities because of a combined fear of violence and of the "other" in increasingly globalized and multicultural cities (Dinzey-Flores, this volume). As the novelist Mohsin Hamid (2015) points out: "The people most often held at bay by our new boundaries, in almost every society, are the poor, the darker-skinned. And yet wealthy citizens and wealthy countries grow ever more fearful. Each wall scares into being another."

The first half of the twentieth century also saw US and British communities using walls to segregate people by class and race. In 1926, residents of Alexandra Crescent, a private road in Bromley, Kent, England, built a seven-foot-high "class wall," capped with broken glass, to block their road (Nelson 2011). They threw up the wall to prevent working-class people living in an adjacent public housing development from entering their neighborhood. In 1940 a Detroit, Michigan, developer built a concrete wall six feet in height and a half-mile long. This wall separated a Euro-American neighborhood from an African American neighborhood and materialized the redlining of the African American quarter (Farley and Mullin 2014).

Easily the most famous internal barricade of the twentieth century was the Berlin Wall. The East German state built the wall to keep its citizens from fleeing to the West, and the fall of this wall, both physically and symbolically, signaled the end of the Cold War (McWilliams 2013). The Berlin Wall no longer exists, but its memory and remnants still shape economic development and social differences in the contemporary city.

Cities have built walls to divide combatants and reduce violence. In Northern Ireland, city authorities assented to demands from neighbors to build walls during the Troubles of the late 1960s to late 1990s, although the walls continue to be erected even in the post-conflict context. These "peace walls" materialize politico-religious difference as they divide Protestants/unionists from Catholics/nationalists. People have embraced them both as sources of security and as powerfully symbolic objects and memorials (McAtackney 2011 and this volume).

The city authorities even have facilitated the decoration and painting of one of the most notable peace walls—between Falls Road and Shankill Road in West Belfast—with bright swaths of color. Town councils market the murals as "dark tourism" with the hope that tourists will spend their money in areas suffering from long-term economic decline (McDowell 2008). In Baghdad, Iraq, the government of Saddam Hussein occupied a section of the city called the Green Zone. After the US Army conquered Baghdad in 2003, it surrounded the Green Zone with blast walls and barbed wire to protect US functionaries and the Iraq government. At the same time, Shia and Sunni neighborhoods raised walls for their own security.

Long Walls or Linear Barriers

Long walls or linear barriers have a history almost as ancient as that of city walls. The earliest example was in ancient Mesopotamia in the third millennium BCE (Mark 2009; Frye 2018, 15–31). These walls did not enclose habitations but rather demarcated territorial, cultural, and political frontiers. The largest of such walls ran for thousands of kilometers. Julia Lovell (2006, 17) argues that in China, the construction of frontier walls was the last option after diplomacy, trade, and punitive military expeditions failed. An unpopular option, they symbolized military weakness, diplomatic failure, political paralysis, and bankrupting policy.

An epic period of linear barrier construction began in the early 600s BCE, when Scythian nomads appeared, and ended in the seventeenth century with the final defeat of steppe nomads (Spring 2015, 1–5). For more than two millennia, Scythians, Xiongnu nomads, Huns, and Mongols threatened and often invaded the agrarian civilizations of the Mediterranean, Near East, and China. These civilizations erected linear barriers consisting of walls, towers, ditches, mounds, canals, and forts in response to these nomads.

Peter Spring (2015, 7) has identified commonalities among ancient linear barriers. Ancient states and civilizations built long walls in two political contexts. Competing polities of similar size and development threw up linear barriers on their frontiers. For example, in China during the Warring States period (475–221 BCE) contending polities built extensive long walls to secure and defend resources. More commonly, however, states, civilizations, and empires constructed linear barriers on their frontiers to counter nomadic "barbarians." Geographic concerns affected the location of linear barriers. Their builders often placed them in strategic topographies to block isthmuses, peninsulas, and mountain passes, and they were used to control access to valued lands and populations.

The Great Wall of China is easily the most famous linear barrier in the world. Despite its fame, no single great wall exists in China (Waldron 1990, 7; Lovell 2006, 1). Rather, the Great Wall of the popular imagination consists of a myriad of border fortifications built over a period of almost 2,000 years. Construction of these long walls began in the Spring and Autumn period (770–476 BCE) and continued through the Warring States period. Competing polities built walls hundreds of kilometers in length (Sawyer 2011, 439; Spring 2015, 45). With the unification of China in 221, long wall building shifted to the northern frontier. Successive dynasties, culminating with the Ming, expanded and connected these walls to a total length of almost 7,000 kilometers (Waldron 1990, 7). The oft-photographed Great Wall near Beijing dates to the Ming dynasty. Julia Lovell (2006, 17) argues that the Chinese border walls never worked well as defenses against steppe nomads. She notes that invaders, such as Genghis Khan, could find weak spots, move rapidly to flank the fortifications, or bribe officials to allow them to transgress the walls. She argues that Chinese frontier walls functioned not to protect land but rather to seize and demarcate territory, control trade, and police people who lived both inside and outside the frontier.

The Red Snake of Gorgan stretches for 195 kilometers from the Caspian Sea to the mountains of northeastern Iran (Nokandeh et al. 2006). People nicknamed the wall the Red Snake because of the color of the bricks used to construct it. Thirty-six forts dot the wall's path, and a deep ditch runs along its front face. It is the largest ancient barrier wall between the frontier walls of China and the Roman *limes* (limits) of Eastern Europe. The Sasanians created the Red Snake in the fifth century BCE to stop the expansion of the White Huns on the steppes to the north. Nokandeh and colleagues (2006, 166) reject critics who question the Red Snake's military function. They argue that such critics focus on catastrophic events that transgressed the long walls and ignore the centuries of successful defense that they supplied.

The emperor Augustus began the construction of the first Roman *limes* in 9 CE after German tribes massacred three legions in the Teutoburg Forest. Between 117 and 161 CE, both Hadrian and Antoninus Pius expanded the *limes* (Cupcea 2015). Hadrian built the most famous of these *limes* across northern England in the 120s CE (Hingley 2012). Stretching 120 kilometers, Hadrian's Wall was 3.6 meters high with a ditch on the north side, a road along the south side, fifteen forts built up against it, and a series of gates and towers; it is now a UNESCO World Heritage site. In Germany, the *limes* consisted of wooden stockades, stone walls, gates, watchtowers, and ditches (Cupcea 2015). They stretched for more than 568 kilometers with at least sixty forts and 900 towers.

As the examples of the Chinese frontier walls, the Red Snake of Gorgan, and the Roman *limes* indicate, a spirited debate continues among academics about the defensive nature and capabilities of ancient linear barriers and long walls. Scholars who question the defensive nature of the long walls note that they would have only slowed an invasion since they would have been easily breached. Instead, these scholars assert that the purpose of the walls was to dominate the landscape, control the movement of people, facilitate tax collection, supervise commerce, and make statements about imperial military and cultural might (Lovell 2006, 17; Hingley 2012; Cupcea 2015). Other scholars argue that researchers should not disregard the "obvious" military function of these barriers (Nokandeh et al. 2006, 166; Spring 2015, 8). They maintain that critics ignore the centuries that walls provided security and instead emphasize the rare times that invaders transgressed them. Champions of defense note that the walls worked well as military technology until confronted by a threat different from or greater than the threats they were designed for. Such elevated threats came fast and furious in the twentieth century.

Twentieth-century changes in military technology made linear barriers obsolete for war. The trench combat of World War I ended with the introduction of tanks supported by airplanes. Armored columns could cross trenches and wreak havoc on the logistical infrastructure behind them. German Panzers supported by Stuka dive bombers swept around the French Maginot Line at the beginning of World War II. During the Gulf War (1990–1991), the US military's rapid transformation of Iraq's sand berms and entrenchments into tombs left no doubt that linear barriers have little value in a modern battle.

By the middle of the twentieth century, the linear barriers that were obsolete for a hot war had become instruments of the Cold War. In Eastern Europe, the Soviet Union materialized the Iron Curtain with walls, fences, ditches, watchtowers, and patrol roads (McWilliams 2013 and this volume). This system of barricades appeared in the 1950s and included the Berlin Wall. The communists put up these barriers in part as a defensive trip line but more to keep people from fleeing to the West. More than 30,000 people, however, managed to transgress these walls and escape. Most of these barriers were torn down following the collapse of the Soviet Union in 1991.

The 1953 armistice agreement that ended fighting in the Korean War set up a demilitarized zone (DMZ) between North and South Korea (Kim 2014). The DMZ is a 4-kilometer-wide, 250-kilometer-long fortified buffer zone between the two Korean nations. The DMZ has been the site of frequent skirmishes. The North Koreans have infiltrated it and tunneled under it, and in the late 1970s, the United States and South Korea built a concrete wall along the southern half of the DMZ. Because of concerns about possible parallels to the Berlin Wall, the United States and South Korea deny the existence of their wall. From a military standpoint the DMZ serves primarily as a trip wire in case of invasion.

And the Walls Came Tumbling Down

Walls inconvenience people. They impede movement, and they interfere with commerce, traffic, and domestic activities. It is therefore little wonder that people abandon and tear down walls as soon as they feel secure and/or when the walls lose their military utility. In the nineteenth century, the Ottoman sultan ordered sections of the Theodosian Wall to be torn down (Tsangadas 1980). In 1911, during the Chinese Republican era, the government tore down the walls and the gates of Shanghai because they were viewed as archaic symbols of backwardness (Choon-Piew 2009, 6). After China came under communist rule, Mao tore down the outer walls of Beijing to signal that the old China no longer existed (Steinhardt 2000, 422).

Leveling walls unlocks a city for expansion and creates open spaces and boulevards in crowded neighborhoods. In virtually any European town or city with a medieval heritage, a contemporary avenue or boulevard around the heart of the city reveals the old defenses (Tracy 2000a; Wolfe 2009; Campsie 2010; Gruen 2010; Donovan 2015). At the end of the seventeenth century, for example, London was bursting at the seams (Donovan 2015). The city authorized the destruction of the city wall in 1760, and five years later little of it remained. By the nineteenth century, a medieval wall greatly limited Barcelona's growth. In 1845, the city received permission to remove the wall, and a major expansion resulted, doubling Barcelona's size (Gruen 2010, 23). The city also built Las Ramblas, its most well-known boulevard, following the route of the wall. Paris had a series of six walls beginning with a Roman construction and ending with a useless 1840s fortification, the Enceinte de Thiers (Campsie 2010). The city leveled the Enceinte de Thiers just after the First World War. Paris built new walls to allow the city to expand and tore down the old ones as it built the latest one. The ghosts of the old walls remain visible because Paris built the Boulevard Périphérique on the path of old walls. The Périphérique divides the city from its suburbs and divides immigrants living in the *banlieue* from the native French living within the boundaries of the Périphérique.

Walls, however, always resist their destruction. These often massive structures require significant effort to build and consequentially necessitate considerable labor to tear down. Sometimes they disappear slowly as the citizens rob them of stone, lumber, and metal. Often, a city must seek permission of a central government or a sovereign to remove its walls. Razing walls raises municipal political issues. These politics revolve around the fundamental question of who will benefit and who will lose as a result of this major change in the city's fabric. What will the vacated land be used for? Who will own it? What will happen to ancient rights, responsibilities, and obligations when walls, towers, and gates come down?

All around the world, we find the remnants and relics of ancient and historic walls. When walls come down, the demolition crews usually leave bits and pieces standing. This most commonly happens when newer buildings incorporate portions of the wall or when the wall has been integrated into the fabric of the city, for example, supporting roads or terraces. Walls tend to survive in towns or smaller cities that have been largely abandoned or become impoverished. For example, people often abandoned medieval communities inconveniently located atop a hill, ridge, or island. They built their new homes nearer to their fields and water, leaving the old town and its walls as relics.

Walls, however, do not simply lose their symbolic power with the loss of their intended military function. They continue to speak with a power and immediacy that few other structures can match (Dey 2011, 4). Thus, ancient walls become modern when they gain a new functionality as heritage and as tourist attractions. As heritage, they define national, religious, and ethnic identities. As tourist attractions, they generate money and define local economies. This transformation from military technology to heritage and tourist attraction can occur with all types of walls, including city walls, internal walls, and long barriers (McWilliams, this volume).

In Europe and China, surviving walled towns and cities invoke heritage, and some have become tourist attractions comparable to Disneyland, promoted through networks of similarly walled places (e.g., the Irish Walled Towns Network). In a modern context, the walls make the communities distinctive and noteworthy. These characteristics attract tourists, who bring money and support the inhabitants, but their numbers can threaten the walls they have come to visit. The walls also make communities seem picturesque and quaint, which attracts settlers to reinhabit and restore the old city.

Carcassonne, France, is one of the earliest and best examples of a city transformed from fortress to ruin to tourist attraction. By the nineteenth century, Carcassonne had fallen into such disrepair that the French government ordered its demolition. In 1849, a decree to do so provoked opposition, and as a result in 1853, the architect Eugène Viollet-le-Duc restored the medieval fortress of Cité de Carcassonne (Lewi 2008). The authenticity and intent of Viollet-le-Duc's restoration remain controversial. He aimed for a "total restoration," reflecting his yearning for historical completion in order to tell and show the whole story about a place. This restoration (coupled with the forces of high-volume tourism) has assisted in the complete eclipsing of the experience of Carcassonne by the consumption of its own representations. UNESCO made the city a World Heritage site in 1997. Today, tourists to the city buy the experience of heritage in what amounts to a spectacular theme park. In France, only the Eiffel Tower receives more visitors than Carcassonne (Lewi 2008).

History and a search for heritage draw people to the Jewish ghettos of Europe as tourist destinations (Ioannides and Ioannides 2002). For example, more than 500 years after Ferdinand and Isabella expelled all Jews from Spain, modern Jewish tourists have returned. They join tours that take them to the ghettos of Girona, Córdoba, Seville, Barcelona, and other Spanish cities. They walk through the narrow, curvy streets to look upon and touch remnants of walls, gates, homes, and synagogues. Such tourism can actively reinforce Jewish identity and make the Diaspora experience real and material for the modern traveler.

Nations preserve the ancient long barriers as symbols of national pride and as places where national heritage can be constructed and performed (Shanks 2013). In China, the so-called Great Wall became important as heritage due to the policies of the nationalist Republican movement of the first part of the twentieth century (Waldron 1990, 194–220). Long barriers no longer regulate who is inside and who is outside by controlling movement. Instead, walls make people insiders or outsiders through their ideological symbolism. Long barriers seem especially well suited for symbolizing nationalist identities, perhaps because nationalist projects use them to define the territory of the state. People can also use them as symbols to challenge the legitimacy of nationalism. For example, the Eighth Balkan Anarchist Bookfair in Mostar in Bosnia and Herzegovina called itself "Over the Walls of Nationalism" (anarhistickisajamknjiga 2014).

One example of long barriers and how they have been anachronistically used to define competing nationalisms can be found in Ireland. Black Pig's Dyke is the popular name for a discontinuous system of linear earthworks and ditches that stretched from County Armagh to Donegal Bay (Ó Drisceoil et al. 2014). Built beginning in the Middle Bronze Age (1500–600 cal BCE) to the Iron Age (ca. 600 cal BCE–400 cal CE), these linear earthworks were monumental in size. They fit Spring's (2015) idea that competing polities of similar size and development build long walls. Starting in the nineteenth century, scholars spoke of the dyke as a unified land boundary that demarcated Ulster from the rest of Ireland. In May 1921, Great Britain ended the Irish-Anglo War by partitioning six of the nine counties of Ulster to form Northern Ireland. In 1948, the rest of the island became the Irish Republic. The partition boundary corresponded very roughly to the Black Pig's Dyke. Unionists who wished for Northern Ireland to remain part of the United Kingdom projected the partition boundary of 1921 back in time onto Black Pig's Dyke. They claimed that Black Pig's Dyke had been a formable barrier that separated Northern Ireland from the rest of the island and that for this reason the region had always been more closely connected by sea to Scotland than by land to the rest of Ireland. More recent research questions the defensive nature of these linear barriers. Archaeologists have concluded that "there is no archaeological or literary evidence to support the hypothesis that a unified/coordinated territorial boundary, formed by a corpus of linear earthworks known collectively as the 'Black Pig's Dyke' (or variants of the name), ever existed across the north midlands" (Ó Drisceoil et al. 2014, 99).

Modern Walls

We do not live in a global culture that is shaped by freedom's
triumph over tyranny. Rather, we live in a global culture where the two
have merged. If we are to speak freely, every word must be monitored.
If we are to roam freely, every entrance must be locked.
—Mohsin Hamid (2015)

At the end of the twentieth century, people began to pull down the Cold War barriers. In 1990, East Germany began to destroy the Berlin Wall (McWilliams, this volume), and all through Eastern Europe the Iron Curtain began to rise. Today, the DMZ in Korea remains as the only major Cold War barrier. With the fall of these barriers, many predicted that humanity would enter a globalized twenty-first century, a world without walls (Jones, this volume).

This has not happened. As Mohsin Hamid (2015) reflects, we live in a world where tyranny and freedom have merged. This merger has compelled nations, developers, cities, and individuals to engage in one of the greatest eras of wall building in the history of the world. This merger also has highlighted a fundamental paradox that exists in all wall building. As Mohammad Chaichian (2014, 1) points out, "Erecting walls on the one hand signifies power and the ability of those who build them to dominate, but at the same time represents the builder's insecurity and fear of the other." Roman city walls resulted from the collapse of Rome's defense in depth. The construction of Chinese frontier walls followed the failure of diplomacy, trade, and punitive military expeditions (Lovell 2006, 17). Rarely, if ever, have walls resolved or eliminated the threats that prompted their construction.

Throughout history, people have built barriers as a standard response to perceived insecurities (Tracy 2000a, 3; Spring 2015, 10). The history of walls demonstrates that people do not lightly make the decision to put up physical barriers because of both the labor and expense of building them and the inconveniences that they create (Reyerson 2000; Tracy 2000a, 3, and 2000b, 75; Spring 2015). People usually build linear barriers in anticipation of a continuous threat rather than in response to a single immediate threat. The great threat of antiquity was the hordes bent on conquest and looting; the most common "barbarians" of the modern world, however, are refugees, the unemployed, and poor people seeking security and economic opportunity (Nails 2015; Jones 2016).

Modern walls physically differ from ancient and historic barriers because of this change in the alleged "barbarians." The old walls sought to defend and destroy the invaders at the gate. Modern walls seek to impede and dissuade the masses that press against them (Jones, this volume). With a few exceptions, such as the DMZ in Korea and modern walls and barriers designed to stop terrorists, modern walls do not use inhumane supplements, such as minefields and electrified fences. Ancient and historic walls usually reflected bilateral tensions, and they confronted similar walls and defenses on the other side. Modern walls tend to be unilateral, the construction of a single nation, neighborhood, or city built to keep the "other" out.

In the past, just as today, policy makers, citizens, and scholars debated the effectiveness of walls for defense (Chaichian 2014, 2; Spring 2015, 6–8). This was especially the case for long barriers, such as Hadrian's Wall (Hingley 2012; Cupcea 2015), the Red Snake of Gorgan (Nokandeh et al. 2006, 166), and the Great Wall of China (Lovell 2006, 44–45). Despite this debate, authors agree that we cannot simplistically reduce the practical, cultural, and historical significance of all walls just to defense (De La Croix 1972, 9; Dey 2011, 110–16; Chaichian 2014, 2). City walls, internal walls, and long barriers have functioned to control the movement of people, collect taxes, mark social inequality and privilege, monumentalize the urban fabric, control urban sprawl, and serve as powerful symbols of identity, wealth, and importance. The symbolic power of walls cannot be underestimated. Many would argue that modern walls exist more as symbols that negotiate ideals of security and sovereignty than as the practical barriers of the past (Brown 2010; Chaichian 2014; Dear and Jones, both this volume).

The nature of the current threats of the poor, the refugee, and the displaced (the modern "barbarians") differs greatly from the militarized threats of the past. Yet many policy makers see walls as the answer to these threats for a variety of reasons. The contributors in this volume ask: how do modern walls succeed or fail at resolving social problems, and what repercussions are created by an increasingly materially segregated world? They recognize that walls have a multifaceted history and that they do not in some simple, physical way create security. They examine instead how modern walls (like past walls) are complex and materialize a host of social relations, how they invite transgression, and how they amplify and polarize social problems and inequalities. Like the critics of the long walls of the past, they question the efficacy of walls to keep people out.

Walls largely embody negative material forces and ideals, but the history of walls should also give us hope. At the most basic level, walls create otherness by physically creating opposing sides and defining who is walled in and who is walled out. They accentuate social and cultural differences, obscure similarities, promote social stereotypes, and magnify the inequalities between who can enter and who cannot. Walls impede freedom of movement and generally compromise commerce, cultural interchange, social integration, social understanding, and internationality. Their materiality breaks bodies. Hope lies in the fact that historically people have torn down walls almost as quickly as they put them up.

Part I
Local Walls

CHAPTER THREE

Race Walls

(In)Visible Codes of Neighborhood
Inequality in Puerto Rico

ZAIRE DINZEY-FLORES

When the forty-fifth president of the United States started spewing about building a wall between México and the United States, the racial contours of the discourse were immediately apparent. Latinos throughout Latin America and the United States quickly denounced the idea of a wall as xenophobic and racist. The way in which this physical national border was immediately seen as racialized contrasts sharply with the way we rarely see local neighborhood walls, such as those surrounding gated communities, as racialized structures. In this chapter, I examine neighborhood walls as built elements of old and new forms of racism—as codifications of specific racial formulations and inequalities, which depend on the built environment as euphemism and veil for their reproduction. Focusing on the neighborhood scale and the walls that surround racialized concentrations of poverty and wealth, I consider how the built environment codifies and cements racial inequality and enforces racial segregation while inconspicuously perpetuating a myth of racial democracy. I argue that walls can be read as materialized forms of racial inequality. They harbor hardly visible significations that physically and symbolically reproduce and exacerbate racism. The walls that fortify neighborhoods and communities effectively "hide race in plain sight" (Harris 2005). They materially disguise the work of racism, displace intent, and sustain racial hierarchies. The walls and gates presume a subject racialized as Black or brown. The architecture of defense in these built forms, in turn, enforces a racial distinction. Moving beyond the scale of nation-state walls, I argue for a greater focus on everyday domestic walls, the ones that exist in neighborhoods, in homes, and on the streets (see McAtackney, this volume, on walls in Belfast). In these everyday spaces, the enactment of race is vivid, even if unreferenced. This codification in space, I argue, is especially useful to negate the real impact of racial distinctions, particularly in places like Latin America, where the role of race on someone's life chances is often denied.

(In)Visible Race in Space

Racial inequality is a fact. Yet specifically in Puerto Rico, and generally in Latin America, race and racism tend to be swept under the rug. When contrasting Latin American racism with a more explicit US racial order, scholars in the mid-twentieth century commonly claimed Latin American racism to be negligible (Babín 1958; Blanco 1942).

The basis for the denial of racial inequality is varied. Many have understood Latin America and the Caribbean as spaces where there has been an extensive mixing of races, creating a racial gradient and putting a variety of people in close proximity and in filial relationships. For a large proportion of Latin America, the issue of race has been intrinsically linked to the unifying concept of nation and culture. As a result, ideologies of *mestizaje* promoted a one-people, one-(mixed)-race perspective, which saw "unadulterated" racial subjects as a threat to national unity. Furthermore, slavery in Latin America and the Caribbean has been presented as being more "benevolent" than slavery in other parts of the world. Early accounts contrast the Hispanic tradition of bondage to a "much more deplorable" Dutch, French, and English system of slavery, and the former created conditions in Latin America favorable to miscegenation (Tannenbaum 1947; Rodríguez Cruz 1965; Díaz Soler 1957, 1974; Williams 1970; Flint 1832 quoted in Betances 1972). Researchers also have cited specific economic circumstances, which allowed conditions that created a racial democracy (Hoetink 1967). Some scholars cite the erratic plantation system of eighteenth-century Spanish colonial Puerto Rico, which resulted from abortive efforts at participation in the international King Sugar trade (Williams 1970; Mintz 1974), as a contributor to a "freer" racial system. It is claimed this permitted racial mixing and continually altered the balance of power between dark and light, enslaved and master (Blanco 1942; Williams 1945; Betances 1972).

Some scholars have claimed that racism is alien to Latin America and is only attributable to the imperialist nation to the north (Babín 1958; Blanco 1942). Wagley (1968) proposed that different criteria for racial classification resulted in varying systems of racial categorization in the Americas. Thus, distinct systems emerged when the three criteria of socioracial classification—ancestry, physical appearance, and sociocultural status—were weighted differentially. Nonetheless, in Latin America the idea of mixture congealed as a continuum, and racial democracy complemented the project of nation building and served as an accessory to avoiding a responsible treatment of racism.

A modern-day Latin American–US comparison, however, might yield a different view of how racial orders in the two contexts really differ. Tanya Hernández (2016) challenges the purity of a "binary" US racial order and a "continuous" Latin American racial order and suggests that these configurations are mythic. Beyond the binary-continuous comparison, the question of how racism is dispersed in the United States and Latin America might yield important insights. From the 1980s to the early 2000s, scholars argued that the mechanisms of racism in the United States had gone from overt to covert. Classified as symbolic, laissez-faire, aversive, or color-blind, covert forms of racisms thrive on their invisibility, which scholars argue makes them harder to redress (Dovidio and Gaertner 1986; Sears 1988; Bobo, Kluegel, and Smith 1997; Guinier and Torres 2002). I suggest that the covert forms of racisms are much like those of Puerto Rico and Latin America, where racism has historically been denied.

Covert racisms are harder to detect and evade measurement. An inability to point to the racist practices and their outcomes, in turn, contributes to the idea that race in Latin America is too complex and ephemeral, which disarms attempts to adequately target racism. The lack of race-based data and a lack of trust in the data that are available are corollaries to the idea that it is hard to measure race in Latin America. These issues have also hampered attempts to identify the consequences of race. Because of the staunch efforts to deny covert racial practices in Latin America, I turn to the material world. The built environment—in this case, residential neighborhoods and their walls—manifests what are new forms of codified racism in the United States, but these forms have been common in Latin America. These walls effectively enact racism due to their ability to veil or hide these forms of racism (Harris 2005, 2013).

Community Gates as Social Artifacts

The history of how housing and residential environments have contributed to racial inequality in the United States is rather well documented (Massey and Denton 1993). Yet we know little about how development and urbanization are implicated in Latin American inequality, where the racialized nature of urban development and segregation is less explored. Still rare in both the United States and Latin America are careful examinations of how race is made concrete, how race is imprinted in the built environment, public and private spaces, and neighborhoods (Dinzey-Flores 2013).

I rely on urban planner Kevin Lynch's work to understand the mechanisms via which gates act socially. Lynch (1960, 6) argues, "The environment suggests distinctions and relations, and observers—with great adaptability and in the light of [their] own purposes—select, organize, and endow with meaning what they see." Complementary to Lynch, sociologist Gerald Suttles (1972) notes the importance of the built environment, underscoring that collective "cognitive maps" are socially applied when social actors activate them to navigate and make decisions about a city. I expand on Lynch's and Suttles's frames to analyze neighborhood fortresses, walls, and gates, thinking about how these built environmental elements help shape the sense of a city.

The gated community entered the repertoire of neighborhood design in the late nineteenth century, when the wealthy in big cities sought shelter from the problems of rapid industrialization (Blakely and Snyder 1997; Newman 1972; McGuire, this volume). It was not until the 1960s–1980s that gates became common in residential communities, retirement developments, resorts, and country clubs, primarily in Florida and California (Blakely and Snyder 1997). The 1980s also saw the rise of gating as a direct response to crime and the fear of crime (Blakely and Snyder 1997). Much of the scholarship on the rise of this physical form has narrated the gate as an intervention of "fear." Privileged residential clusters gate themselves in the quest for a sense of security—from crime, from fear of crime, from declining property values (Davis 1990; Dillon 1994; Blakely and Snyder 1997; Caldeira 2000; Frantz 2000; Rivera-Bonilla 2003; Low 2004; Romig 2005).

My ethnographic work and my book on Puerto Rico (Dinzey-Flores 2013) expand the view of gated communities beyond the gates of privilege to examine the relational roles of gates in both privileged and underprivileged communities. Based on 2003 and 2004 ethnographic research and interviews with residents in four adjacent Puerto Rican communities—two public housing and two private subdivisions, one of each gated—I argue that residential gates support the social branding and distinction of communities. The gate becomes an efficient "imageable object" (Lynch 1960) that shapes the social distance between communities and how they are perceived to enforce and reproduce social distinctions and inequality (Dinzey-Flores 2013).

One of the primary qualities that shapes the meaning of a gate is its unique form, which becomes an imaginable object of distinction (Dinzey-Flores 2013). The public housing gate and the private subdivision gate have different shapes, and these morphologies have meaning. The government designs the gates of public housing to be uniform and functional. In the private residential developments, the residents pay for gates with decorative elements. In Puerto Rico, these built environment symbols repeatedly invoke perceptions that fit into four categories of meaning or image: (1) safety and security; (2) liberty, freedom, and control; (3) private versus public lifestyles; and (4) social class and prestige. I briefly discuss these social distinctions and how gates enact them below.

Whether spaces are perceived to be sites of potential harm or violence is communicated by the community gate. While the decorative gates of private subdivisions bring prestige, the functional gates of public housing communities send a warning sign to stay away. Gating is perceived to increase the status of a private subdivision relative to an ungated private subdivision, while a public housing gate has the opposite communication: it suggests danger in ways that ungated public housing does not. The changes to the physical environment further distance public housing communities from private subdivision communities in both social perception and social segregation. Furthermore, they serve to create nuanced distinctions between the perceptions of those neighborhoods that are gated and those that are not gated.

The desirable gate is the private subdivision gate; this gate affords a greater freedom. The gates that surround public housing, on the other hand, make these developments look and feel like prisons, because the gates create barriers for movement, access, and liberties. As Foucault (1975) did for institutions of power, the metaphor of Jeremy Bentham's panopticon has been utilized to describe the types of monitored spaces that have been devised by middle- and upper-class communities to control the environment (Romig 2005; Dinzey-Flores 2013). However, nowhere is the metaphor more applicable than in gated public housing sites. After all, that gating is implemented not by independent, private homeowner associations, but by government policy. This is a reality that we see in other social housing throughout the Latin American and Caribbean region. Thus, in contrast to the gates of private subdivisions, which are portrayed as features that increase security and that feed the privilege of the private subdivisions, the residents of public housing experience their environment as one that is externally controlled with limited movement and liberty (see McAtackney, this volume, for walls in working-class communities in Belfast).

Research on neighborhood gating and urban development has pointed out that in modern society, interventions that seek to control and secure the environment increasingly privatize public space (Davis 1990; Young 1990; Dillon 1994; Blakely and Snyder 1997; Low 2004). Residents of public housing similarly express that private residential areas privatize their spaces through gating. However, there are specific features of the gates of private enclaves that point to the private character of those communities. Residents note the aesthetic and technological features that contribute to the gates in private residential areas being private. While electric gates increase privacy in private subdivisions, public housing residents' lack of everyday control of their own gated infrastructure makes their environment oppressive. In other words, the self-controlled electric gates that allow residents of private subdivisions to gain access with beepers or being permitted access by private police both indicate "privacy" in private housing. In contrast, residents of public housing perceive their gates, which are monitored by the Puerto Rican police force, as putting them under control and limiting their privacy.

There is a level of resentment expressed by public housing residents toward the private subdivisions' control of access. Residents of public housing communities feel that their lives are more visible to the wider public in comparison to the private, self-determined lifestyles indicated by the gates in private subdivisions. Furthermore, it is clear, at least to the residents of public housing, that the private gating's purpose is to control them. What the gates do for the private residential areas is identify who their neighbors are. They mark who belongs to their community, their class, and their social circle.

Gates in Puerto Rico's neighborhoods shape the way that people perceive, experience, and interact with the urban residential built environments. In turn, the gates define social interaction, and specifically social distance, between neighborhoods. With high-status gates, private subdivisions become even more prestigious and more segregated, while the militarized, gated public housing becomes a hyperfeared version of the already stigmatized, but now relatively harmless, open public housing. The gated public housing thus becomes the ultimate representation of the negative qualities of public housing and a contributing factor in the process that Massey and Denton (1993), Wilson (1987), Venkatesh

(2000), and others describe whereby neighborhoods become isolated "ghettos." In private subdivisions, both those that live inside the neighborhood and those that live outside, despite some reservations, see the gate as a positive structure. The elaborate, well-kept, and clearly marked gate denotes safety, prestige, and the value of the neighborhood. Affirmation of the gates in private subdivisions is also found among public housing residents. Many envy the gates in private subdivisions, although others complain that the gates signal the desire of those communities to be apart from them, to distinguish themselves from the residents of public housing.

Yet even if we recognize the four dimensions of distinction mentioned above, the racial aspect of the gate can blend in and remain obscure, subservient to other social qualities, most prominently class. Below, I explicitly discuss how these four qualities extend a racial logic and reconstitute racism in Puerto Rico and, by extension, Latin America. Community gates, I argue, are artifacts that enact and establish racial distinctions. Their violence is codified as they render invisible the racially marked subjects and the racially impressed social significations.

The Race of Gates

Race imbues the four sets of images or meanings: safety and security; liberty, freedom, and control; private versus public lifestyles; and social class and prestige. These are all social constructions, and they also are racial formations and racial structures. Perhaps because gated community scholarship has largely focused on elite communities, with few exceptions the racial and class distinctions being elaborated through gates are rarely explicitly discussed (Dinzey-Flores 2013). Looking at both sides of the gates, and looking at different gates, exposes the racial geography of their production. Their racial aspects are activated socially when residents describe how the gates operate in their everyday lives. And they also are activated as we consider the social context in which they are physically and socially erected and reinforced.

Hartigan (1999, 4) suggests that scholars should "pay attention to the local settings in which racial identities are actually articulated, reproduced, and contested, resisting the urge to draw abstract conclusions. . . . We need to take these situations as examples of a different sort—as insights into the daily processes by which people make sense of racial matters in particular locales." In Puerto

Rico, the application of the gate to public spaces, and to public housing in particular, was partly due to the perception of crime as being a production of public housing communities and their residents. The face of public housing is Black.

A 1997 political cartoon—published in a San Juan newspaper at the apex of when public housing was being gated—denotes that most media reports associated crime with young Black men who resided in public housing. The caricaturist, Miche Medina, demonstrates the hierarchical, power-laden existential binary of race in the context of the criminal justice discourse in the island. At the top center of the cartoon, the governor of Puerto Rico, Pedro Rosselló, a white man, is in conversation with the director of corrections, a white woman, Zoé Laboy. At the top right, we see El Pueblo (the people) represented by an older white (in the context of Puerto Rico) man with a traditional folkloric *pava* (a broad-brimmed straw hat). At the bottom of the page is a visibly Black inmate. To the left, under the dynamite, is a visitor, represented by a brown woman with curly hair, exhibiting the racialized gender dynamics of criminality in Puerto Rico (Dinzey-Flores 2011).

This cartoon makes the claim that crimes were either occurring in public housing or being perpetuated by public housing tenants. Furthermore, the concurrent hemispheric war on drugs and the identification of public housing—with its Black and racial "others"—as the primary sites of the drug industry consolidated the image of public housing as crime-producing estates.

The perception of which spaces are considered dangerous or safe, and the racialized aspects of those perceptions, become articulated in built environments. Researchers have found that rather than actually leading to declines in crime, gates in neighborhoods mostly create a sense of safety—safety from violence but also safety in property values and being in a "good neighborhood" (Fowler and Mangione 1986; Taylor 1988; Atlas and LeBlanc 1994; Blakely and Snyder 1997; Wilson-Doenges 2000). Thus, a sense of safety is linked to ideas of race, poverty, and who is the "other." Research in the United States confirms that the racial and class demographics of a neighborhood have a significant impact on the sense of safety, the desirability, and the value of a neighborhood (Frey 1979; Harris 1999). With a few exceptions (Costa Vargas 2006; Fusté 2010; Alves 2014; Godreau 2015; LeBrón 2017; Rivera-Rideau 2013), not much research has been conducted in Latin America directly on this matter, but I found that ideas about what makes a good neighborhood were informed by imagery of who are the "good" people and who are the "bad" people. In "good" neighborhoods, the "bad" people were often implicitly characterized as "not white" (Dinzey-Flores 2007).

In 2000, the US Census asked Puerto Ricans to racially identify themselves for the first time in fifty years: 80.5 percent of Puerto Ricans in the island identified as "white," 8 percent identified as "Black or African American," 6.8 percent identified as "some other race," and 4.2 percent identified as "two or more races." The results of the census surprised those who thought that Puerto Ricans would reject the racial categories proposed by the census question. However, the responses suggest that Puerto Ricans were willing to identify themselves under the racial categories provided by the census. In Ponce, the racial identifications were similar to those across the island: 83.8 percent classified themselves as white, 9.5 percent identified as Black or African American, and 5.1 percent identified as some other race. Comparing the four communities of my field research, it is evident that there were some differences in how the residents of

Table 3.1. Race Statistics by Census Tract

	Public Housing 1 (Dr. Pila + 9 Alhambra houses)	Private Subdivisions (Alhambra + Extensión Alhambra)	Public Housing 2 (Gándara)
Census Tract Number	704	705.03	719
Total Population	3,289	4,317	5,729
Race			
White	78.5	92.2	73.3
Black/African American	7.0	3.1	11.3
American Indian or Alaska Native	0.8	0.2	0.4
Asian	0.0	0.5	0.1
Native Hawaiian or Pacific Islander	0.0	0.0	0.0
Some other race	11.0	1.9	3.6
Two or more races	2.6	2.1	11.3
Hispanic or Latino	99.5	96.3	99.4
White alone, not Hispanic or Latino	0.4	2.8	0.4

Source: US Census 2000.

Table 3.2. Race Statistics by Block Group

	Public Housing 1 (Dr. Pila)	Public Housing 1 (Dr. Pila)	Private Subdivisions (Alhambra + Extensión Alhambra)	Public Housing 2 (Gándara
	Block group 1, Census tract 704	*Block group 2, Census tract 704*	*Block group 1, Census tract 705.03*	*Block group 1, Census tract 719 (no data available)*
Total Population	1,731	1,558	760	—
Total Population Race	1,702	1,587	704	—
White	81.3	78.4	97.7	—
Black/African American	8.0	7.0	2.1	—
American Indian or Alaska Native	0.0	0.0	0.0	—
Asian	0.0	0.0	0.0	—
Native Hawaiian or Pacific Islander	0.0	0.0	0.0	—
Some other race	5.7	14.1	0.0	—
Two or more races	4.8	0.8	0.0	—

Source: US Census 2000.

private subdivisions and public housing identified racially. Whereas 92.2 percent of residents of the two private subdivisions that I examined identified as white (above the island average), the proportion of residents in the two public housing developments who identified as white was between 73 percent and 79 percent (below the island average). A greater percentage of residents in public housing identified as Black or African American or "other" when compared to the private subdivisions. Thus, residents of the private subdivisions identified almost exclusively as white, while one-fourth of residents of the public housing sites identified as Black, as being of two or more races, or as being some other race. These patterns hold using different spatial statistics.

These patterns of racial identification were also visible in how participants in focus groups identified themselves racially. The public housing communities and private residential communities chose divergent ways to identify racially, with the residents of private subdivisions leaning toward lighter racial identification and public housing residents making darker selections. When filling

Table 3.3. Race Identification by Community

Public Housing	Moreno/a, Negro/a, Trigueño/a, De Color, Piel Oscura	Blanca	Hispana, Puertor- riqueña, P.R., Hispánica	Other	Blank	Totals
Dr. Pila	13	4	6	2	7	32
Gándara	3	7	5	0	3	18
Public Totals	*16*	*11*	*11*	*2*	*10*	*50*

Private Housing		Blanca, B, Cau- cásica, Caucasian	Puerto Rican, Puer- torriqueña, Hispana, Latina			
Alhambra	0	1	6	0	1	8
Extensión Alhambra	0	7	0	0	0	7
Private Totals	*0*	*8*	*6*	*0*	*1*	*15*

Public + Private Housing	Black	White	Ethnic I.D.	Other	Blank	
GRAND TOTALS	16	19	17	2	11	65

Source: Author's focus group interviews, 2003, 2004.

out the form that asked for respondents' "race/raza," all of the respondents of one of the private subdivisions self-identified as white, using several different terms: "Blanca," "Caucásica," "B." Interestingly, residents in a second private subdivision tended to identify themselves as Puerto Rican, Hispanic, or Latino/a. Only one qualified their racial identity as white.[1] In the public housing sites, the racial identification patterns were rather different. In one, respondents loosely paralleled the census race responses. Out of eighteen respondents, seven identified as white ("Blanca"), three identified as Black ("Negra" or "Trigueña"), three identified as Hispanic ("Hispana" or "Hispánica"), two identified as Puerto Rican, and three did not identify racially by leaving the question blank. In a gated public housing community, the racial identification pattern was inverted from both the census pattern and the results in the other communities. Out of thirty-two respondents , thirteen identified as Black (four as "Moreno/a," two as "Trigueño/a," five as "Negro/a," one as "De Color," one as "Piel Oscura"), six identified as Hispanic or Puerto Rican, four identified as white ("Blanca"), one identified as "India," one as "Amarillo" (yellow), and seven left the question blank.

As racial attitudes in the United States increasingly resemble those of Latin America, with similar inequality outcomes based on race in both locations, it is important to consider how inequities are reproduced in covert ways. In Latin America, for example, as data on race become more and more available due to political commitments, there is growing empirical evidence of inequality based on race and skin tone (Andrews 2004, 2016; Telles 2014). As I have argued elsewhere (Dinzey-Flores 2013), there is a duality or dialectic of concreteness and vagueness in space that fixes social distinctions and dynamics (particularly with regard to race) in a highly effective manner. It's vague, so invisible, hard to pin down, and easy to deflect. It conforms to what Isar Godreau (2015) notes are conflicting and imprecise articulations of race. Nonetheless, these seemingly imperceptible, invisible cementations reproduce social inequalities and sustain race (Dinzey-Flores 2013).

Who is privy to seeing, and naming, these racial markers is as important as noting that they exist. For given actors, moving in different spaces at specific times, the imprints of race become visible, mediated, and at times fully exerted by the built environment, the very places where race can be hidden and codified. The privileges or violence of racial subjectivities, thus, are easily encoded; their inadmissible distinctions are built into the walls, the fences, the surveillance technologies. In these spatial configurations, schools, libraries, and other public spaces become loci of racial surveillance and enactment (Dinzey-Flores 2013).

Norbert Elias (1939) has argued that as Europe experienced a change from a decentralized feudal society to a system of states, there was a need for increased centralization, peace, and cooperation. To impress these elements into the social structure and so that knights could become the bourgeoisie, class separation was aesthetically imposed through "manners" and appearance. Similarly, Bourdieu (1986) proposes that cultural resources and practices are constituted in social class and act as mechanisms to distribute power. This power, however, is held only as long as it is codified. The built environment, including gates, has a strong material and symbolic impact on status, social class, and race and distributes power in the guise of cooperation. Racially dominant groups benefit from these codified built environments and their qualities of privilege.

These easily overlooked built environments of race and class privilege enact race in very forceful ways. Gates define who is an insider and who is an outsider, who belongs and who does not, marking some as more deserving, and allocating access and privilege in racialized ways (Dinzey-Flores 2013). In turn, whiteness in neighborhoods—marked by "good" schools, a helpful police presence, "safe" neighborhoods, gates—affects those who do not fit the new demographics in salient ways. This is especially important to understand when considering a Latin American society, where race inequality is often denied and where there is reliance on mythic representations of democracy that serve to uphold the very real racial violence of a racialized structure.

Racial Reflections in Everyday Built Environments

If we look closely, dig up the artifacts in the context of racialized societies, we cannot help but see the built environment's racial dimensions. For example, Puerto Rican and Latin American walls only reveal themselves to be racialized upon close examination and contact: the surveillance cameras in stores, the metal detectors in schools, the racially selective private parties of nightclubs (Williams Castro 2013), the unsanctioned entries into a neighborhood, the verified authorizations required to enter social sports clubs, the required codes of dress or comportment at libraries (Dinzey-Flores 2013). While superficially they appear to be raceless, they are all imbued with race, as are the neighborhood walls throughout Latin America, such as the ten-foot wall that divides the communities of San Juan de Miraflores and Surco in Lima, Peru (Robinson 2015). A political cartoon of this distinction by the Peruvian caricaturist known as Carlin pictures the poor residents as brown in contrast to the lounging white residents on the other side of the wall. Caricatures like this are especially effective in relaying the underlying meanings of the built environment. Similarly indicative of racialized walls is the now-famous image of the gated segregation between a favela and a condo with pool and balconies in Brazil, the racial aspects of which are captured implicitly (though not explicitly) in Teresa Caldeira's (2000) work.

The ethnographic contact with these artifacts reveals their racial calculations (see Bishara, this volume), particularly when the observer is Black (for example, Valle 2017). I, for one, am always a Black woman traversing these gated communities and social fortresses. Much academic research on walls has largely focused on borderlands (Dear, Dorsey and Díaz-Barriga, Jones, Papadopoulos, all this volume). But as walls are deployed rhetorically and physically to reinforce social boundaries and exaggerate differences, it is of great importance to pay attention to their functions not only at the nation-state level, but at smaller scales (Bishara and McAtackney, both this volume). That is, we must examine their effects in the home and community spaces that characterize all people's lives. This includes those who are near, but also the many that are far from nation-state borders, because they can be very close to visible or invisible borders in their everyday built environments. At this scale, the reproduction of social inequality, and particularly race, often goes unnoticed as walled environments are taken for granted and recede into the background (McAtackney, this volume). I also wish to highlight the importance of paying attention to the neighborhood scale and equipping those who intervene with our domestic built environments—policy makers, planners, architects, community residents—to consider the racialized subjects of our society and how "softer" new forms of racism can continue to circulate harshly, possibly violently, via community gates.

In 2008, French artist JR embarked on an art project in a Brazilian favela (Day 2010). The objective was to trouble the stigma attached to these locations by pasting giant-size pictures of the faces of favela residents onto the structures themselves. Huge images with large eyes looked down upon Rio de Janeiro, explicitly highlighting the dark faces of the residents of the otherwise "racially neutral" constructions of the favelas. We might consider how such racial codification might help deconstruct the built-in inequities of space if eyes, and researchers, and policy makers "see" and render visible the racial inequality in Latin America, in the hopes that seeing it will lead to it being addressed.

Note

1. The avoidance of the term "white" is surprising given that in the US Census in 2000, around 92 percent of residents of these two areas identified as white. The difference in this identification, I conjecture, comes from the fact that most of the respondents that I interviewed in one of the subdivisions I either knew before my fieldwork or I got in touch with through acquaintances from my high school. Their knowledge of my participation in school activities and my

emphasis on race and racial equality may have affected the responses. Thus, I think the avoidance of certain racial terms was informed by respondents' preexisting impressions of me and how they perceived my race. In addition, the respondents knew that I was coming from a US university and had familiarity with the racial system in the United States, and some discussed what the true meaning of the word "raza" in the questionnaire was. Disagreements emerged regarding whether I meant "race" in the Puerto Rican sense or in the US sense. The responses that specified "Latino/Hispanic," I believe, reveal attempts to provide what participants considered the "right" response, given my affiliation with a US university.

CHAPTER FOUR

Segregation Walls and Public Memory in Contemporary Belfast

Intersections with Gender and Class

LAURA MCATACKNEY

Contemporary archaeologies increasingly emphasize the fruitfulness of exploring our material worlds in order to answer questions relating to social justice. The focus is often on unearthing material indicators of unequal and marginalized lives in our various presents, particularly when those experiences are otherwise undocumented, bypassed, forgotten, or silenced. Inspirational studies include Shannon Dawdy's (2006, 2015) work on post–Hurricane Katrina New Orleans, Courtney Singleton's (2017) immersive explorations of urban homelessness in the United States, and various attempts to understand the "refugee crises" in Europe through an archaeological lens (including Papadopoulos, this volume). In this chapter I argue that using a contemporary archaeological perspective embedded in the places we study enables us to explore the localized repercussions of the global tendency to materially divide (see Bishara and Dinzey-Flores, both this volume). I argue that by engaging with both the materiality of dividing walls and their repercussions on the construction of public memory, contemporary archaeology has the potential to reveal the subtle manifestation of marginalization and polarization in urban environments. In particular, I contend that our emerging archaeological preoccupations with the contemporary world too frequently conflate the everyday experience with the middle class and androcentricism. In this chapter I focus on class and gender repercussions in terms of conflict and memory in the "post-conflict" but still divided city of Belfast in Northern Ireland.

In order to provide a localized lens on the global phenomenon of ideological walls intended to divide, I focus on the Newtownards Road in East Belfast. The need to narrow an investigation of walls to a particular part of Belfast is dictated by necessity: there are too many political walls to discuss in detail in one chapter. The Community Relations Council (2009) claimed that there were at least eighty-eight separate peace walls (so-called because they are monumental partitions constructed to keep antagonistic ethnic communities apart) in situ in Belfast a decade after the conflict ended with the signing of the so-called Good Friday Agreement (1998). Although these walls take various material forms and have multiple and evolving meanings, they have a particular local context due to the long-standing sectarian geographies of the historical city of Belfast, which shape its contemporary life. The Newtownards Road was selected because it includes a number of peace walls; there are a wide variety of official and community projects that decorate the walls or the areas around them; and there are a number of narratives projected from them into the micro-communities these walls create.

Before I proceed, a note on terminology: everyday words are frequently political, loaded, and problematic when experiencing, but also explaining, Northern Ireland and Northern Irish society. Long-standing divisions have heightened the role of symbols and signifiers of sectional identity to the extent that they have a direct impact on how most facets of society are understood by the "two communities": Protestant/loyalist/unionist and Catholic/nationalist/republican. This means that seemingly mundane preferences—such as the football team one supports or the school one attends—are read as signifiers of political and religious identity. Many aspects of everyday experience can be conflated with ethnicity, politics, and religion, and there are few who can escape such associations. Even some recent migrant groups are considered more associated with one of the two communities by Northern Irish people (e.g., the sizable Polish community, which is from a majority-Catholic country, is often perceived as being more "nationalist").

In this context, terms such as PUL (Protestant, unionist, loyalist) have emerged and are sporadically used by politicians and social commentators as an easy, cover-all term to demarcate and collectivize one of the two traditional communities. Its coining coincided with a perceived "crisis" in loyalist identity (Monaghan and Shirlow 2011), which was precipitated by perceived losses by working-class loyalist communities in terms of the "peace dividend" from the end of the conflict in comparison to the other community (Clarke 2013). However, their experiences also follow global trends in reflecting the depressions associated with the long-term decline of an urban, industrial working class into postindustrial mass unemployment in Global North countries. The term is problematic in that it obfuscates and flattens what are in reality fluctuating forms of identity that intersect with other facets, including class, gender, and geography. The equivalent term, CNR, is not as frequently used for the Catholic/nationalist/republican community as they do not collectively perceive themselves as negatively impacted by the peace process, and due to structural sectarian discrimination they did not have a significant industrial base for employment. However, the impact of a lack of devolved assembly for a number of years and the perceived threat of Brexit have heightened tensions in ways that are reemphasizing and solidifying traditional divisions. For the sake of brevity, in this chapter I use "loyalist" and "nationalist" when identifying the two communities because despite the terms' evident problems the communities themselves most frequently use these labels.

Societal Background

For a society of its size, Northern Ireland has been the subject of intense academic scrutiny. Indeed, it has been claimed there is a danger of overanalysis to the point of exceptionalism (e.g., Whyte 1990). Much of the research has centered on social relationships in urban areas that have been impacted by sectarian internecine conflict. This conflict afflicted the province in the mid- to late twentieth century during a period commonly known as "the Troubles" (1968–1998). However, as the post-conflict period is now more than two decades old, academic focus has shifted to the enduring problems of how conflict persists or has ongoing impacts on what is supposed to be a more normative society. Some of the major issues that have potential archaeological undercurrents include: How do we deal with the material boundaries created by enduring segregation and sectarianism? How can we live with material remnants from the conflict without overemphasizing them or, conversely, diminishing the experiences of the past? How can we explore contemporary Northern Ireland beyond the lens of two communities and with intersection beyond ethnicity, politics, and religion?

In the arena of civic politics, progress has been made in the post-conflict context even if it has been nonlinear, afflicted by setbacks, and at times in danger of complete derailment. This is especially the case with the destabilizing impact of Brexit since 2016 (Hayward 2017; Parr and Burke 2017) and with the long-term lack of a power-sharing government in Northern Ireland since early 2017 due to increasing tensions between the two main parties, the Democratic Unionist Party and Sinn Féin (Hain 2017). The focus of much of the recent academic analysis on high-level political crises, especially the perceived need (subsequent to Brexit) to explain Northern Ireland and its special constitutional status to a previously disinterested UK audience (see O'Toole 2018), has led to less of a focus on experiences at the everyday community level.

One notable remnant of the Troubles that has endured and proliferated in the peace process is the placement of separation barriers between the two communities in the form of peace walls. These structures are not inert walls placed to simply mark and bound properties, as in more normative societies; they are innately political and ideological (see Bishara, this volume). They were not designed into the landscape when the buildings and roads were put in place. Rather, they have been implanted at a later stage at the request of those who live alongside them in order to create separation (Community Relations Council 2009). At a subtle level, the concept of separation has been inserted into the urban built environment in Northern Ireland for decades via the replacement of traditional terraced housing with defensive cul-de-sacs, inertias, and major roads strategically placed to divide communities (Esposito De Vita, Trillo, and Martinez-Perez 2016). Peace walls, however, remain the most obvious materialization of separation. The most common form of peace wall is a monumental structure wedged into the interface between the two communities. However, these walls can also take the forms of landscaping, fencing, and/or facilitated dereliction, which are ambiguous and therefore have a wider impact than simply a monumental wall (McAtackney 2011; McWilliams, this volume). Clearly, enduring segregation and separation in post-conflict Belfast take material form—and are most complete—when they appear as monumental walls. But separation extends beyond the materially impassable into the psychologically impenetrable.

While material and psychic sectarian separation has persisted from the conflict into the official post-conflict city, the impacts of that segregation have changed since the Troubles ceased and society has embraced a post-conflict status. Twenty-first-century media attention has increasingly acknowledged that a negative repercussion of enduring divisions is the rise of other forms of intolerance, including racist, homophobic, and misogynistic attacks (e.g., Mercer 2014). These attacks most notably occur with the heightened tensions associated with the annual cycle of commemorative events in the summer months.

It was media reporting of the innovation of burning election posters of female candidates for the European elections (in 2014) on bonfires that prompted my investigation. I contend there is an enduring link between materialized segregation (especially peace walls) in parts of contemporary Belfast and the ability to create micro-communities that facilitate valorization of particular groups that reside within them. In this context, peace walls are not anachronistic symbols or materializations of sectarian separation associated with a previous conflict. Rather, these ideological walls have evolved in ways that have a contemporary context, and there has been little analysis or critique of their changing meanings. In particular, in this chapter I argue that walls facilitate very localized forms of place identity that allow partial memories of the past to be propagated by those who hold the power to materialize memory inside the communities created by walls. In post-conflict Belfast those in power are almost always men with long-standing connections to paramilitary organizations, and they were usually active during the conflict. They almost always remember themselves and their comrades and in doing so exclude or marginalize those whom they do not consider to have been actively involved. This includes those who were not resident during the Troubles, those who opposed the violence, and many of the women and children who were impacted by the conflict. The enduring presence of separation walls facilitates and propagates this practice.

Segregated Belfast: An Abridged History

The relative lack of wider social and academic engagement with the evolving, contemporary context of societal discord in Northern Ireland deserves critique. The acceptance that Northern Irish society is essentially a problem of two communities bound to a deep history of unfathomable antipathy means that conflict is considered ahistorical and essentially irresolvable (Vaughan-Williams 2006). Such an implicit assumption is not only deeply conservative but also lacks engagement with the temporal, spatial, and socioeconomic context of communities in Belfast today. It ignores the localized material realities of an increasingly divided city where separation has proliferated rather than dissipated since the official end of the conflict. By ignoring the contemporary context of Belfast, Troubles narratives dominate, and their assumptions are maintained. These narratives are almost always gender-blind since they tend to focus on men as military and political figures with agency: perpetrators of violence as well as statesmen who resolve it. Women and children, if they are referenced at all, are passive and victims (Murphy 2015). Conversely, this assumption also ignores that Belfast exists within a global context of what we label in this volume "walling in and walling out": a world of walls across various scales and arenas. Due to Belfast's long history of living with ideological walls, it can act as a warning to other cities on the long-term and unforeseen repercussions of erecting walls to separate, regardless of whether they are intended to separate in terms of politics, religion, or economics.

Before I consider how enduring material segregation impacts contemporary Belfast, a brief history of the city will explain how and why separation became segregation and how segregation took a material form. There are innumerable books written on Northern Ireland, on Belfast, on the history of the Troubles, and on why this low-level conflict occurred and continued for so long (e.g., Edwards and McGrattan 2010; Hennessy 2005; Mulholland 2002). This context is important, but the concentration on the Troubles without an analysis of the intersection with other facets of the city has unintentionally skewed our understandings of the past (and, by extension, the present). The emphasis of historians and political researchers on high-level politics and the acts of men of violence and their repercussions ensures a narrow understanding of the society and, therefore, how it potentially moves forward. The focus solely on sectarian conflict does not allow sufficient weight to be attached to other social, economic, and cultural factors that have fed into the contemporary city and how they continue to evolve and impact the present.

An archaeological lens can provide an alternative reading of Belfast. In 1613, the city's founder, Sir Arthur Chichester, conceived of Belfast as a place apart, a "loyal" city within a disloyal island. Urbanization was a central policy of the English Crown's colonial plantation of Ulster, and the planters intended the planned city of Belfast as a mercantile town (Horning 2013). Since the planned city took material form, it had defended, if unwalled, boundaries (unlike military cities, such as the walled settlement at Londonderry) that provided a spatial distinction between the loyal planter Scottish and English Protestants residing "inside" and the Gaelic-Irish Catholic populations who were initially only allowed to settle "outside." These divisions established Belfast as an officially planned segregated city. However, archaeological evidence reveals that the material reality of separation in Belfast was not as complete as the decrees declared and the boundaries proclaimed. Excavated artifacts show that the intermixing of "planter" and "native" material culture was common (Horning 2013). Furthermore, although distinctions existed between those who lived inside and those who resided outside the city, these fluctuated over time and only solidified with the influx of lowland Presbyterian Scots, who arrived in the city in the late eighteenth century. From this time on, the loyal subjects regarded the native Irish with suspicion, and the Irish were ghettoized (Boal 2002, 690). Boal (1994, 31) has convincingly argued that it was in this later period that Belfast took the form that is recognizable today: a materially divided and "polarized city."

The association of different communities with distinct areas of the city stems from this late eighteenth-century rearticulating of Belfast from a mercantile colonial plantation to an industrial imperial powerhouse. During the Industrial Revolution, Belfast was the center of the industrialized zone in the northeast of Ireland. It increasingly differentiated and isolated itself from the "rural peripheralization" of the more Catholic, "Irish," and agricultural areas beyond its immediate hinterlands (Cebulla and Smyth 1996, 40). Internally, the city also increasingly differentiated between the various workers in the large industrial manufacturers. In the shipbuilding industry, for example, the majority of employees were working-class Protestants (mainly self-identifying as loyalists) who resided close to the docks near the Newtownards Road in the east of the city. The connection between industrialization, segregation, and sectarianism was more complete for men than women. Indeed, the link between industrialization and segregation in Belfast was a predominantly male phenomenon, with owners and managers of shipyards and manufacturing plants often deciding to ensure that tensions remained low by employing predominantly Protestant workers (Cebulla and Smyth 1996). Some of the biggest industrial employers of women, such as Gallaher's cigarette factory, hired women from both Protestant and Catholic backgrounds despite the tensions that inevitably existed during troubled times (Multimedia Heritage n.d., 18). These differences had an impact on the geography of Belfast. The more complete sectarian segregation experienced by men, especially in relation to shipbuilding, shaped wider loyalist identity and their understandings of themselves and "industrial Belfast" as being both a male experience and entwined. As a result, the more transgressive experiences of loyalist women were sidelined and ignored.

The Government of Ireland Act (1920) created the state of Northern Ireland within the United Kingdom and constitutionally separate from the rest of Ireland. The partition of the island was a legal solution to the increasing spatial delineation of religious identity on the island—Catholic in the south, Protestant in the northeast. Partition legally enshrined the ability of the majorities in both parts of the island to maintain territorial control. In Northern Ireland, it facilitated the retention of political power (and economic prosperity) for loyalists in an economy they controlled, which focused on particular parts of the industrial city of Belfast and continued for many decades (Cebulla and Smyth 1996, 45). Hitherto, there has been a lack of academic research into how industry and conflict intertwined and shaped Belfast in various ways postpartition but also how this situation evolved. It is infrequently noted that those who benefited from industrialization the most—the loyalist urban working classes—have been most negatively economically impacted by its waning. Despite government grants to attract investment, deindustrialization hit Northern Ireland at the same time that it affected similar areas in the United Kingdom (Brownlow 2015). This experience of the Global North was just as decisive a factor in the relocation of international companies as the issues of civic conflict (Frey, Leuchinger, and Stutzer 2004, 17). Through most of the twentieth century, the shipbuilding, linen, manufacturing, and aeronautics industries in particular dramatically scaled down and ceased to be mass employers. While deindustrialization has occurred throughout the Global North, the peculiar form it has taken in Belfast—it has differentially impacted one community—reflects the sectarian nature of its development.

The advent of the Troubles around 1968 accelerated and heightened preexisting divisions in the industrial city and allowed segregation to take material form. Preexisting psychic divisions were increasingly materialized and solidified through the erection of peace walls. These monumental walls have taken a number of forms, making them hard to define in terms of materials, but they often have different planes of increasingly transparent elements up to four meters tall (McAtackney 2011). They first appeared to divide loyalist and nationalist West Belfast in the late 1960s (Mulholland 2002) and initially took the form of temporary barricades, which eventually transitioned to being permanent. In East Belfast, roads and walls act as sectarian interfaces and barriers that have psychic as well as physical implications. They act in a number of ways, which are both planned and have evolved over time. Those who live along community interfaces have increasingly withdrawn to *their* side of the road, and this has been facilitated by the Housing Executive, which allocates government-owned housing (figures from 1999 show almost 100 percent segregation of HE areas in Belfast;

Figure 4.1. Murals on the large peace wall that divides Falls Road and Shankill Road, Belfast. This is at Cupar Way on Shankill Road. Photo © Laura McAtackney, 2010.

Jarman and O'Halloran 2001, 4). Town planners have extended and added lanes to many of the major thoroughfares—including the Newtownards Road—to enhance the sense of separation. At Bryson Street off the Newtownards Road, the original row of terrace houses that marked the interface was bought by the Housing Executive in the 1970s so it could be demolished; a peace wall was constructed in its place.

All these official planning decisions have incrementally added to the creation of various forms and scales of micro-communities and enclaves in this area. The Newtownards Road is a predominantly Protestant, loyalist area, but within it is an enclave of mainly Catholic nationalists: approximately 3,500 people who live in Short Strand (Wainwright 2010). This nationalist community has continued to live close to the shipyards while being largely excluded from mass employment. At the micro-level, a one-street enclave—Cluan Place—persists within Short Strand. It is a highly decorated loyalist street that continues to defiantly remain behind monumental peace walls (figure 4.1).

The interconnections among deindustrialization, the residual impacts of sectarian conflict, and the more recent emergence of signifiers of intolerance demand fresh insights and new perspectives into the changing nature of identity and how it links to material segregation in contemporary Northern Ireland. Current interpretations that overfocus on the Troubles legacy do not consider how the maintenance and enhancement of walls created during the conflict not only continue to have impacts on sectarian identities but also intersect with other forms of identity to account for divergences in contemporary experiences across Belfast. Contemporary East Belfast can be read not only as a landscape of conflict but as a local manifestation of global experiences of the malaise of deindustrialization, which is being configured as an overwhelmingly loyalist and male experience articulated through murals and memorials.

Peace Walls and the Enduring Materiality
of Division in Northern Ireland

In contemporary Belfast, peace walls occupy an ambiguous place. They do not simply exist; they are monumental structures that are designed to separate and allow only sporadic and controlled physical interactions between those who live on either side of them. For those who do not live near them, they are unseen, and they are largely absent from maps. During the conflict, they played both positive and negative roles, but essentially they were situated to control movement and to create a sense of security and belonging for those who lived beside them. While walls play a significant role in directing the lived experiences of any city, they are particularly important in post-conflict but still divided cities, such as Belfast (see McWilliams, this volume, on Berlin). In those cities, security and belonging have heightened importance, and so walls have ideological meanings connected to separation that are not perceived as negative by local communities, especially for children who do not remember a time without walls (Wainwright 2010).

In most cities, walls are largely unseen because they perform normative roles: they define property and space (see Dinzey-Flores, this volume, for how these normative facades can be discriminatory). Their ubiquity ensures that people barely see them and consider them a mundane, commonplace, and unremark-able phenomenon. However, walls in divided cities fundamentally act as bar-riers. They shape access, and they can play a heightened role during conflict in channeling violence since they can become a focus for unleashing tensions (see Jarman and O'Halloran 2001). As well as having roles and meanings for the *other side* of the wall, they can also act as canvases to communicate opinions and maintain identity internally (especially through graffiti and Belfast's famed wall murals). Walls can have many enduring, evolving, latent, and even contradictory meanings, which can be activated or recede depending on circumstance. Therefore, there is a need to engage with temporality in discussions of Belfast's walls—not only to recognize changing community forms and intercommunity relationships but also to consider walls' changing role in a post-conflict society. When the threat of violence is largely absent, how do the meanings of walls change, and do they contribute to what Colin Knox (2016) has called "negative peace"?

Walls as barriers in a long-divided city like Belfast are often psychic as well as physical; the divisions are not located only in the monumental constructions. Dividing walls are infrequently complete: they often are built with room for expansion at either end, and most have doorways or openings (official or unofficial) that allow movement and the possibility of transgression. Despite their claims of monumentality, they are not static, and they are not impenetrable. Furthermore, they do not equally affect everyone who physically experiences them; one has to come from the communities that live around them to know what the rules are—and which to abide by or transgress—and to make a decision as to how to engage with them. While they are created as unambiguous means of controlling social interaction, they are not always obeyed. More insidiously, the long-term maintenance of walls that explicitly act as material barriers prohibits the development of understanding and empathy between near neighbors. They act to visually block the everyday experiences of similarly disadvantaged and conflict-torn communities from each other. The communities that live along these walls do not see and therefore do not know the issues, material realities, and critiques of those who live on the other side. This means that in times of relative peace, communities—or their self-appointed protectors—are left within the enclaves created by walls to proclaim their own identity and publicly commemorate as they see fit without comparative or external critique. This ensures that very particular and skewed views of the past develop, which alongside the othering of the hidden community on the other side allows misrepresentations of the past to be propagated. In the post-conflict context, I argue, the proliferation of community memorials alongside these walls is an important means of reading how communities engage with and reproduce their understandings of *their side* of the peace wall.

Memorialization, Commemoration, and Gender

Unofficial community memorials commemorating the Troubles are a growing phenomenon. They have proliferated in the shadows of peace walls, enabled by the relative isolation created by material separation. Micro-communities—or, more precisely, members of the ex-paramilitary groups that maintain control within those communities—design and place these memorials throughout their communities. They are most frequently found in working-class, urban areas of Northern Ireland (see Dinzey-Flores, this volume, for class walls in Puerto Rico). This phenomenon has been relatively underresearched in the context of the peace process (although see McDowell 2008; Graham and Whelan 2007; Viggiani 2006), however, it is clear the proliferation of unofficial community memorials follows global as well as local trends in materializing memory. Erika Doss, writing about the contemporary United States, has noted how memorialization is increasingly being used to remember a wide variety of people, events, and occasions. She argues that such actions are important because of their ability to "evoke memories, sustain thoughts, constitute political conditions and conjure states of being" (Doss 2010, 71). They are inherently political and reflect the power to materialize particular memories and claim certain narratives as representing the places where these memorials are located. As in the United States, community memorials to the Troubles at this point in the peace process cannot be disconnected from their wider context. In East Belfast, they cannot be separated from the enduring presence of peace walls.

In Northern Irish civic society, contentious aspects of "the past" (meaning the Troubles) continue to be deliberately bypassed at a political level, considered too difficult to confront without potentially reigniting conflict and reinforcing divisions (McGrattan 2009, 164). In the areas of Belfast most impacted by the conflict, which are also those most likely to have peace walls, the public is disengaged from the "authorized heritage discourse" (Smith 2006) of official museums and the decision to gloss over *their* past. Instead "the past" that is meaningful to these communities is remembered and materialized on the streets through memorials. Many of these memorials are placed against peace walls, or alongside them, tacitly confirming both the presence of barriers and their reason for existence. Community memorials act to remember the community they reside in; they do not aim to represent the past across sectarian divides. They are facilitated in this role by the peace walls, which keep out the eyes and potential critique from the other side. These memorials are not attempting to articulate the broad or representative history of the Troubles associated with official heritage; they aim to communicate very localized and often one-sided readings of the past. On the Newtownards Road in East Belfast, community memorials rematerialize aspects of the Troubles into the place where they are most meaningful. This gives them heightened effectiveness especially since those places most connected to the violence of the Troubles are often the interfaces now materialized by peace walls.

The creation of these memorials acts not only to present local narratives of what happened in the past but also to present hierarchies of who deserves to be remembered and what form this memory takes in a particular place. Memorials placed alongside peace walls in Belfast are made spatially significant because both the walls and memorials have often been implanted into places that were significantly relandscaped over the course of the conflict. This means that peace walls act as enduring materializations of memory for places that have otherwise been planned out of existence. These spatial and temporal connections to the Troubles can be important to local communities, especially at a time when peace walls are increasingly under threat due to the official desire to "normalize" the city. Due to the ambiguities surrounding their roles and meanings, they often evoke connections to lost lives, fear of change, and an enduring desire for security. These multiple and even contradictory meanings of peace walls have ensured that generations have grown up with what Bryonie Reid (2005, 489) has called "a psychology of spatial confinement" that is internally normalized. In this respect, the walls and their associated memorials reveal a disjuncture in experience and memory for different people in Belfast: they are a normal and everyday backdrop for the communities that have always lived beside them whereas they are an anomaly for those who grew up in places without peace walls and had a very different experience of the conflict (and peace). While the liberal press can deride the continued existence of peace walls as anachronistic from the safety of their broadsheet newspapers (e.g., Geoghegan 2015), those who live beside the walls can have different feelings. For those communities, the walls are often considered an enduring and necessary form of protection as well as a form of *lieux de memoire* of lost family and friends (Nora 1989).

Due to their form and placement, community memorials can reflect a complicated array of experiences and understandings — sectarian conflict and segregation but also deindustrialization, class, and gender. The latter connections are often overlooked in analyses of contemporary Belfast. Academic analysis tends to focus on studying the places most linked to sectarian violence, especially nationalist West Belfast (Viggiani 2006; McAtackney 2011, 2015), and on the narratives constructed by those who have created the memorials. Memorials tend to be analyzed by academics individually and hierarchically—with most attention given to them as stand-alone monuments with the biggest and most ornate and those at the most prominent locations discussed the most. They are often interpreted as articulating singular claims of victimhood and/or victories, and the nuances of presentation and absences are infrequently explored. Often unremarked are what is implicitly being claimed, what is deliberately or accidentally being omitted, the link of historic grievances to contemporary conditions, and the subtle interplay of the memorial with its wider landscape.

A close examination of community memorialization practices in contemporary East Belfast reveals complex and entangled narratives of place, identity, and conflict within the micro-community materially bounded by peace walls. The myriad of material forms and symbols that contributes to place identity in East Belfast is particularly varied, as evidenced in a report on the role of flags and emblems and how they are read by the wider public (Bryan et al. 2010). However, such reports do not explore the landscape in its fullest context. The tendency to focus on paramilitary or reimaged murals located on the gable ends of houses and the flags on streetlights ensures that the main thoroughfares are examined. But these analyses do not often venture into all of the aspects that make up the more convoluted landscape, which includes peace walls, community memorials, and council-funded public art on and alongside arterial roads. An even more holistic investigation of the many facets of identity reveals the importance of historic conflict, industrialization, and the experiences of the Troubles in creating an inward-looking place identity that is also unremittingly androcentric. Women's experiences and contributions to the area are excluded from almost all materializations of public memory on and around the Newtownards Road. The focus is firmly connected to a paternalistic view of men working in and protecting the enclosed area.

East Belfast: The Newtownards Road

The Newtownards Road in East Belfast links the unionist middle classes to the more neutral city center of Belfast via the Lagan River. The lower part of this road is a working-class and predominantly loyalist area, which has suffered in recent years due to deindustrialization. Peace walls abut the road on one side due to a small nationalist enclave (the aforementioned Short Strand area) located where the road meets the city center. Over the decades, clashes between the two communities have resulted in an almost complete separation by peace walls and road expansions. Only the small enclave of Cluan Place—a self-identifying loyalist street—breaks the separation as it continues to exist in walled isolation in the Short Strand area. The peace walls in this community continue to have multiple purposes: to separate both communities at all times, to protect the nationalist area from the wider loyalist community at times, and to separate and at times protect the one loyalist street from the enclosing nationalist area.

The Newtownards Road is important in the history of Belfast. It housed the industrial working classes that manned the shipbuilding, engineering, and aeronautical industries; they were predominantly loyalist and Protestant. Despite the negative impacts of deindustrialization, a nostalgic view of this past is emphasized in official heritage narratives, including a commissioned bronze sculpture of three men walking home from work from the Harland and Wolff shipyard. Local artist Ross Wilson created *Titanic Yardmen 401* as a high-profile and spatially significant addition to the urban landscape. The accompanying plaque refers to "East Belfast's shipbuilding force" and calls the sculpture "a tribute to their culture, life and legacy." Dedicated "to the memory of men who built giants" (figure 4.2), it has been placed on the loyalist side of the main road with the famous Harland and Wolff cranes as backdrop.

The Newtownards Road displays a variety of official and unofficial symbols and identity-affirming representations. Alongside sculptures such as *Titanic Yardmen 401* are street art, murals, and community memorials as well as flags and painted curbstones. These adornments, placed on or near walls, come from a number of sources, including the city council, the Housing Executive, private foundations, and paramilitary organizations. They jostle for recognition and attention in this busy streetscape. By examining the mix of official and unofficial forms, one can ascertain hierarchies of importance. Of those placed alongside the arterial road, some official examples have been retained and even maintained over the long term and are evidently accepted by the local communities. (This is not always the case with reimaging mural projects or the insertion of public art sculpture; Crowley 2011.) However, reading the Newtownards Road as a wider landscape, it is clear that the narratives of public art initiatives are not uncontested. They compete with unofficial graffiti, murals, flags, and memorials, which create their own sense of community identity as bounded by the surrounding

Figure 4.2. *Titanic Yardmen 401* by Ross Wilson. These three bronze statues depict men leaving the shipyards in East Belfast. The artwork was unveiled in time for the centenary of the sinking of the HMS *Titanic* in 2012. Photo © Laura McAtackney, 2013.

peace walls. The public art wall murals and sculptures on Newtownards Road largely address two themes: the *Titanic* (the famous ship that sank on its maiden voyage in 1912) and the Battle of the Somme, a major battle of World War I. Due to the number of men from the province who died at the Somme, it is considered a foundational act of the Northern Irish state (Jeffrey 2011).

The *Titanic* became an increasingly popular motif in East Belfast in the run-up to the centenary of its sinking in 2012. Harland and Wolff had built the ship, and so the centenary was viewed by the city council as both a potential tourist attraction and as a nonsectarian symbol for the still materially segregated area. The *Titanic* murals and sculptures that have been implanted on the New-townards Road by the city council tie in with evolving processes of post-conflict place making in Northern Ireland. They are not simply random diversions from previous sectarian images; they attempt to meaningfully reconfigure place meaning by referencing preexisting associations of place. Whereas the *Titanic* may seem an unlikely identity-affirming symbol more than a hundred years after its sinking, it has been deployed as a means of articulating a broader nonsectarian identity for Belfast and, more specifically, the loyalist working classes of East Belfast. The negative aspects of its wider associations—the obvious significant loss of life, the historic sectarianism at the shipyard, the lack of representation of women in choosing such a subject, and the impact of deindustrialization on the area—have been largely ignored. In this context, the *Titanic* memorializes a proud industrial heritage, but it also unintentionally reinforces feelings of lost male supremacy, which loyalist working classes connect with the terminal decline of the nearby shipyards. It also excludes women from the "authorized heritage discourse" of the area (Smith 2006). These messages are writ large due to the nature of the built environment, and the material divisions of the monumental walls that project this identifier ever larger to the micro-community.

The implicitly androcentric nature of official place making is even more problematic when one engages with the wider context of the loyalist community on the Newtownards Road. The unofficial symbols and identifiers that reside alongside the *Titanic* are almost completely overtly paramilitary and masculine. Examined holistically, the *Titanic* represents a minority theme on the Newtownards Road, and therefore its real impact on place making is questionable. The majority of murals and memorials that abut this road and line its associated peace walls reference contemporary paramilitary organizations, commemorate the dead from these groups, or revere their historical predecessors back to World War I (see McAtackney 2017). This saturation of paramilitary imagery, symbolism, and material memory is particularly notable because it reflects enduring contemporary paramilitary activities and competition in this community (McDonald 2017).

The contemporary nature of the memorials means they not only are commemorating past actions and events, but they are used as a means of reflecting the ongoing jostling for position among the paramilitary hierarchies in the area. As the official membership of loyalist paramilitary organizations is exclusively male, this means their murals and memorials are unremittingly masculine in character. The murals are highly elaborate, colorful, and monumental. They engulf the reimaged *Titanic* murals and sculptures in the wider landscape setting and neutralize their attempts at place making. Following Bryan and colleagues (2010), the Newtownards Road, in particular, is a place where the wider public perceives murals, memorials, and flags as explicitly linking to contemporary paramilitary activity. The symbols, identifiers, and images—even if not explicitly paramilitary in subject—are viewed as territorial markers due to the saturation of similar symbols in a bounded and relatively contained space.

Moving on to community memorials, there are at least half a dozen memorials located in close proximity to the Newtownards Road and its associated peace walls. These memorials originate from different organizations and commemorate different aspects of the past, with some more directly related to sectarian conflict. They have strong material similarities (they are often brick structures with gates and metal railings), and they universally represent men's perspectives and experiences. Alongside memorials dedicated to Ulster's war dead from World War I—who are presented as ancestors of the contemporary community and by implication as their contemporary "defenders"—are memorials for loyalist paramilitary organizations and their exclusively male members. Memorial gardens to both the Ulster Defence Association and the Red Hand Commandos have been placed in side streets that are physically and visually accessible from the Newtownards Road. These memorials display similarities: they both take the form of monumental structures placed within walled environments with metal railings around the periphery to allow visual, if not physical, access at all times. The gates of the memorials are padlocked, presumably by the organizations they commemorate, ensuring that they act as exclusive spaces. Plaques with paramilitary insignia and lists of local members who died during the Troubles adorn the memorials (figure 4.3). In contrast to many of the republican memorials of the Troubles that remember civilians (McAtackney 2011), the memorials in East Belfast exclusively commemorate active combatants from paramilitary organizations from their micro-community. They are all men. Women are completely excluded from the public memory of the conflict. Peace walls in this location enable singular, particular, and partial representations of the past that exclude not only external perspectives but also internal noncombatants.

In contrast, nationalist working-class areas and the more neutral areas of the city center have been particularly careful to include women's experiences in both public art and community interpretations of the past. There are many reasons for the differences in experience and representation of identity in loyalist and nationalist areas—too many to discuss in this chapter—but the most obvious difference is that women were not excluded from being combatants on the nationalist side (see Bishara, this volume, for the role of women in Palestinian resistance). While nationalist memorials still overfocus on the (predominantly male) paramilitary dead from their areas (although civilian dead, especially women and children, from the communities are often included on memorials), the roles and experiences of women have been consciously included. For example, for the centenary of the Easter Rising (1916), a foundational event for

Figure 4.3. Community memorial in East Belfast (located in a side street off the Newtownards Road) for the Red Hand Commandos. Photo © Laura McAtackney, 2013.

nationalists in Ireland, women were strongly represented in the posters, flyers, and murals in nationalist West Belfast. Beyond the built environment, there were also events that allowed the sharing of individual stories and the inclusion of women in communal commemorations. Indeed, there was a conscious attempt during the Easter Rising commemorations to locate previously sidelined historical women. This included the representation of the Corr sisters (Morrison 2016) and Winifred Carney (McCormack 2016), women who were absent from murals and public memory before the 2016 Easter Rising commemorations.

The large mural of Countess Constance de Markievicz (long the only named republican woman who adorned a significant mural site in West Belfast) near the Falls Road and Whiterock Road intersection was replaced by a large composite mural of Mná na hÉireann (Women of Ireland in Gaeilge), which includes a number of historical and contemporary women. This attempt to insert women's experiences into the Easter Rising commemorations for a distinctly local Belfast audience followed the creation of a mural (still intact) dating from 2014 at the junction of Falls Road with Beechmount Avenue. This mural celebrates Cumann

Figure 4.4. Wall mural of Constance de Markievicz at the junction of Falls Road and Beechmount Avenue in nationalist West Belfast. Photo © Laura McAtackney, 2016.

na mBan (Group [or Council] of Women in Gaeilge), the women's organiza-tion that was militarily involved in the Easter Rising. The mural foregrounds Markievicz on the left side with the women of Cumann na mBan from the later Troubles (1968–1998) on the right (figure 4.4). Of course, critique can be made of the mural's construction and content (with the ubiquitous Markievicz in front of the faceless rank-and-file women; McAtackney 2018), but at the very least these murals reveal a number of women being implanted into public memory in significant spaces in working-class nationalist areas. In contrast, there was no significant input of female figures in the painted memorial landscapes of the Newtownards Road in the summer of 2016, whether connected to the Battle of the Somme, loyalist paramilitaries from the Troubles, or the *Titanic*.

Dealing with the Past and Heritage in Contemporary Belfast

The issue of "dealing with the past" in Northern Ireland remains sidelined despite the region being almost twenty years into a peace process. It has become clear that Northern Ireland as a society is on a dual track: it is officially a post-conflict state attempting to move forward while dealing with difficult legacy issues, such as defining victims, while at the grassroots level communities are left to articulate their identities on the street and away from sanitized, authorized heritage discourse. Within segregated communities, this means the past is being re-remembered in highly localized and selective ways. While official heritage institutions, such as the Ulster Museum, have been critiqued for avoiding representations of difficult or contentious issues of the past (Jones 2010), communities are creating and living alongside self-selected representations of "their" past in materially segregated isolation.

Against this backdrop, community memorials in East Belfast are important for a number of reasons. For the community, they have a significant role in filling the official vacuum that has arisen from politicians and civil society bypassing the difficult issues from the conflict. They are often monumental, highly public, in spatially significant locations, embedded in their communities, and situated alongside materialized divisions that have allowed partial histories to be articulated without criticism. These memorials are at a considerable physical and conceptual distance from the sanitized official heritage. Furthermore, these bottom-up memorialization practices are not discrete entities. They are constituent parts of what are becoming memorialscapes. They reveal that public memory remains sharply divided as they both reflect and sustain material barriers that ignore and bypass potential "shared" histories. In contemporary Northern Ireland, public memory is being unofficially curated in an echo chamber with enduring peace walls facilitating it. Finally, these memorials and their concentration on dealing with the past that has been bypassed by official heritage are implicitly androcentric and tend to emphasize stereotypical gender roles in their focus on war and their attempts to articulate the connection of the (male) individual to the nation (McDowell 2008).

Conclusions

Exploring manifestations of public memory in East Belfast reveals materialized segregation in the form of walls that demarcate more than land. Despite being more than twenty years post-conflict, peace walls continue to stand, but their roles and meanings have evolved. In contemporary East Belfast, peace walls act not only to prevent violent interactions but to facilitate the creation of memorialscapes that remember only local, male combatants. In such micro-communities there is no place for intersectional identities or complicated, layered histories. At the same time, public art and unofficial murals attempt to counter paramilitary symbols by celebrating historical industries without considering how this also acts to exclude women's experiences and deny the impacts of deindustrialization. This situation means that when one reads the Newtownards Road in East Belfast as a place, there are mixed messages, but essentially it communicates an aggressively male place identity that is being further enforced.

Examining community memorials in Belfast reveals that there are differences in how working-class communities remember, which is facilitated, as well as determined, by the material barriers between them. These differences are impacted as much by misguided official policy as by unofficial community dynamics and claims on space. They are the result of the economic problems of postindustrialization as experienced in the Global North and of the particularities of post-conflict experiences in Northern Ireland. Therefore, despite the unique issues Belfast faces, it does provide an important warning to cities that wish to materialize their divisions: once walls are erected for long periods of time, they become more difficult to bring down, and the psychic divisions can remain (see McWilliams, this volume). The repercussions of such barriers are not always foreseen. Clearly, in Belfast there is not just one form of working-class, inner-city, post-conflict community surrounded by peace walls and remembering "their past" in isolation. Through analyzing the collection of community memorials, murals, and public art on Newtownards Road, we can see clear attempts to manipulate and direct who is remembered. Official public art projects promote largely unreflexive memories of past industrial glory whereas unofficial murals and memorials maintain claims of authority through reinforcing an enduring paramilitary identity. Neither considers women worthy of public commemoration.

In order to address these negative and problematic materializations of identity on the ground, there is a need to move beyond the blinkered focus on the Troubles and androcentric experiences, which peace walls have facilitated. Instead, we must broadly conceive the various associations and impacts of class, gender, and other experiences and publicly question how enduring materialized segregation allows partial views of the past to emerge and remain unchallenged. Ultimately, we need to ask not only why there are no women in public memory in East Belfast, but how can we open up what the past means, and continues to mean, so that we can begin to find other ways and forms to remember?

CHAPTER FIVE

An Ongoing Violence, a Sustained Resistance

Israel's Racist Separation Wall at Aida Refugee Camp

AMAHL BISHARA

While building the wall in Aida Refugee Camp, Palestine, took Israel's soldiers and contractors years of intermittent work during the day, piercing the wall took young Palestinians weeks of clandestine work at night just a few years later. Palestinians living in Aida Camp used drills and fire to physically puncture the eight-meter-high concrete wall. They saw their efforts as a fitting response to the violence of the wall that has confined them and dramatically militarized their community. After so many decades of Israeli military occupation, the wall made visible in a new way the carceral and necropolitical workings of that occupation. In turn, Palestinians' demonstrations drew on Palestinian traditions of popular protest—direct, unarmed confrontations with the army—to make visible and tangible their opposition to the wall and its violence.

In her book *Walled States, Waning Sovereignty* (2010), Wendy Brown analyzes the recent spate of state-constructed walls as props to sovereignty, questioning why they are so popular when they do not effectively stop people's movement. She asserts that wall building in a wide variety of contexts, including in the Palestinian West Bank, should be considered "a single historical phenomenon, despite their formally disparate purposes and effects" (Brown 2010, 26). Walls are part of a symbolic and material infrastructure upholding the fiction of the nation-state, she writes, since this fiction has been "severely compromised by growing transnational flows of capital, people, ideas, goods, violence, and political and religious fealty" (22). Her argument that walls "constitute a spectacular screen for fantasies of restored sovereign potency and national purity" (9) is consistent with arguments that sovereignty is often imagined (Hansen and Stepputat 2001), though Brown is focused more on what she sees as sovereignty in decline rather than on its necessarily imagined qualities.

It is certainly worthwhile to consider the ideological and material work of such walls as interrelated and to conduct a comparative analysis of walls as a way of investigating the role walls play in contemporary sovereignties (see Jones, this volume). It is also essential to ground an analysis of such walls in their material qualities and to investigate how they operate in specific locations (see Dinzey-Flores, McWilliams, and McAtackney, all this volume). With this approach, one can consider what kind of sovereignty walls uphold. Is it the neutral sense of a normalized nation-state, or is it sovereignty as "the power and capacity to dictate who may live and who must die," in Achille Mbembe's (2003, 11) words (building on Michel Foucault)? Israel's wall may not stop movement entirely, but it does have deeply material effects, including confining Palestinians to ever-smaller pieces of land and militarizing Palestinian space. The wall materializes the violence of Israel's rule in a spectacular and solid form. This becomes especially clear when the wall is analyzed from the perspectives of people living closest to it, like the residents of Aida Refugee Camp.

The Racial Logic of Building a Wall

In 2002, Israeli prime minister Ariel Sharon announced that Israel would build a barrier in the West Bank, ostensibly to prevent Palestinian attackers from entering Israel. The argument that the barrier was about Israeli security is part and parcel of a prevailing logic of security that is a dominant discourse in Israel (Ochs 2011) and increasingly around the world (Goldstein 2010; Vallet 2014). The idea of a West Bank barrier had been floated years earlier by Prime Minister Ehud Barak. Sharon and others on the Israeli right wing had initially been against the plan because it seemed to suggest giving up territory. This politics may be one reason that the Palestinian Authority (PA) was initially so subdued in its opposition to the idea. It seemed in some way consistent with the PA's goal of a two-state solution, in that it separated out an area for Palestinians, however fragmented. As the barrier has been built, it indeed has materialized the "politics of separation" that is very popular among Israelis (Weizman 2007, 162), but it does not do so in a way that has promoted Palestinian statehood. In fact, a 2004 International Court of Justice decision declared the wall illegal under international law because it compromises the Palestinians' right to self-determination (Falk 2005; Shi 2004).

Instead the barrier has entrenched Israeli settler colonialism and its related racial logic. Israel's wall is consistent with other Israeli policies of confining Palestinians (Pappé 2017). Indeed, a scholar of settler colonialism, Patrick Wolfe, observes that Israel's wall is quintessentially an instrument for the elimination of the native, and specifically it is a technology for warehousing surplus populations. He writes, "There could hardly be a more concrete expression of spatial sequestration than the West Bank barrier" (Wolfe 2006, 404). Israeli authorities have constructed the wall in a manner that at once fragments Palestinian territory and maintains Israeli sovereignty over the entire West Bank. This strategy advances a right-wing vision of a perpetual Israeli presence because 85 percent of the wall is built not on the Green Line, which divides Israel and the West Bank, but instead well inside the West Bank. The final path of the wall will leave 9.5 percent of the land of the West Bank on the western, or Israeli, side of the wall (B'Tselem 2017). When complete, the wall will be 709 kilometers long, more than twice the length of the Green Line. The wall undermines Palestinians' access to agricultural land and water and cuts off access to schools and hospitals (OCHA 2013), and thus continues Israeli policies of pressuring Palestinians to leave their homes and give up their lands.

As Sari Hanafi (2009) sees it, Israel uses various tactics to dispossess, occupy, and destroy Palestinian living space, and the wall is part of this project of what he calls "spacio-cide." Rema Hammami (2010, 33) writes about the immediate and long-term effects of Israel's wall as part of Israel's system of closure:

> Movement, itself, has become central in the struggle between Palestinian survival and Israeli domination. . . . The system of spatial control is not simply about controlling and containing resistance but is primarily a mechanism of disinheritance. It both enforces inequality and attempts to make it permanent by creating the means to defer and detour around what is necessary to end the conflict. That is to say, it has made a two state solution based on the 1967 armistice lines, a geographic impossibility. Instead, it relegates Palestinians to a series of disconnected ghettoes, locked behind high walls[,] unable to make sustainable livelihoods in the present and unable to foresee a viable and independent national future.

In short, the wall is an instrument of confinement and dispossession of Palestinians both individually and collectively.

An anthropology of policy sets the state's assertions of policy and various theoretical perspectives in dialogue with the perspectives of those upon whom policies are enacted (Tate 2015). An ethnographic and materialist approach to a phenomenon like the wall pays attention to the conceptual unity of the wall, but also it attends to the local specificities of lives lived in the shadow of the wall (see Dinzey-Flores, this volume). A close ethnography of one location is important because it allows us to home in on the specificity of the barrier's material qualities and also to examine the newer effects of the wall in relationship to the long-standing system of military occupation. It can highlight how the wall is perceived by those who live closest to it: as a violence inflicted upon them, as a way of treating them only as threats to be neutralized, cordoned off, or made invisible rather than as people to be consulted. Indeed, in this sense the wall is a material analogue to military occupation itself. An anthropological perspective allows us to investigate Palestinians' responses to and theorizations of the wall in terms of the embodied dimensions of lives lived next to it and also in terms of popular action in response to it.

A first step toward centering Palestinians' experiences and the materiality of the barrier is to consider the terminology used to describe it, especially since this has been a subject of some controversy over the years (see McGuire and McAtackney on fence versus wall, and McAtackney on Northern Irish peace walls, both this volume). The barrier is no neutral, two-dimensional piece of infrastructure. It includes access roads, coils of barbed wire, and military watchtowers. It runs as fences over hills and through farmland of the West Bank—and near Palestinian towns, cities, and refugee camps, it is usually a concrete wall, often eight meters high. This is one reason that Palestinians refuse the term "security fence," which Israeli officials prefer to use as they defend the barrier. It is hardly designed to offer Palestinians security, and Palestinians experience it most directly as a wall. The term "barrier" is useful in its open-endedness, encompassing the fact that it is more than just a wall. Yet the word lacks affective and political weight. The term that Palestinians in Aida and elsewhere often prefer is *al-jidār al-faṣl al-ʿunṣuri*: the racist separation wall. In this chapter, I use both "barrier" and "wall," though I always refer to the parts of the structure that are made of concrete as a "wall." I aim to clarify some of the reasons that the wall is considered to be an instrument of racist separation by those who live with it.

Aida Refugee Camp

Aida Refugee Camp has an official population of 3,150 (many residents believe this to be an undercount; UNRWA n.d.) and is located on the northern edge of Bethlehem. The families of these refugees originally lived in villages in the western Jerusalem and western Hebron areas, many of which are just a twenty-minute drive away inside what is now Israel. Villagers were dispossessed of these lands in 1948, and Israel has never allowed them to return. Aida Camp was established by the United Nations Relief and Works Agency in 1950. For years, refugees lived in tents. By the mid-1950s, UNRWA provided families with concrete rooms and small plots of land. In the decades that followed, residents built larger homes around or in place of these rooms. The camp gradually grew more and more permanent, with electricity, a sewage network, and piped water. As families grew, they enclosed the small plots of land and narrowed the streets. They also built story on top of story to accommodate new generations, since many Palestinians prefer to have the families of their married sons continue to live close by. Throughout these changes, the camp remained distinct—both socially and physically—from areas around it (see Papadopoulos, this volume, for a similar discussion of a refugee camp in Greece). Some residents of Bethlehem have regarded it as something like a ghetto. For many of Aida's residents, its status as a refugee camp has continued to be an important marker of their history and an integral site from which to claim their collective rights as refugees to return to their pre-1948 villages. Aida's residents are also proud of their strong local tradition of resisting Israeli occupation.

Aida Camp has witnessed several political transformations since its establishment. After the 1948 war, the West Bank was under Jordanian rule until the 1967 war, when Israeli military occupation began. By the 1980s Aida, like other refugee camps, was a site of frequent resistance to Israeli rule; confrontation only intensified during the first Intifada (1987–1993), a mostly unarmed resistance in the tradition of "popular uprising" (*intifāḍa shaʿbiyya*) throughout the occupied territories of the West Bank and Gaza Strip. Following the establishment of the PA in 1994, Israeli troops redeployed to the edge of Bethlehem in 1995, and the PA took over the administration of many internal matters, while UNRWA continued to have responsibility for services like primary education and trash collection in Aida Camp. During the second Intifada, which started in 2000, Aida Camp again became a center of resistance. Because of Aida's location on the edge of the city, its residents experienced intense attacks from the Israeli army. UNRWA reported that Israel destroyed twenty-nine houses during this period. Israel also badly damaged an UNRWA school in the camp. As Israeli closures of the West Bank intensified (Berda 2017; Hass 2002; Peteet 2017), unemployment in Aida skyrocketed to 43 percent (UNRWA n.d.). Yet through it all, families continued to grow. According to UNRWA statistics, 60 percent of residents are under the age of twenty-four.

I have been spending time and doing fieldwork in Aida Refugee Camp since the fall of 2003, when I began volunteering in a local community-based organization. As I walked through the camp in the early years of my fieldwork, it seemed that nearly every house needed or had recently undergone repair, whether of broken windows or bullet holes that had pierced walls or water tanks. Since then, much of this damage has been repaired, and families have continued to add to their houses to accommodate new generations. Aida Refugee Camp has become a second home while I am conducting research, the place where I experience the day-to-day flow of events and daily forms of Israeli violence.

I had recently returned from a field trip when in November 2012, Palestinian protests against an Israeli attack on Gaza began. I followed events in Aida closely, especially since even when protests waned in the rest of the West Bank, they continued in Aida. Over the next several months, I gleaned information from Facebook, stayed in touch with friends through phone and text, and conducted phone interviews. Facebook was thus both a way for me to follow events from afar and a subject for analysis, though I address the latter dimension less in this chapter. I also conducted interviews on the movement against the wall, especially in the summer of 2013, and did participant observation over several subsequent summers.

The Violence of Construction and of the Wall Itself

Infrastructure, writes Brian Larkin (2013, 335), is "the means by which a state proffers . . . representations to its citizens and asks them to take those representations as social facts." Infrastructure is inextricable from violence. In Aida, the violence of the wall was evident to residents from the first days of its construction, since the start of construction was inextricable from an Israeli military invasion of Bethlehem. On April 1, 2002, the Israeli military surrounded the city. Many tanks then entered through Aida. At the time, there was nothing but

Figure 5.1. The wall under construction near Aida Refugee Camp.
Photo by Amahl Bishara, 2004.

a field of olive trees and a bypass road separating Aida Camp from the nearby
Israeli settlement of Gilo, which is today home to about 40,000 people. During
the 2002 invasion, residents recall, with Aida under an extended Israeli curfew,
the army unfurled coils of barbed wire in triplicate down the middle of the field
that separates Aida Camp from the Israeli bypass road, which is known as the
Tunnel Road (Weizman 2007, 181). This road is notorious among Palestinians
because it runs under and through the Palestinian town of Beit Jala, but Palestinians are not allowed to travel on it. On April 14, Sharon announced his plan
to build the wall, although nothing happened for some months. Soon, though,
it became evident that the path of the barbed wire was to become the path of the
wall. That path would have been about 100 meters from the houses of the camp.

Construction ensued in fits and starts (figure 5.1) because Palestinian youths
immediately protested with stone-throwing demonstrations that halted work on
several occasions. A court case raised by the owner of the land on which the wall
was being built also stalled construction. Still, it always resumed. The process
of construction intensified the militarization of space around the camp. By day,
Israeli soldiers and contractors dug holes and erected the wall, panel by panel.
By night, the army arrested teens who protested the wall, raiding homes in the
middle of the night (Bishara and Al-Azraq 2010; Cook, Hanieh, and Kay 2004,

Figure 5.2. The minaret of Aida Camp's mosque can be seen above the separation wall. In front of the wall is the olive grove to which residents lost access. Photo by Amahl Bishara, 2015.

31, 52). As one youth commented from a balcony that overlooked the new wall, "Our whole generation is in prison" (Bishara and Al-Azraq 2010). Both in tours that I watched Aida Camp residents give to visiting political tourists and in less formal settings, people spoke of how, with the new wall being built, imprisonment meant simply moving from the larger prison of Aida to a smaller one. This popular theorization joins other critiques of the blurred boundary between the "inside" and "outside" of prisons and of the relationships among imprisonment, walls, and racialized settler colonialism (Hernandez 2017; Loyd, Mitchelson, and Burridge 2012; Pappé 2017; Turner 2016; Wacquant 2001).

Israeli authorities proceeded to construct the wall on a path much closer to the camp than those initial coils of barbed wire had been. They built it just ten meters from houses of the camp. This happened without any consultation or direct informing of residents of the camp. Though Aida's residents did not own the land next to the camp, it had always been significant to them (figure 5.2). Camp residents often recall that the name of their community is linked to that land. Aida, it is said, was the name of a woman who ran a coffee shop on that land in the early years of the camp—and it also means "one who will return"

(*'Aida*), a profound name for a refugee camp. Over the decades and through the early 2000s, that land was not only a means of passage into Jerusalem but also an escape from the throng of the camp. Some people remembered studying there when electricity was weak or a house was too crowded with siblings. Others remembered playing soccer there. Many people had memories of picking olives on that land as hired labor. In villages like Beit Sourik and Bil'in, residents raised court cases and built vibrant popular movements around the cost of losing agricultural land to the wall. In contrast, the refugees of Aida did not legally own the land that they lost to the wall, so they had no such route for appeal. Nevertheless, they regarded it as an important public space for the community as well as part of the Palestinian homeland. Yet their emotional and practical connections to the land were even less important to Israeli authorities than was Palestinian property ownership.

The wall shifted in the vicinity of Aida to incorporate into its structure the contested holy site known as the Bilal bin Rabah mosque (and generally referred to by Aida's residents as *qabar raḥīl*, Rachel's Tomb), a site dating back to the fourth century CE (Bowman 2013). For decades, this site had also been a small Israeli military installation. This shrine, believed by many to be the burial place of the biblical matriarch Rachel, is on the northern outskirts of Bethlehem, perhaps 100 meters from Aida Camp. The shift allowed Jewish worshippers to enter Bethlehem while staying on the Israeli side of the wall (Weizman 2007, 169). The enclosure of the site, which had once been the location of intercommunal Jewish, Muslim, and Christian religious practices (Bowman 2013), further cut off Aida Camp from the main entrance to the city and from an important and once bustling neighborhood. Even worse, Rachel's Tomb became an entrenched and expanded Israeli military base, with a watchtower overlooking the camp, a gate used by soldiers to enter to harass or arrest residents, a space for short-term detentions, and a storage area for military vehicles. Such is the palimpsest of religious, national, and military layers in contemporary Zionism.

The wall, it was clear to residents from these beginnings, was no neutral technology of separation. It was an aggressive military structure, initiated during a major military invasion, and constructed under what amounted to a prolonged military operation. Simultaneously with the construction of the wall, Palestinians could see cranes behind it, building houses in the neighboring settlement of Gilo. Camp residents saw that their happiness and well-being were utterly inconsequential to the state, which was so profoundly changing the landscape of their community. While the wall was under construction, Palestinians in Aida sensed that Israeli officials saw Palestinians as objects or threats to be immobilized or defused, but never as people to be consulted. Viewing Palestinians as subordinate subjects to be ruled or managed, rather than as citizens to be consulted (see Dorsey and Díaz-Barriga, this volume, on the US context), is of course at the heart of Israel's project of military occupation.

By 2005 the wall around Aida was complete. The wall—eight meters high and made of gray concrete, with an army road on the side not visible to Aida—abuts two sides of Aida. Embedded into the wall are one full military base and about five watchtowers. Coils of barbed wire top the wall, especially around the watchtowers. By then, it was already plastered with a riot of graffiti and murals. Some referred to Bethlehem in the language of Christmas carols ("oh little town"), some were colorful imaginations of alternatives to this architecture of segregation. But Palestinian opinion was already beginning to solidify against murals that beautified the wall, with many activists saying they preferred to work for the destruction of the wall, rather than to adorn it (Bishara 2013). This opposition to painting the wall stands in contrast to the many murals that are found on peace walls in Belfast (McAtackney, this volume), the Berlin Wall (McWilliams, this volume), and the US-México border wall (Dear, this volume).

For me, one mark on the wall near Bethlehem stood out: a great black-and-white mark, perhaps four meters wide and extending to the full height of the wall (figure 5.3). The black was from tires burned next to the wall in 2005, and the white was from paint thrown at it in the months after. Such fires serve the purpose of shielding protesters. Lit immediately next to the watchtower, as these were, the fires would have blocked the views of the soldiers on guard and made their post very uncomfortable. The point of the fires was not, then, to leave the mark or, at that stage, to destroy the wall, but rather to play a strategic role in the protests.

Yet the mark became significant, a giant reminder—perhaps even a promise—of resistance that one did not need to read Arabic to understand. In Peircean terms, it was an index of resistance, a sign that signifies because of its physical relationship to what it represents (Peirce 1985). Writing the conclusion to my book in early 2012, I noted that this mark was "an eloquent and fitting way to express [residents'] rejection" of the wall (Bishara 2013, 249). It answered in kind the wordless and violent way in which the wall had been built and its violent effects on Palestinian life in Aida. The mark remained long after the protests

Figure 5.3. The black mark of protest on the wall near Aida Refugee Camp, as seen from the rooftop of a nearby house. Photo by Nidal Al-Azraq, 2009.

ended, layered later with a huge mural of a boy throwing a stone. The mark was located at the point at which the wall was closest to the houses of Aida. Only a street and a narrow space that was, at the time, a small garbage dump separated the watchtower from the multistory houses of the camp. Every day, residents of Aida saw the mark, and probably Israeli soldiers did too.

The wall has had profound effects on camp residents. Lost is any sense of open space and access to Jerusalem. Residents of the camp who have always felt a social isolation from Bethlehem are now more spatially isolated from it as well. People sense when they are in the sight lines of the watchtowers: when they are walking home from school or work, or even if they are sitting on a patio or next to a window. These sight lines enable something other than a simple Foucauldian panoptic surveillance (Foucault 1975). In the Foucauldian model of the panopticon, camp residents might expect that their compliance would prevent punishment meted out from a site of surveillance. Instead, Israeli soldiers inflict violence capriciously, knowing that they face little risk of punishment if they err (Amnesty International 2014). We can think of this instead through the lens of necropolitics (Mbembe 2003), a politics of sovereignty revolving around the state's ability to kill. For example, on December 8, 2006, soon after the wall was completed, Miras Al-Azza, a twelve-year-old boy playing with his cousins on their balcony, was shot in the stomach with live ammunition on an otherwise completely calm afternoon (Al-Azza 2016). Perhaps soldiers had mistaken a play gun for a real one and shot him. Perhaps, as some camp residents suggested, they just regarded violence against Palestinians to be a kind of a game, and they did not care whether the gun was a toy. No soldier was held accountable for the injury. The wall and its watchtowers transformed even domestic spaces into potential sites for military violence.

For many years after the construction of the wall, the protest movement was in a hiatus in Aida. Many people later explained this as being a result of the wave of arrests in 2005, which left youths in prison for months or years (Cook, Hanieh, and Kay 2004). After their release, many faced additional years of suspended sentences that would return them to prison for any infraction. The periodic presence of PA forces also limited popular protest. By late 2012, the situation felt grim. Despite the positive ruling against the wall from the International Court of Justice, Palestinians saw no changes on the ground. Everyone in Aida, young and old, noticed the many delegations of international visitors who came to see the wall, bearing witness to its violence—and yet, they also saw, none of this made a difference.

Traditions of Resistance

Popular politics have a long and rich history in the Middle East (Chalcraft 2016). Stone throwing and tire burning are by no means distinct to Palestinians, but Palestinians name them as part of their heritage of popular resistance (*muqāwima sha'biyya*). We can think of this opposition as part of what Charles Tilly (2006) calls a "repertoire of contention," a mode of resistance that has a specific cultural history and is also cultivated in relationship to a particular regime. Popular resistance is part of a Palestinian repertoire of contention that dates back many decades to even before the popular revolt of 1936–1939 (Anderson 2017; Banko 2016; Bishara 2010; Collins 2004; Lockman and Beinin 1989; Swedenburg 1995). For Palestinians it indexes the asymmetry of colonial rule, because it pits Palestinians armed only with homemade weapons, like slingshots, against well-armed colonial police or soldiers. It is performative in that it makes visible relations of power that Palestinians experience across all realms of life.

Popular resistance famously propelled the Palestinians of the occupied territories into the center of the Palestinian struggle and onto global television screens during the first Palestinian Intifada (1987–1993) (Lockman and Beinin

1989). Yet the establishment of the PA in 1994 led to a hollowing out of Palestinian civil society, as the new authority consolidated power. The "NGOification" of the occupied territories and the entrenchment of a donor economy and donor politics also sidelined the possibility of popular resistance (Alazzeh 2014; Hanafi and Tabar 2005). For various reasons, Palestinian resistance during the second Intifada (2000–2005) was more armed than during the first (Bishara 2010; Hammami and Tamari 2001; Johnson and Kuttab 2001). This militarization made it harder to summon the disciplined collective energy necessary for popular resistance on a national scale. Spatial politics and sociocultural changes have also made popular resistance difficult to sustain (Alazzeh 2015).

While Aida Camp was relatively quiet between 2005 and 2012, resistance against the wall occurred in dozens of villages around the West Bank, the highest profile among them Budrus, Bil'in, and Ni'lin near Ramallah (Norman 2010; Hallward and Norman 2011). Palestinians carried out performatively nonviolent actions, such as chaining themselves to olive trees threatened with destruction. This move toward nonviolence was an effect of the NGOization of the West Bank and of the PA's state-building project, which had committed the Palestinian Authority to denouncing violence (Alazzeh 2014). International groups led many of these nonviolent initiatives, and they garnered coverage in the United States (Bacha 2009; Davidi and Burnat 2011). For international observers, the stone throwing—which tended to happen at the end of even "nonviolent" demonstrations in the villages—was a problem, even though this was clearly not armed resistance and it rarely injured soldiers (though it did push them back). As *New York Times* columnist Nicholas Kristof (2010) wrote, "I don't know whether Palestinians can create a peaceful mass movement that might change history, and their first challenge will be to suppress the stone throwers and bring women into the forefront but this grassroots movement [in Budrus] offers a ray of hope for less violence and more change." I imagine many Palestinian activists would respond that Palestinians' first challenge in building a nonviolent movement was overcoming Israel's violent suppression of nonviolent protest.

The village-based activism thrived due to strong familial networks that overlapped with local forms of political organizing and the high stakes faced by villagers regarding a loss of agricultural land and livelihoods because of the wall. The PA and the Fatah leadership expressed support for this nonviolent resistance, though their backing came late and was symbolic when there was an imperative for more substantive support (Alazzeh 2014, 32; Lagerquist 2004, 26).

However, Palestinian activists were often ambivalent about how to name their movements. As one activist from a village campaign said, "When we started we used the language of popular resistance. We did not want to use the term nonviolence—we practiced it but did not talk about it. We try to internalize it, so that it becomes part of our culture, but the word itself sounds strange" (Darweish and Rigby 2015, 4). While popular resistance (*muqāwima shaʿbiyya*) has a clear and proud history in the Palestinian context, nonviolence (*al-lā-ʿunf*) has been marked as an import that seeks approval from Western audiences. Perhaps many in Aida were especially critical of the discourse of nonviolence because they had seen so many international visitors coming and going from their communities (Bishara 2013, 167–96). They were ready to refuse outside support and frameworks if they did not anticipate them being productive.

Popular Resistance Renewed in Aida

On November 14, 2012, Israel began a major military operation in the Gaza Strip. A few days later, fierce Palestinian protests began in Bethlehem and elsewhere in solidarity with Palestinians in Gaza. During demonstrations, protesters with stones and Molotov cocktails confronted helmeted soldiers armed with automatic weapons, often in armored jeeps near the Rachel's Tomb military base. Protesters used burning tires and burning dumpsters as their defense. The Israeli soldiers used tear gas (firing multiple canisters at once), rubber bullets, and sometimes live ammunition. The participants were boys and young men, including many who had been imprisoned during the 2004–2005 wave of arrests. After the Israeli operation ceased in Gaza a week later, the situation calmed in most of the West Bank, but protests roared on in Aida and came to take on an extraordinarily local orientation. Through the experience of protests carried out with great frequency, activists discovered that the tire fires next to the watchtower, where the black mark was, had begun to eat away at the concrete of the wall (figure 5.4). In essence, the density of their protests had revealed a new strategy. By late November, activists talked of breaking through the wall.

In the weeks that followed, many camp residents posted images of a burning watchtower on Facebook. Dramatic photos showed billows of smoke encompassing the tower. The fires eventually accomplished a noticeably crumbling wall: concrete chipped away and the metal network underneath showing through. Young men, in the dead of night, employed a large drill to expedite the

Figure 5.4. Protests against the wall at Aida Refugee Camp included fires lit next to it. Photo by Mohammad Al-Azza, 2012.

process of puncturing the wall. Even though this was a new method of protest against a relatively new structure of oppression, camp residents recognized and valued a basic continuity in this form of protest. As a man who had come of age during the first Intifada told me in an interview, "The generation who came after Al-Aqsa Intifada [from 2000 to 2005] hadn't had the experience of throwing stones. . . . Now this was an opportunity for them to participate and resist. There is an old song that says, 'Each generation learns from the previous one.'" He saw these protests as tradition in action.

Still, camp residents felt a tension between their sense that they were undertaking something significant and their sense of isolation in their resistance, because the rest of Bethlehem and even the West Bank was by then quiet. They thought they might be on the verge of starting a new national movement. One teenager from the camp posted on Facebook alongside a photograph of the exposed metal network inside the concrete wall: "Soon your wall will fall, Israel." This was an ambitious threat, given that perhaps the most they could hope to do was to pierce one segment of the long, high wall. What infiltrating the wall did do was strengthen the sense of a collectivity and pride in resistance in Aida

Camp, which built on a longer Palestinian tradition of resistance. As one person wrote on Facebook, "A thousand salutes for your steadfastness, sons of Aida Camp." Steadfastness (*ṣumūd*) is a cherished value for Palestinians that points to the necessity of persistence and strength in the face of decades of Israeli rule (Meari 2014).

The primary participants in these protests were boys and young men between the ages of fourteen and twenty-five. This was a shift from earlier waves of popular protest when more women participated, as during the first Intifada (Peteet 1991). The tradition of women's resistance had been lively and strong in Aida Camp, which I knew because women still spoke of these formative movements. The reasons for women's waning participation in street protests have to do with the increased militarization of resistance during the second Intifada, which limited participation from both genders (Johnson and Kuttab 2001). It also had to do with other sociocultural changes in Palestinian society. During the years of the Palestinian Revolution and the first Intifada, roughly from the 1960s through the 1990s, much of the Palestinian movement was proudly radical and working for liberation, and this meant an alignment with feminism. During the Oslo years, the modality of state building was much more conventional, and it focused more on a neoliberal feminism, if any at all, that did not prize women's participation in street protests. One woman in her early thirties explained to me in the summer of 2013 why she and other women did not participate in the protests: "Families don't allow it. . . . A guy, he knows how to run, and defend himself. What would you [a young woman] do? You'll get scared." This explanation would not have sat well with women from Aida in their forties and fifties who had thrown stones and Molotov cocktails before and during the first Intifada and even gone to prison for it (see Gorkin and Othman 1996 for some of these stories of resistance). Notably, a few years later in Aida, photographs of protests did feature women throwing stones, so this dynamic continues to shift.

As during the first Intifada (Jean-Klein 2000; Peteet 1991), popular politics involved more than throwing stones and relied on broader participation than just young men, even if these forms of participation were less public. A woman in her twenties confirmed to me in 2013 that while women's participation was different, it was important too: "Everyone was resisting in their way. We women would, for example, tell the guys where the army was, shouting from the windows or on the phone." Men who were culturally regarded as too old for stone throwing—or unable to risk arrest—also served as lookouts. Some women and children too young to throw stones gathered stones, and some community members helped to procure the great number of tires needed to degrade the concrete of the wall. Many men and women also contributed ideas about strategy. Sometimes this advice was gathered from a previous generation that had participated in uprisings, and sometimes it came just from being observant of the current positioning of the army. One woman in her twenties told me more than once how she had casually speculated on how best to confront the army in front of a male relative; later, she saw him put her idea into action. She was ambivalent about her contribution: her relative was eventually arrested, though not specifically for doing what she had mentioned.

Tear gas permeated the camp during these protests. Managing the large quantity of tear gas also required labor, especially from women, who are often engaged in creative strategies for resistance on the front lines of military occupations as they occur in domestic spaces (Shalhoub-Kevorkian 2008). In many households, women were more often at home due to child and elder care commitments. Women often held jobs in education or health care that had shorter hours or faster commutes. So they were most often responsible for closing windows at the first whiff of tear gas, and they cleaned up patios littered with spent canisters. Another way that people supported the protests without throwing stones was by helping youths to resist arrests, something that Palestinian women have been famous for since at least the first Intifada (Sharoni 1995). They stood in the street as barriers between soldiers and youths. They even occasionally counterattacked soldiers with stones during arrest raids. Especially when the boy arrested was particularly young, they approached the military base to negotiate with soldiers for the child's release. Women opened their homes to youths running to escape soldiers or tear gas. Just as the wall affected everyone in the camp, a wide variety of people involved themselves in various ways in the protest movement.

After a lull, in early January 2013 protests against the army began again, and they seemed to be intensifying. A soldier was injured in the face by a stone. A youth managed to hoist a Palestinian flag on top of a watchtower, generating another of the locally iconic images of the protests. Finally, on the morning of January 14, the camp awoke to what felt like a new reality: the young men had drilled a hole in the wall large enough for a child to squeeze through (figure 5.5). On Facebook and in phone calls, people were elated and proud.

These protests, it should be clear, were dramatically different from the carefully nonviolent protests occurring against the wall in West Bank villages, which

Figure 5.5. Activists succeeded in drilling a hole in the wall at Aida Refugee Camp.
Photo by Mohammad Al-Azza, 2013.

attracted more Palestinian, Israeli, and international news coverage and also
involved many Israeli and international (primarily American and European)
solidarity activists. Many of the Palestinian activists in Aida explicitly repudi-
ated the idea of nonviolent resistance, because they disliked the history of the
terminology. It was precisely the unruly quality of Aida's resistance that one of
the prominent protesters especially prized. He emphasized to me that no one
had issued any decision about what methods of resistance were appropriate.
Moreover, the many non-Palestinians who visited or even lived in Aida Camp
would not be central players in these protests because of the risk of being shot
or arrested and because few would have the physical skills to be effective in
them. Perhaps the mode of resistance was partly a means of underscoring to
those non-Palestinians—who tended to be researchers, NGO workers, or seekers of political adventure, many of whom were good friends with camp residents—who was really on the front lines of the struggle. It was a reaction to the
intense militarization of space brought about by the proximity of the wall and
the military base it housed. In the coming months, as the protests went on and
became more and more dangerous—both in terms of shootings and in terms

of nighttime arrests—other community members became more critical of the lack of organization of the protests.

Experienced protesters tried to be clearer that stone throwing was appropriate for demonstrations while other weapons were not. Still, even people critical of some aspects of the protests continued to emphasize the importance of popular resistance and to eschew the term "nonviolence." One camp resident noted in an interview during the summer of 2013, "I support the popular resistance more than the nonviolent resistance. . . . We might only disagree on the name. If they would call it 'popular,' then it would be better." In his late thirties, he had been active only in the earliest days of the protests. He went on to note that he supported stone throwing and Molotov cocktails, but not the throwing of pipe bombs, because the latter rendered the protests too dangerous.

Another community leader in his early forties told me during the summer of 2013 that the goal was not physical damage to the Israeli army and that protecting Palestinian lives was crucial: "The goal [of] protest is not to kill or injure Israelis. These protests are a rejection of the occupation policy and a way to send a message to the world that we are still under occupation, even if we have the PA. . . . Any losses among our youth, whether they be deaths, injuries, or arrests, are serious losses for us." But he also contrasted the movement in Aida with nonviolent protests, which in his mind did not send a strong enough message to the Israeli army. They were, he said, "limited to a weekly event for an hour or hour and a half. The Israelis know about it before it happens, and so they prepare for them. . . . These events in the name of nonviolent resistance are courageous, but they lack a sense of long-term goals. In some areas, Israel changed the path of the wall, and protesters considered that as a victory." In his view, moving the wall from one Palestinian location to another was not a victory. Clearly, while he viewed a purely military victory against the Israelis as unlikely, he also saw confrontation itself as sending an important message, and he believed that making military occupation costly was itself important.

Back in January 2013, drilling a hole in the wall in the middle of the night felt—to me, and I gather also to those involved—like a discovery of a new kind of physics, a whole new way of confronting the violence that surrounded Aida. Participants knew that they were at risk of arrest for stone throwing, but they had a strange feeling of impunity about the hole in the wall. They quipped, "What will they charge us with? Destroying cement?" It was as though they saw their tactic as so new that it had not yet been made illegal, or as though—despite the hundreds of tires they had burned, despite their smuggling in of a drill under cover of night—they imagined that what they had done would not be regarded as "violence" by the Israeli authorities. They were against the label of "nonviolence," but they also thought their protests were strategic, smart, and sound in that they did not target soldiers.

After the protesters' success in penetrating the wall, the Israeli response came quickly. The army closed the opening the youths had created, but it was not easy for the Israelis to operate in the midst of Aida Refugee Camp. Four soldiers were stranded in a house of the camp for several hours as protests continued below. Residents said that the army brought in a new and more ruthless (*sharis*) unit of soldiers. Then, on January 18, just four days after the young men had busted open the wall, an Israeli soldier standing right in front of the separation wall at Rachel's Tomb shot an unarmed sixteen-year-old boy, Saleh Al-'Amareen, in the head with live ammunition (Beiler 2015; B'Tselem 2013b; DCI Palestine 2013). While there had been protests going on that day, Al-'Amareen posed no threat at the time he was shot. He died on January 23. It was the second time in a week that a Palestinian teenager had been murdered by Israeli soldiers near the wall in the West Bank: Israeli soldiers had killed Samir 'Awad, seventeen, near the barrier in Budrus on January 15, 2013 (B'Tselem 2013a).

Protests in Aida slowed. A wave of nighttime arrest raids led to widespread sleeplessness among teenagers and their families, an ordinary dread that exhausted everyone. Each time soldiers entered the camp, they did so from the military base embedded in the wall. When soldiers arrested boys and young men, they were disappeared into the wall itself. The first stop for those arrested was the Rachel's Tomb military base, where people often experienced beatings (Addameer 2017) before they went on to interrogation centers or prisons.

Over the next several months, Israeli soldiers arrested dozens of young men and boys. The documentary *We Have a Dream to Live Safe*, produced by a lifelong resident of Aida Refugee Camp, shows both the potential of the arrest raids to escalate into direct confrontations with the army and the ways in which they instigate a pervasive anxiety. As eleven-year-old Shahd Awais, a resident of Aida, says, "Very often I wake up to the sound of bullets in the camp. When I wake up every day, I open Facebook to check the news of the camp because I am afraid that the soldiers will have taken someone from my family or a friend" (Al-Azza 2016). A new generation of mothers and fathers has assumed a familiar role: managing the care of those in prison.

During the months and years that have followed, as protests and arrest raids surged and subsided and surged again, tear gas has become a part of the environment as much as the wall is. Israeli soldiers have shot tear gas so often that it has tuned people's senses; they can sense just the slightest acrid whiff of it in the air. It has coated the pavement and sunk into the soil. Most horrifically, it killed a woman, Noha Qatamish, a mother in her forties who was suffocated in her own home when the gas flooded in (Beiler 2014). The military base in the wall means that the Israeli presence is pervasive.

In 2013, I asked many of my interviewees if and when they experienced a sense of victory during the protests. By that time, the first wave of arrests had happened, and soldiers had already killed Al-'Amareen. Many of my interviewees returned to the same moments. One of the leaders of the protest movement told me, "The way I see victory is that the wall was breached, and Israel even admitted that its army could not control the camp [for a short period of time]. . . . That instills in them a great fear." Likewise, a woman in her thirties declared that the most successful moment in the protests was "when they burned the tower and made a hole in the wall, and when they trapped the soldiers inside the camp. . . . The army had to call for backup. . . . Look, when you see four heavily armed soldiers in a room who cannot protect themselves, afraid of stones—it is a small thing, but it was a good feeling." She said that the protests sent an important message: "We are doing something, so that Israel can't say, 'Look at the Palestinians, they are asleep, despite the fact that we are still taking their land.'" A man in his early forties confirmed, "The new generation's rejection of the wall, of the watchtowers, and of life under occupation—this is important. They decided to burn the tower or drill a hole in the wall. Even though they know the Israelis will fix the wall and the watchtower, it was a message to the occupation." He argued that the action had inspired other similar operations to destroy similar walls, including the separation wall in Al-Ram and even in Al-Lydd (Lod) inside Israel, where a wall separated a poor Palestinian neighborhood from a wealthier Jewish one. Still, one interviewee, a man in his fifties, harshly criticized the protests because he could not stand the heavy black smoke the fires brought into his house.

Habits of Protest

Campaigns to damage the wall and the related stone-throwing protests were connected to the Palestinian national movement in that they drew on Palestinian repertoires of contention (Tilly 2006). Sometimes these actions were correlated with events outside of Aida, such as the war on Gaza, but they were only tangentially connected to a broader movement against the wall. This was because there was little coordinated leadership capable of making collective strategies and appeals. After the International Court of Justice decision in 2004, the PA did little to press Israel to take action based on it. Palestinians in Aida could not bring a court case, as villagers had done in other instances, because they did not own the land that they had lost. Instead, participants and community members valued protests as an ongoing practice of confronting the army and resisting the wall—the latest manifestation of Israel's violent rule over their community. The frequency of these protests is analytically important both because it was the initial frequency of the protests that led to the insight that fires might degrade the concrete of the wall and because it points to the significance of resistance as a practice for young protesters. The violence of the wall is ever present, so they made their resistance as persistent.

For Palestinians in Aida, the wall is no dispassionate infrastructure of separation but rather a looming infrastructure of racialized militarization—an edifice that targets their space, their bodies, their lives. The wall is the most proximate, visible piece of the Israeli occupation, inflicting the structural violence of enclosure (Peteet 2015) and also facilitating outright military violence in Aida. It has made Aida Refugee Camp into what Israeli journalist Gideon Levy has called "the lowest point in the occupied territories" (Levy and Levac 2014). Busting a hole in the wall was a blunt way of remaking a carceral space that, Aida's residents saw, had been manufactured around them specifically to degrade and threaten their lives.

Palestinians in Aida live with the pervasive and relentless violence of dispossession as refugees; they endure social and geographic isolation from the rest of Bethlehem; they cope with the threat of outright Israeli military violence at all moments of the day and night. These problems have beleaguered Aida for decades as its residents have lived with Israeli settler colonialism, but the wall has exacerbated them all. Foucault (2003, 254–55) defines racism as "a way of introducing a break into the domain of life that is under power's control: the break between what must live and what must die . . . a way of fragmenting the field of the biological that power controls." The wall is an instrument of such division, containing a military base that always threatens the camp. It has made starker than ever the separation and distinction between Aida Refugee Camp, a space of confinement and endangerment, and the nearby Israeli settlement of Gilo, a space of ongoing expansion.

The confrontations with soldiers to protest against the wall—the rounds of demonstrations that overwhelmed daily routines and made almost any moment a plausible time for resistance—responded to this violence with the same pervasive, everyday quality that the protesters saw in front of them in the form of the wall. The protests were a kind of theory in action. But this was a dangerous kind of theory. Though protesters were unarmed and though their goal was not to hurt people, they made no claims of nonviolence. Even though these protests have not, as protesters hoped, ignited a national movement, in some ways they have maintained the possibility of such a movement, in that they have ensured that new generations learn the tactics of popular resistance. In general, resistance is conditioned by many factors, including tradition, the possibilities for repression and retribution, and global validation or invalidation of protests. All of these factors came into play in Aida Refugee Camp, but especially relevant here are the material conditions of living in the shadow of a military base and surrounded by the separation wall. As a long-term visitor to Aida Refugee Camp, I know that some years may be calmer than others, as people recover from tragedies and imprisonments. But I also know that Palestinians there will not cease their resistance until the wall falls.

Part II
National Walls

CHAPTER SIX

The Materiality of a Metaphor

The Cold War and the Berlin Wall

ANNA MCWILLIAMS

When I started my research into the archaeology of the former Iron Curtain, I had never been to Berlin. Even though I had not seen the Berlin Wall, I was still very aware of it. Images of graffiti-painted concrete walls, guards patrolling, and barbed wire filled my head. I had heard the stories of people trying to get across the wall—some succeeding, others not. I remembered the news coverage following November 9, 1989, when the wall was opened up. As I started my background reading about the Berlin Wall, I noticed the ever-present metaphor of the Iron Curtain and the use of the Berlin Wall as a symbol of the Cold War separating communism and capitalism.

My research on the Iron Curtain revealed that this was only one image of the Berlin Wall. There was also a more practical side to this metaphor that was a lot more mundane and functional: a physical manifestation of a border that restricted people's movements and that altered the urban landscape through which it stretched (see Dinzey-Flores and McAtackney, both this volume, for other examples of restrictive urban walls). Maybe this should have been obvious to me because the main aim of a border is to restrict, to keep in or out, and to control, but I was still surprised by the materiality I encountered. I asked myself why the impression I had before I started my research looked the way it did. It soon became clear that the photos of barbed wire, border guards, and graffiti-covered walls were heavily affected by the images produced during the Cold War, reinforcing the idea of the Berlin Wall as a symbol of a divided world. On the streets of Berlin, both a metaphor of the Cold War and the physical remains of a divided city confronted me. Sometimes they told the same story; sometimes they did not.

In this chapter I discuss how the physical wall, the border structures, the military presence, and the metaphors of the Cold War divide became so inter-twined and how they influenced each other. I also discuss why, even after the Cold War, the Berlin Wall remains such a strong symbol of this period of division. The remnants and the memorials of this border are still important today for the people around it as well as for the knowledge and remembrance of the Cold War. Why is this?

Historical Background

Following World War II, Germany and Berlin were divided into four zones by the Allies, and Great Britain, the United States, France, and the Soviet Union each managed one of the zones. The inner German border was developed as a response to unrest in the areas between the Russian zone and the zones controlled by the other three nations. This was a slow process that advanced in stages from 1952, becoming more and more militarized with time. The border between East and West Germany was closed in 1952, but the border within the city of Berlin remained open. Leaders of the German Democratic Republic (GDR) considered it a bleeding wound. After studying previously secret documents, historian Hope Harrison (2005) has shown that the Soviet Union turned down several requests from East German leader Walter Ulbricht to close the Berlin border. The Soviets worried that it would be too disruptive to Berliners and to the peacekeeping forces from the four nations, which were still present in the town. They also thought that it would "place in doubt the sincerity of the policy of the Soviet government and the GDR government, which are actively and consistently supporting the unification of Germany and the conclusion of a peace treaty with Germany" (Harrison 2005, 20).

Soviet leader Nikita Khrushchev eventually approved the plan to close the border in June 1961. This was only a few weeks after his meeting with US president John F. Kennedy in which the two parties failed to solve the so-called Berlin issue, which likely influenced his decision to support building a wall (Rottman 2008). As soon as this agreement between the Soviets and East Germans was reached, the plan, given the code name "the Rose," was set into motion. At 2:00 a.m. on the thirteenth of August, work started on what was called the "anti-fascist protection wall" (for terminology on walls, see McGuire and McAtackney, and McAtackney, both this volume). GDR troops moved into position to guard the border, and at 4:00 a.m. truck upon truck began to arrive, loaded with pre-fabricated concrete blocks. Workmen erected the first section of the wall across Ackerstraße near Bernauerstraße. Photographs from the time show that the wall was poorly built using large stone blocks that were cemented together without much precision or care for aesthetics. Stones were not aligned, and the mortar was used in large quantities to hold the wall together. This demonstrates that the builders considered speed of more importance than robust construction. Other structures were soon added, such as watchtowers, death strips, anti-vehicle obstacles, and searchlights. The wall cut through 192 streets and could only be crossed at one of the thirteen official gates (Rottman 2008).

The GDR upgraded the border throughout its existence, especially in 1975 when the nation carried out a major reinforcement operation. Local improvements were carried out continuously, often in response to threats or attempted breaches. The border through Berlin is usually called just "the wall," but its material presence extended far beyond this. By 1989 it had become a major, well-thought-out barrier. It consisted of L-shaped reinforced concrete slabs reaching three and a half meters high with sewer pipes cemented on top, making climbing almost impossible. In addition the border included anti-vehicle obstacles and ditches, other anti-climbing measures, control strips, patrol roads, trip flares, searchlights, dog runs, signal fences, and an inner, three- to four-meter-high wall (Rottman 2008). West Berlin had become a fort to which access was almost impossible from the surrounding GDR without the correct paperwork (see Bishara, this volume, on the West Bank). However, there was one major difference from a typical fort: it was the surrounding area—the East, not West Berlin itself—that had constructed the fortifications that surrounded it.

The wall became an established feature in the city until 1989, when it suddenly became porous at a speed that was not foreseen. Although the general tone of the East German socialist party had been starting to soften, the fall of the wall was still highly unexpected. Indeed, a misunderstanding and a lack of communication were major factors behind the fall. At a press conference, one of the Socialist Unity Party officials, Günter Schabowski, read aloud information just handed to him stating that East Germans would be able to cross the border with proper permission. As he had not been informed of the regulations surrounding this decision, he answered the reporters' questions about when this would be effective by saying: "As far as I know—effective immediately, without delay" (*Frankfurter Allgemeine Zeitung* 2014). The news spread quickly, and soon thousands of East Germans demanded to be let through at the Berlin crossing points. Eventually, border guards stepped aside and allowed people to cross.

Getting past the wall does not appear to have been enough, however, as people started to hack their way through the border structures. The expression "fall of the wall" therefore has both a metaphoric and a physical reality behind it. Sections of the wall were chipped off by people nicknamed *Mauerspechte* (wallpeckers), who worked their way through the fabric of the wall (see Bishara, this volume).

Metaphor and Material

As the physical barriers in Berlin were being built and upgraded, the metaphor of a divided Europe developed and became connected to the physical Berlin Wall. The city was one of the few places where this Cold War division could be seen physically. The Iron Curtain in the rest of Europe, especially along the border of the former Czechoslovakia and Hungary with Germany and Austria, was heavily militarized, but because the border structures were several kilometers inside the actual border, they were very difficult to see. In contrast, when the GDR constructed the Berlin Wall right through a bustling city, the division immediately became acutely obvious to the world. In a city, it is impossible to hide border fortifications within vast areas of farmland or forest. Right in front of the eyes of Berliners, as well as the international press, a wall rose out of the ground. For the first time for most people in the West, it suddenly became possible to see and even touch the division between East and West. An intangible metaphor had taken a tangible form (see McGuire and McAtackney, and Jones, both this volume).

Over the years the Berlin Wall became a frequently used image in discussions about the Cold War and a common backdrop for political speeches and agendas, especially for Westerners. Photographs of President Kennedy's visit to the Berlin Wall in June 1963 were spread throughout the Western press as were images of President Ronald Reagan's June 1987 speech in front of the wall by the Brandenburg Gate (figure 6.1). In the Western world, the Berlin Wall had become the sign for the division between East and West, what Manghani (2008, 59) refers to as a sort of shorthand by media professionals: a situation in which an image has become so symbolic of something else that the image and broader

Figure 6.1. Ronald Reagan speaking in front of the Brandenburg Gate and the Berlin Wall on June 12, 1987. Courtesy of the Ronald Reagan Library.

meaning become inseparable. Whenever TV reporters or newspapers required an image to represent the Cold War or the Iron Curtain, photos of the Berlin Wall were used to great effect. They became an important part of the historical writing of the Cold War, and as such were always skewed by subjectivity and, in this case, camera angles. In this ambiguous conflict with no battlefields, which stretched all the way into space, the Berlin Wall became its most obvious physical manifestation. The material Berlin Wall helped to make sense of the concept of a divided Europe since witnessing something physical and visual makes an idea seem more real (Manghani 2008, 103). In this way the Berlin Wall became a focal point as people tried to make sense of the Cold War.

For official East Germany, the fortified border with the capitalist West became the focal point during celebration ceremonies. However, the majority of people in the East considered the border more like a prison wall (see Dear and Jones, both this volume, for other analogies to prison walls). The actual border was generally not accessible to the population because of the security zones, restricted areas, and surveillance in the areas closest to it (see Dorsey and Díaz-Barriga, this volume, on access to the US-México wall). Instead, the border extended conceptually as well as materially into society with informants keeping track of the population not only in the border zones. One estimate of how many informers there were within the GDR, including both Stasi officers and part-time informants, is one informer for every six and a half citizens (Funder 2003, 57).

In "Life in the Shadow of the Wall," Ulrika Poppe (2005, 28) describes her upbringing in the GDR: "During my schooldays in the 1960s, we called it the border, only amongst confidants could the term Wall be occasionally heard." In the East, referencing the materiality of the wall was considered a Western approach, and anyone using the term could be considered a Western infiltrator. She continues: "Later the taboo disappeared: we spoke of the Wall as such; however, we talked about it less and less because the world on the other side of it had faded" (Poppe 2005, 28).

In an article about humor and graffiti in a divided Berlin, written only months before the wall came down, Mary Beth Stein (1989, 86) used humor as a way to study people's views of the wall. She concluded that in the West there were fewer jokes about the wall, but there was a lot of graffiti with political and personal statements placed on the wall itself. In contrast, on the East side there was very little graffiti but a lot more jokes about the wall. She suggested that the act of writing graffiti was more obvious, and the person carrying it out was more likely to be punished than if they told a joke, which was a more subtle criticism. One thing Stein did not discuss was the accessibility of the border, which would have made graffiti on the East side a lot more difficult because people were generally not allowed to come close to it. In fact the East Germans had very little interaction with the actual border at all.

Stein's article described and reflected upon the wall as a then-functioning border, and her work can now be seen as source material in itself. She described the wall from several perspectives, including international views, in particular through tourism and media reports, and local views. The latter in fact contains two different perspectives: the wall viewed from the West and from the East. For West Berliners, the wall became such an everyday image they stopped noticing it, but for East Berliners, who were not allowed to see or speak of it, it became a much bigger issue: "the Wall in the West is visible, everyday. It is not a topic. The Wall in the East is invisible, everyday and a topic — which is very much taboo" (Stein 1989, 86). The idea of the wall as a divider and as a metaphor was therefore a lot stronger in Western rhetoric than in East Germany, where it was viewed more as a physical divider that limited movement. This is also, at least in part, reflected in how Berliners today show different attitudes toward the memorials of the wall (see McAtackney and Dear, both this volume, on memorials at walls). Several former East Berliners have commented that the memorial at Bernauer-straße does not mean that much to them because they never got to see the border during its time as a functioning frontier (Axel Klausmeier, pers. comm. 2009).

The Berlin Wall was therefore not just one thing but was seen in different ways depending on a person's point of view. There was the local perspective that saw the wall in its more practical and functional aspect: the border struc-tures or fortifications produced by the East in order to control the movement of people and goods. Beyond that, the local perspective also depended on if you were from East or West Berlin. The international perspective mainly followed the Western perspective in which the Berlin Wall was highly connected to the metaphor and rhetoric of the Cold War division of communism and capitalism. The wall helped to visualize the abstractness of the Cold War and the division between East and West.

The images of the Berlin Wall being torn down beginning in November 1989 added to the symbolism of the wall: it was referred to from the start as a historic event and became what Manghani (2008, 60) calls "instant history." After its fall, the Berlin Wall became a symbol of freedom and the victory of the people on both sides. This meaning of "freedom" has also come to extend outside the Cold War context, and images of the fall of the Berlin Wall have found their way into other settings, such as during the 2003 invasion of Iraq: images of the fall of the Berlin Wall were used in news coverage to convey liberation (Manghani 2008, 59). It is a well-known adage that history is written by the victors, and the victors in this case — Westerners — have held onto their images and metaphors in their history writing and in their treatment of the heritage of the wall. In the next section I explore how this heritage looks today and how the metaphor and physical remains are still connected.

Berlin Today: Remembrance and Education

The idea that material remains can embody aesthetic, historic, educational, and social values and therefore communicate these values in order for us to learn from people's previous experiences is prevalent in the Global North heritage industry (although not without criticism; see Smith 2006). The types of physical remains and sites connected to the former Berlin Wall vary, and so do the purposes behind their preservation as heritage. I have shown how the wall was not just one thing but had different meanings to different people depending on their experiences, or lack of experience, of the wall as a border. This also affects how Berliners view the remains and sites connected to the wall that still exist in Berlin today.

When I arrived in Berlin for the first time in 2009, I soon realized that the border was still highly present. It may not look like it did during its time as an active barrier, but it most certainly still remains an important aspect of the Berlin cityscape. In fact, the first thing that struck me about the wall was how much of it was still there despite twenty years having passed since it was "torn down." Even though I had come to Germany to study its remains and was fairly well informed about their existence, their frequency still took me by surprise. The second thing that struck me was the variety of remains (see Dinzey-Flores, this volume, on the variety of gated community walls). During my walks along the former borderline, I encountered remains of the "enemy-facing wall" (i.e., the face that was closest to the West). I came across vast open spaces that were leftovers of the death strip; smaller remains of the former border installations, such as anti-climbing measures; and signs to keep people away from the border areas or anti-vehicle installations. There were also many memorials that in different ways commemorated the former border and particularly the people who died trying to get across it. The remains today consist of everything from small bits of leftover border infrastructure, installations, and plaques to large memorial structures. Some of the latter are intentional memorials raised after the wall came down while others are remains of the border structure that became memorials after the fall of the wall. Here, I take the same approach to memorials as Rodell (2007, 66), who suggests that although the origins of monuments may vary, depending on whether they were raised intentionally or if they are the remains of a structure, object, or feature that has subsequently changed purpose, they may be studied in the same way because they have taken on the same meanings.

There are also remains of the wall that cannot be described as monuments — either intentionally erected as such or as part of this process of change — and they mainly continue to exist with the same purpose they had when the wall was a border (see Papadopoulos, this volume, on the persistence of northern Greek border materials). An archaeological documentation of the remains of the border was carried out by the Department of Architectural Conservation at the Brandenburg University of Technology in Cottbus, Germany, for the Berlin Senate Department for Urban Development in 2001–2003 (Klausmeier and Schmidt 2004). This is an important record of the residues of the Berlin Wall because many of the remnants have disappeared since this documentation project, and they will continue to do so over time. The material from this study was published as a tourist guide, which means that it can be used to visit sites as well as acting as an archaeological record. The majority of the remains recorded as part of this study were smaller features connected to the former border structure. Those parts of the wall that have become monuments were also included.

There are many examples of how the monuments of the wall focus on remembrance, including the lists of names of the people that were killed trying to cross the border by Bernauerstraβe, where the Documentation Centre is now located. At Strelitzerstraβe there are plaques commemorating the tunnel that was built in 1964, which allowed fifty-seven people to get over to West Berlin and led to the death of one East German border guard, Egon Schultz. Near the Reichstag building the memorial Weiβe Kreuze (White Crosses) has been installed to commemorate people that died trying to cross the border. Other sites are more abstract in character, such as the painted sections of wall at the East Side Gallery or the Parlament der Bäume (Parliament of Trees). These kinds of artistic installations, some permanent and some temporary, often reuse the material of the wall as part of their fabric. Farther from the city center there are other, possibly less visited but still important memorials and installations, such as plaques and monuments at Tempelhof Airport commemorating the Berlin airlift.

In terms of education, remains of the former wall are used to inform visitors, especially the younger generation that did not experience the wall themselves, about the period, the political context, and the border itself. There are two main museums: the Documentation Centre at Bernauerstraβe, which is the city of Berlin's official museum of the Berlin Wall, and the private Haus am Checkpoint Charlie. The stories told in the different places include factual information about the wall itself and personal stories of people affected by the wall. The Documentation Centre, where research is also carried out, has a more academic mission. There is a clear focus on scholarship, and since it was established in 1998 research has been undertaken on the history of the wall "and the history of the people in both the East and West who suffered because of it—or who helped to sustain it. . . . To do this the relevant facts have to be

collected, organized and made accessible to the public" (http://www.berliner
-mauer-gedenkstaette.de/de).

The Haus am Checkpoint Charlie was established in 1962 by human rights
activist Dr. Rainer Hildebrandt next to the recently erected Berlin Wall (http://
www.mauermuseum.de). It was moved in 1963 closer to Checkpoint Charlie due
to its high number of visitors. It provided views over the Berlin Wall into East
Germany and became a place for escape organizers, protesters, and journalists to
meet. After the death of Hildebrandt, his wife, Alexandra Hildebrandt, ran and
expanded the exhibitions, including more general exhibits focusing on human
rights globally. The museum is privately run and has been accused of becoming
increasingly commercially focused; critics also claim that the exhibitions are
created without any scholarly advice (Harrison 2011, 85).

Although some of the stories told at these two museums are based on the
same basic facts, the different approaches make for two very different institutions. At the Documentation Centre, there is an exhibition in which visitors are
facilitated in bringing their own thoughts in order to process the information
provided through information boards, photos, and films. The Haus am Checkpoint Charlie is more focused on a popular culture audience. The stories at
Haus am Checkpoint Charlie are told in a less objective way, but through doing
this they also manage to convey more emotional responses. The museum's aim
of providing an "experience" of the Berlin Wall does not always take complete
authenticity into account, especially in the exhibited material, but it is centered
on telling the stories to visitors. Often it succeeds well in this aim, and the exhibit
is very popular.

Checkpoint Charlie itself has become a tourist spot and, some claim, a "Dis-
neyland-version of its former self" (Paterson 2012). On the street by the former
checkpoint, students dress up as American, British, French, or Russian border
guards and pay to pose for photographs in front of a guard hut that has been
built to look like those at the site in the 1960s (the 1980s huts were demolished
in 2000, and none of the original structures remain). Vernon Pike, a former
US Army colonel who was stationed at the checkpoint during the Cold War,
wrote in a letter to Berlin's city government in 2008 that the spectacles that were
being performed at this historical site were "inappropriate for the location and
its historical importance" (Paterson 2008). A Cold War museum was planned
there, but because this caused major political arguments the plans were changed,
and a small, temporary Cold War exhibition was installed instead.

Different Attitudes toward the Past

The various discussions, arguments, displays, and exhibits about the wall clearly demonstrate different attitudes toward the recent past and how it should be retold, presented, and remembered. It cannot, however, be denied that despite its possibly dubious relationship to facts and its commercialized and Disneyfied development, Checkpoint Charlie attracts a staggering number of visitors per year. It is a success, at least on a commercial level. Haus am Checkpoint Charlie presents a history that corresponds to the image or idea that many people in the West have about the Iron Curtain and the Berlin Wall. It is likely that it receives so many visitors because it is in line with the image created by Western propaganda, and therefore the museum does not require people to modify the view they already have of the Berlin Wall (Schmidt 2005, 16).

During my research I spent time at the different heritage sites and museums connected to the wall, interviewing and observing visitors. The success of Checkpoint Charlie in particular shows that many people come to Berlin not to experience the Berlin Wall as it is nearly twenty years after it came down but to find support for a preexisting idea of what this wall should look like as shaped by the Cold War media. Schmidt (2005) points out that a different history about the Berlin Wall can be found, but for many people the idea they have is sufficient, and having this image reaffirmed through the material—albeit a reconstructed image built on inauthentic materiality—is considered enough. The most well-known heritage attractions related to the wall are located in the heart of Berlin, and that location is important because it makes particular versions of the wall easily accessible. However, I believe that the connection of this place and the image of the Berlin Wall as it has developed during and after its fall in Western rhetoric is an important factor guiding what tourists expect from their visit. The materiality and events at sites like Checkpoint Charlie represent an image that tourists expect when they visit Berlin. That image corresponds with the history of the Berlin Wall as written from a Western perspective, a history that has become the prevailing one.

The commodification of the wall itself also demonstrates the dominance of the Western narrative. The perimeter wall, the section facing West Berlin, is the most well-known part of the Berlin Wall, and portions of it have become artifacts to buy and sell. Large surviving sections are considered collector's items and sell for a high price on the art market. In 2008, an auction house in Berlin

Figure 6.2. Monument of reconstructed Berlin Wall at Bernauerstraβe. Photo by Anna McWilliams, 2009.

Figure 6.3. East Side Gallery, Berlin. Photo by Anna McWilliams, 2009.

was reported to have sold one section of the perimeter wall for 7,800 euros (BBC News 2008). Smaller pieces of the wall are sold in souvenir shops or on the internet, and they come with a certificate to authenticate them. As the smaller pieces are easily moved and there are no restrictions on taking them out of the country, they have contributed to the wall being distributed all over the world. I am an archaeologist, and it is a new concept for me to buy my artifacts, but as the tourist shops are full of pieces of the Berlin Wall, I have purchased a selection. I received a certificate of authenticity with some of these pieces, and I asked the saleswoman: how can you know that the pieces are in fact authentic? She claimed that they know they are because they buy them from a reliable source. She then lowered her voice somewhat so that the other people in the shop would not hear her and acknowledged that the paint on them was generally not authentic. It had been applied more recently. She explained that without the paint, people would not think the pieces are real. This is one example that shows how the tourism industry, closely related to the heritage industry, adjusts to what it thinks tourists want, and in this case they want a piece of the kind of wall that faced the Western side, the side that has mostly occupied popular memory.

Although academic publications such as Klausmeier and Schmidt (2004) take into account many of the different types of remains, this is less often the case with more popular tourist and heritage literature or on-the-ground tours of the Berlin Wall. There are a few specific locations that are generally promoted as official "Berlin Wall sites": the East Side Gallery, Checkpoint Charlie (figure 6.4), the Topography of Terror (which also includes history from the world wars), a former East German watchtower at Potsdamer Platz (although not in its original position), the Palace of Tears, and the Berlin Wall Memorial and Documentation Centre at Bernauerstraße (see http://www.visitberlin.de/en/article/tour-along-the-berlin-wall). What is interesting is how these selective remains of the former border are highlighted and given a more prominent role in the commemoration and telling of the history of the Berlin Wall. They show that although remains from the former border are still clearly visible in many places for those with enough interest, time, and background knowledge to find them, many sites are overlooked within the tourism and heritage industry, which tends to promote only a few.

In other places, and in particular for other types of Cold War remains, the situation is very different. Even if some physical remains are still present, little is known or remembered of them. This is often the case with the less obvious remains of the functioning Berlin Wall, such as anti-climbing features, electrical wires, lamps, fencing, lanes drawn on the streets at crossing points, and concrete obstacles in the River Spree. In the documentation of the border remains carried out in 2001–2003 (Klausmeier and Schmidt 2004), these were the most common materials that remained in situ, yet in the representation of the Berlin Wall in commemoration and heritage narratives they play a very small role. These material forms of the wall have not received a lot of attention in the media or in the tourist narratives created about the Berlin Wall.

One type of place that has received little attention is the voids that are still visible in the landscape (figure 6.5). In some areas, even close to the center of town, large areas of the death strip have not yet been redeveloped; rather, they run like a wilderness straight through the townscape. During the Cold War these areas, including the vegetation, were kept under total control. This previous control has kept larger plants, such as trees, at bay, but the complete lack of attention to them since 1989 has allowed green corridors to form. These corridors through central Berlin are now slowly being developed and will soon be eradicated as a material reminder of the wall.

One especially interesting commemorative site is the crossing by Sonnenallee in southeastern Berlin. During the time of the active border, this site did not receive much attention compared to other crossings, such as Checkpoint Charlie, and stayed out of the limelight until 1999, when it was made famous through the film *Sonnenallee*. In the film this crossing provided the backdrop to the story of a group of young boys growing up in East Berlin. Therefore, what made this site famous is not the events that took place there during the Cold War but rather a fictitious representation of the wall produced ten years after it fell.

The range of remains and sites connected to the Berlin Wall, and their various fates, can be seen as representing different attitudes toward the evolving heritage of the former border. While physical remains are believed to be able to communicate heritage values through their fabric and therefore promote remembrance of and education about the Berlin Wall, this is inconsistently found in practice. Exploring a range of sites does, however, demonstrate that the communication of the wall is only one side of the process since the receivers—the visitors—also have a major impact on how the sites are treated and remembered and how they change.

The more everyday objects that remain of the Berlin Wall are not hard to find, especially with a bit of background knowledge. For those who choose to stay on

Figure 6.4. Checkpoint Charlie. Photo by Anna McWilliams, 2009.

Figure 6.5. A void turning into a green corridor just outside central Berlin.
Photo by Anna McWilliams, 2009.

the official Berlin Wall tourism track, however, there are clearly a few sites that are more accessible, both physically and in terms of gaining information about them. Only through understanding people's perceptions and experiences, or lack thereof, of the Berlin Wall in a historical perspective can we understand why the physical remains that still remain today look the way they do and are treated and used the way they are.

Berlin Scars

Sites connected to dark heritage are often given less room than are the remains of a more glorious past in the "authorized heritage discourse" of official tourism (Smith 2006). In this respect, Berlin and Germany as a whole have plowed deeper than many other places in addressing their less than glamorous twentieth-century past and letting their heritage reflect not only the good but also their darker history. We have to remember that the heritage of the Berlin Wall and Cold War division is only one part of Germany's traumatic twentieth century. Berlin is full of material scars that demonstrate a turbulent hundred years. How to confront a past that is connected with conflict and trauma in the present is highly problematic. The monuments in Berlin today are to a large part the results of more or less conscious decisions about what to keep, restore, rebuild, or redevelop (see McGuire, this volume).

Heritage of conflict is particularly difficult to present as it can have many different aspects of trauma connected to it but also feelings of victory, heroism, and great achievements. What side of the conflict a person was on will make a major difference to their memory of it and how they move through the subsequent post-conflict period. Just as history writing is highly selective, so are the material records we decide to keep and display, and the decisions as to what we retain can be dependent on what we want to portray as "our past." A walk around central Berlin demonstrates the various layers of the city's history through its monuments, such as the Brandenburg Gate, the only surviving city gate in Berlin, which has been a stage for political struggles since Napoleon first transported its statue to Paris. Other examples are the Holocaust Memorial, which was created to acknowledge the horrors of World War II, and the Marx-Engels Monument, a communist leftover in what was once the heart of the GDR.

Since Germany was highly involved in European wars during the twentieth century, handling the heritage from this period in its capital is a complex undertaking. The material remains of the Nazi period, for example, have caused discussions and controversies since the end of World War II. Macdonald's (2009) study of the Nuremberg Nazi rally grounds, for example, demonstrates the complexities involved when dealing with such loaded material, the attitudes to which have changed dramatically since the 1950s. Perspectives on how to handle material remains related to these histories have varied greatly through time and have led to materials from other periods being ignored, trivialized, removed, commemorated, reconstructed, and used for educational purposes (Macdonald 2009). How to deal with a heritage colored by conflict is far from clear-cut. The need to maintain the material in order to keep the memories alive and make sure we remember the lessons learned has to be weighed against worries that some places, like former Nazi sites, can become places of pilgrimage for neo-Nazi groups. The need to face up to one's own past has to be weighed against the need to move forward. Discussing monuments dedicated to the Holocaust, Forty (1999, 6) claims: "The difficulty was to know how to remember the atrocity without lessening its horror, without somehow sanitizing it by making it tolerable to remember."

Changing Heritage

As times move on, the knowledge about, attitudes toward, and relationships with monuments change. Some places are kept as monuments while others disappear or are altered, having lost their original sense of importance. The retention of monuments, such as statues, memorials, and sites intimately connected to particular events, is therefore highly dependent on the attitudes of later generations. The remains and the memorials of the Berlin Wall are in a process of constant change. When the wall first came down, and as Germany was reunited, the immediate reaction was to remove all traces of the wall. Large-scale demolition was carried out in 1990–1991 to destroy traces of the former border. Although some voices called for parts of the border structure to be kept as a reminder and to act as a memorial, the majority of the remnants were successfully removed (Klausmeier and Schmidt 2004, 11; Harrison 2011). As time progressed, attitudes changed, and more and more sites became protected and recorded, including several sites and structures that were considered of such high importance to have become scheduled (given heritage status). Thus the Berlin Wall has changed from being a functioning border, to a demolition site, to a recognized heritage

site. It is clear that the remains of the Berlin Wall are now governed by what
Laurajane Smith (2006, 13) has called an "authorized heritage discourse," which
is the official discourse about sites that decides their legitimacy, rather than by
the content of the sites themselves (see McWilliams 2013, 190). This has both
pros and cons. As with many managed heritage sites the choices regarding what
to promote also affects those not chosen, often meaning that less desirable sites
disappear or are forgotten. So how do we understand this process of the Berlin
Wall moving from a functioning border to a memorial of division and terror?

There are already many different views and images of the Berlin Wall. Our
understanding of it is affected by the way that we have learned to perceive it.
The perception of the wall was very different in the West and the East. For the
Western world the image of the border was the large, outer concrete wall since,
apart from a few observation platforms, this was really the only viewable part
of the border structure (Schmidt 2005). In the West the wall became the symbol
of the Cold War (see Jones, this volume). As Schmidt (2005, 14) writes: "Only
at this border were the superpowers in such close contact and frequent conflict
that the Wall became the most potent symbol of the Cold War worldwide." In the
East the border went under the official name of Antifaschistischer Schutzwall
(antifascist protection wall) and was claimed to have been installed in order to
protect the East against its capitalist neighbors. Although people in the GDR
did not believe this to be true, the restrictions and high surveillance of people
led to it being visually inaccessible and rarely spoken of unless possibly as part
of a joke.

The image of the wall from the West was presented to the Western world as
a showpiece in the propaganda against the communist East. The high levels of
media coverage, partly as a result of the easy access to the physical form of the
wall, demonstrated clearly the material division between East and West, and
this image spread fast and efficiently. It soon became a tourist attraction, aided
by viewing platforms that provided a glimpse over the wall and into East Berlin.
The Berlin Wall became a popular feature in films and books, especially in the
increasingly popular spy genre. The remains of the Berlin Wall that are highlighted in the heritage and tourism industry today are still based on this image.
Just as the physical wall helped to make the Cold War and the idea of the Iron
Curtain more tangible, the remains of the border now are equally important to
the history writing of Berlin, the Cold War, and the Iron Curtain.

Conclusions

In a world where walls are increasingly seen as a solution to controlling the movement of people and to protecting ourselves against the "other," it is important to remember the walls that have existed in the past (McGuire, this volume). It is especially important to understand the full history of these walls, not just selected parts that fit our version of the past, even if this forces us to revisit the sources and keep challenging what we believe to be established narratives (see Papadopoulos, this volume). The Berlin Wall has started to take a further step away from its Cold War setting—it has now been "down" longer than it was "up" (Krämer 2018)—as it is compared to other walls being constructed in the world. It is often used in discussions of walls and division, but it is used in a metamorphosed way as an institutionalized heritage, the physical face of a metaphor.

The materiality of the Berlin Wall has been important throughout its history. During its time as a functioning border, it had the role of controlling movement and keeping people on the correct side. The physical features of the border were imperative in keeping the border working efficiently and for it to fulfill its purpose. Signs and roadblocks stopped unauthorized people getting near the border areas; high walls and anti-climbing features stopped people from scaling over; watchtowers helped monitor the areas around the barrier; large open death strips with barbed wire and mines made sure it was almost impossible to get through the border. This was a highly physical barrier in depth designed to kill rather than let transgressors through. The physical border structure was continuously updated as time went on, almost always in response to perceived threats.

The materiality of the Berlin Wall was also important for the metaphor of the Iron Curtain and the Cold War. When the Berlin Wall was constructed, it was one of the few places where the Western world could see and even touch the border between East and West. The image of the wall was broadcast and used in news coverage, in political and ideological rhetoric, and in popular culture. Just as the physical border helped to reinforce the metaphor, the metaphor also helped to reinforce the physical border, especially following its fall.

In a world after the Cold War, the materiality of the wall remains important, but now as an expression of remembrance and for education purposes. Looking at the border structures through a longer perspective, from functioning border to memorials and heritage sites, it becomes clear the wall is not a monolithic site; it has continuously but partially changed throughout its existence and continues to do so (see Papadopoulos and Dear, both this volume). Of course, not all of the remains of the former border structure have gone through the same development or these different stages. Some remains, often those that fit well with the idea of the Berlin Wall as a Cold War metaphor, appear to have become more memorialized. Those physical remains have an important role to play in keeping this memory and history alive. Many of the more mundane objects and sites that reflect the everyday reality of living alongside this border, however, have disappeared or are less promoted and visible because they do not fit the authorized heritage discourse. This has resulted in the version of the Berlin Wall as a metaphor of the Cold War and German division (heavily influenced by Western narratives) becoming the more prevailing story while the everyday side of the border is becoming increasingly forgotten.

Let us not forget that behind the idea of the Berlin Wall as a metaphor of the Cold War and the representations of it in places like Checkpoint Charlie, there is a hard physical reality of control, damage, and death, which stretched far from the border itself into every part of East German life. By highlighting certain parts of the story, we are simultaneously forgetting other parts, the more mundane stories represented in anti-climbing features, roadblocks, lanes through which to control traffic, patrol paths, and informants reporting people for using words like "the wall." These are the places or experiences that are less represented in today's heritage discourse in Berlin. What happens when all that is remembered of the Berlin Wall are the iconic images and moments? How can we learn from experience when we select a limited part of it to remember and represent a whole section of our history?

CHAPTER SEVEN

Boundary Work

Invisible Walls and Rebordering at the Margins of Europe

DIMITRIS C. PAPADOPOULOS

I discuss here the ways in which the Greek border, embodying fears of external—or even internal—threats, has operated, when required, as an effective
if not necessarily physical or visible wall on both land and water. I examine
how this function of the Greek border has been made possible through the
use of multiple spatial strategies and infrastructures, including the building of
walls or fences in "weak" locations. This involves the instrumentalization of
border landscapes and seascapes as physical barriers in a logic of continuous
zones of deterrence and division. Ultimately, in this chapter I show how the
complexities, materialities, and temporalities of such a process extend beyond
the border-as-wall metaphor. In that respect, the Greek case offers poignant
insights into moments in which borders acquire walling-in effects, are made
solid, or are extended and internalized, often in accelerated ways. These materializations always have a political context, and in the case of Greece they have
come in response to post-conflict anxieties or emergencies, from the postwar
Iron Curtain condition (McWilliams, this volume) to the current Fortress
Europe project (Jones, this volume).

Currently, Europe is actively proliferating the construction of walls and is amplifying its borders in parallel with wall-building projects globally (Brown 2010;
Dear 2015; Jones 2012, 2016, and this volume) and in contrast to the vision of a
"borderless" European Union. From 2015 to 2018, new heavily guarded walls or
fences were raised, extended, or reinforced from Greece and North Macedonia
to Serbia and Hungary (figure 7.1). This new project of raising walls comes as a
"defensive" response to refugee and migration flows, more specifically to the so-
called Balkan or eastern Mediterranean route leading from the Greek-Turkish
border to Central and Northern Europe through the Western Balkans. There

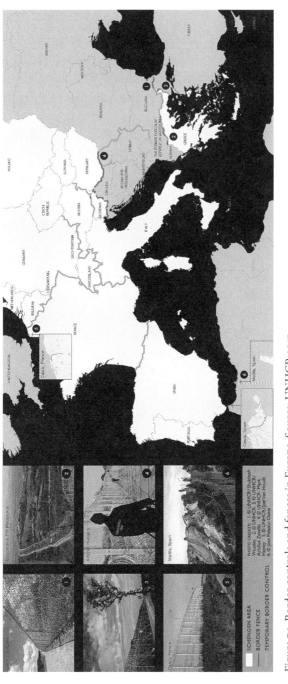

Figure 7.1. Border controls and fences in Europe. Source: UNHCR 2017.

were 856,723 migrants and refugees in 2015 and 173,450 in 2016 (UNHCR 2018) who followed this route in an attempt to reach—through Greece—Central and Northern European countries. The EU-Turkey agreement signed on March 18, 2016, explicitly aimed to stop "illegal immigration" and managed to limit sea arrivals to Greece in 2017 (table 7.1). But it caused an increase of flows through the deadly central and western Mediterranean routes, while simultaneously leaving thousands of migrants and refugees in limbo in camps dispersed on the Aegean islands and on mainland Greece.

Greek Aegean islands, such as Lesvos, Chios, Kos, and Samos, have been the first landing points of the eastern Mediterranean refugee route from the Turkish shores to Central Europe. After a first wave of refugee arrivals in Austria and Germany in late 2015, and a subsequent failure of European policy to implement reception quotas, most Balkan countries completely shut down their borders to constrain the refugee flow. In October 2015, just a month after Germany announced that it would reestablish border checks at the German-Austrian border, Austria announced the construction of a fence at its border with Slovenia. Almost at the same time, Hungary raised fences on its borders with Serbia and Croatia, redrawing the Balkan route along new paths through Croatia and Slovenia. In a domino effect, Slovenia built a fence with Croatia, and North Macedonia strengthened the security forces at its border with Greece while completely

Table 7.1. Refugee Sea Arrivals in Greece, 2015–2017

	2015	2016	2017
January	1,694	67,415	1,393
February	2,873	57,066	1,089
March	7,874	26,971	1,526
April	13,556	3,650	1,156
May	17,889	1,721	2,110
June	31,318	1,554	2,012
July	54,899	1,920	2,249
August	107,843	3,447	3,584
September	147,123	3,080	4,886
October	211,663	2,970	4,134
November	151,249	1,991	3,215
December	108,742	1,665	2,364
TOTALS	856,723	173,450	29,718

Data source: UNHCR 2018.

denying entry to most refugees, especially those not coming from Syria or Iraq. Thousands of refugees found themselves trapped in limbo in Greece.

The refugee flows, imagined through metaphors of "intrusion" as a European security crisis instead of as a reception crisis (Christopoulos and Souvlis 2016), fueled discourses of exclusion, division, and separation. In political terms, this has led the long-term vision of an integrated, borderless Europe to seamlessly transition into the "ill logic" (Gourgouris 2017) of the project Fortress Europe. In material terms, new walls and fences are being raised and constructed,[1] and existing fencing and border checkpoints are being reinforced with the explicit objective of blocking immigration and constraining refugee flows (see Dear, this volume). This is a project of exclusion, separation, and rebordering that violently shuts down, at a deadly cost, existing routes and passages, such as the Balkan refugee route. It facilitates the building of new infrastructures and creates new spatial categories, such as the so-called refugee hot spots, which usually serve as camps and registration sites for new arrivals.

This project of border securitization, which has turned Europe into the "world's deadliest border" (Jones 2016), involves sophisticated monitoring and data collection systems (see Dorsey and Díaz-Barriga, this volume), sea operations by Frontex (the EU border agency), and even pushbacks of migrant boats. The Greek national border has a special place in this project. It serves as a frontier stronghold of the European "fortress" in ways that are similar to how it was used to project European border security anxieties in the past. It is, therefore, critical to contextualize the current transformations of the Greek border in response to the refugee crisis within the historical trajectory of its past bordering moments (see McGuire, this volume, for a broad history of wall building).

Through a historical perspective, I examine two Greek border regions: the island of Lesvos, a few miles off the coast of Turkey, and the Prespa lakes at the triple border of Greece, Albania, and North Macedonia. Lesvos has emerged in recent years as one of the Mediterranean hot spots of the refugee crisis. In 2015, more than 500,000 migrants and refugees landed on the shores of the island. The border shutdown along the Balkan refugee route and the agreement between Turkey and the European Union stranded thousands of migrants and asylum seekers in refugee camps on the island. Prespa, a wetland area shared by Greece, Albania, and North Macedonia, witnessed a different kind of displacement related to the Greek Civil War (1946–1949), which ended dramatically with the government defeat of the communist Democratic Army. The war caused a mass exodus of thousands of civilians and political refugees to Eastern Bloc countries and established a postwar condition of division, separation, and securitization that essentially remained in effect until the signing on June 17, 2018, of the Prespa Agreement by Greece and North Macedonia, which ended the long-standing dispute over the name of the latter. Despite their local specificities, both cases encapsulate the tensions, desires, and anxieties of Europe's imagined margins and provide a historical depth to examining European borders that materialize at times of crisis.

By juxtaposing these different border episodes, I aim to problematize the idea that the current European border crisis, triggered by increased migration flows, is an isolated or exceptional moment. Through historicizing the Greek national border, I show that in fact these entities are in a perpetual process of creating multiple material lives, layers, and enduring effects of separation and division. I am interested not just in highlighting key border making and unmaking biographical moments but also in revealing the mechanics of loosening or amplifying border infrastructures, which do not necessarily occur in a linear fashion. Drawing from Adrian Little's (2015, 432) notion of the "complex temporality" of the border focusing at "different speeds" on "different aspects of bordering," I use these two cases not just as chronological moments but also as thresholds that accelerated, condensed, or interrupted different ways of bordering. I see these moments within a multitemporal, multilayered continuum: they are triggered or conjured up depending on bordering needs, capacities, and conditions. If the border-crossing refugees in the Aegean have triggered what Reeves (2016, 168) calls a "tempo of bordering that is characterized by emergency," we should look at other nested, critically differentiating events, haunting anxieties, and accumulated capacities that enable changes of pace and intensity.

Following this problematic, I examine the national borders in these two regions not merely as lines or walls on the ground but rather as a set of (1) shifting spatial and material configurations, including both built structures and geomorphological features, which often produce enduring ruins with long-lasting effects; (2) infrastructures and apparatuses of surveillance and control, some of which are mobile; and (3) processes of bordering, unbordering, and rebordering that are not limited to the nation-state border but also include the making and propagation of multiple internal boundaries and divisions. Borrowing from analyses of the border as technique and process (Green 2005, 2013; Van Houtum and Van Naerssen 2002) and from Yael Navaro-Yashin's (2009) concept of borders as both rooted and rhizomatic, I use the term "bordering" to emphasize boundaries both as anchored divisions and as ever-active instruments of propagating fragmentation and internalizing differentiating relations. Also, following Sarah Green's (2005) discussion of bordering within a project of relocating Europe and Saskia Sassen's (2006) analysis of new border capabilities in multiple sites and on different territorial scales beyond the nation-state, I argue for an understanding of current border security tensions in Greece and Europe within the historical trajectory of an unfinished, still-unfolding project. In this respect, borders must be viewed within Europe's physical and imagined terrain, which mobilizes designed features and built infrastructures, utilizes "soft," data-driven capabilities of surveillance and monitoring, and weaponizes landscapes and seascapes from the Balkan Mountains to the Aegean Sea.

Twenty-first-century works in border studies have complicated the notion of the border by challenging its often taken-for-granted materiality, complicating its temporality, and diversifying its forms of presence and effect, including border patrols, drones, databases, and software (Johnson et al. 2011; Little 2015; Green 2005, 2013; Reeves 2016; Demetriou 2013; Potzsch 2015). At the same time, there is an acknowledged need to flesh out stories of where and how the border is seen, materialized, and felt (Johnson et al. 2011; Reeves 2016). Told together, the two border stories discussed in this chapter can be seen as a contribution to destabilizing monolithic views of solid walls and borders and moving toward a more fluid and nuanced understanding of boundary making within a diversified repertoire of spatial and material strategies of exclusion, separation, and division. These stories also bare the sensorial depth and the often-traumatic impact of boundaries that have been felt and experienced as impenetrable walls of family separation, fragmentation, and loss (see Bishara, this volume, on the West Bank).

My discussion of these two border cases draws from ethnographic fieldwork at refugee camps and sites on Lesvos (Stefatos, Papadopoulos, and Haralambous 2015) and from a much longer (2002–2010) ethnographic project on landscape history and perception in the Prespa lakes area (Papadopoulos 2010).

(In)visible Walls: Materialities of the Greek Border

The border forms of Lesvos and the Prespa lakes are not primarily physical walls or extensive built barriers. Their morphology includes border checkpoints, partial fencing, military outposts, sea patrols, mountain ridges, and miles of water.

Except for a narrow stretch of land on the Greek-Turkish boundary along the river Evros, the Greek border lacks the monumentality of a massive border wall or a continuous built barrier (see Dear, this volume, on the US-México border). Its hinterland is dotted, instead, with the traces of the border's supportive infrastructure and long-term impact: abandoned checkpoints and outposts, mine-filled areas, ruined villages, and personal items left behind by border crossers. The reimagined built structures and designed interventions work in synergy with the physical features of the landscape and the diverse and often unwelcoming geomorphology. In this sense, the spatial strategies and apparatuses of division, separation, and walling, including the strategic use of vacated and deserted areas as buffer zones, often serve as a continuation or extension of actual wall building, as in the case of the US-México border (De León 2015). In the Greek case, it is the landscape or seascape itself—operationalized by the border security forces as part of European deterrence tactics, reinforced with built structures where needed, and supported with soft or mobile surveillance tools and infrastructures—that functions as a wall (Kourelis 2017; Dorsey and Díaz-Barriga, this volume).

The interlocking function of landscape features and built components is best illustrated in the security priorities materialized on the Greek-Turkish border. In 2012, the Greek government started the construction of a security fence along the Greek-Turkish land border. The barbed-wire fence, more than ten kilometers long and three meters high, is enhanced by twenty-five thermal cameras and the Border Surveillance Operations Center. The Greek minister of internal affairs described the fence as having "both practical and symbolic value" to discourage "illegal migrants and smugglers." "We will not allow," the minister added, "Greece to become a transit country for migrants on their way to other European Union countries" (TVXS 2012). Of course, this is exactly what happened in the following years with Greece becoming the European entry point to the Balkan refugee route. While the fence succeeded locally in reducing the influx of migrants, it created the need for refugees to choose alternative and even more dangerous routes across the Aegean Sea.

The securitization shift from the land border to the sea border, made possible with the involvement of European and international forces, such as Frontex (the European Border and Coast Guard Agency) and NATO, turned the Aegean into a critical zone for implementing migration surveillance and deterrence policies. The liquid Greek-Turkish border in the Aegean lacks built walls, gates,

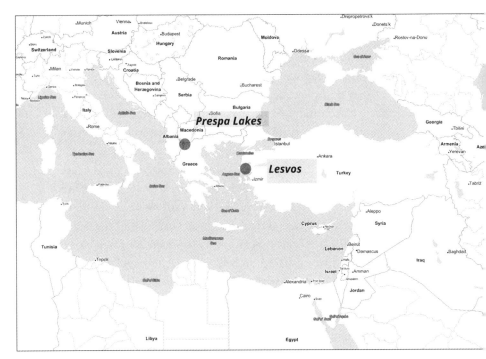

Figure 7.2. Border regions discussed in the chapter. Map created by Dimitris C. Papadopoulos with data from OpenStreetMap and map tiles by Stamen Design, under CC BY 3.0, 2017.

or checkpoints, much to the frustration of some European countries, which see the lack of monumental borders along the sea as a security vulnerability. Yet, enhanced sea patrols and military surveillance and, most important, more than 1,800 dead and missing migrants from 2014 to 2018 in the Aegean demonstrate the effectiveness of the instrumentalized landscape—or, in this case, seascape— as an unspoken but effective deterrence infrastructure (UNHCR 2018).

The Greek national boundaries, in all their geographic diversity, challenge a conventional understanding of the border as a—thick or thin—wall and of the built wall as the exclusive or quintessential material form of division (figure 7.2). The Greek case favors a conceptualization of boundaries that materialize and dematerialize in different forms, at different times, and at different scales beyond a border-as-wall or border-as-line perspective. As Reeves (2016, 179) observes: "The study of borders is perhaps still too wedded to considerations (and critiques) of the fact of exclusion (the 'border-as-wall') than to how and for whom and with which tempi [a] 'border' comes to materialize or dematerialize." Below, I trace some key transformations, moments of materialization and dematerialization, walling, and permeability of the Greek border in its historical trajectory from the early twentieth century to the current moment.

The "Wall" on Water: Lesvos and the Aegean as a Securitized Seascape

The European border security measures and migration deterrence policies have turned the Aegean into a highly monitored and increasingly militarized seascape. The EU-Turkey agreement stated that stopping "irregular migration" was the key objective. Donald Tusk, the president of the European Council, has been explicit in trying to discourage migrants from crossing the European borders: "Do not come to Europe. Do not believe the smugglers. Do not risk your lives and your money. It is all for nothing" (Sky News 2016). This is a strategy aiming to repel, detain, deport, "sanitize," and keep out the "other" (see the introduction to this volume). It is not a victimless strategy, as the rising death toll in the Mediterranean attests. The EU-Turkey agreement and the shutdown of the Balkan route led to a limited flow along the eastern Mediterranean route but also caused a rise in deaths along the central Mediterranean route from North Africa to Italy (table 7.2).

These measures have also inspired a series of new internal walls, boundaries, and spatial units of detention, separation, or limited access on the Aegean islands that receive the highest numbers of migrants and refugees (table 7.3). Despite the global interest, media attention, and spectacle of life in refugee camps from Lesvos to Lampedusa (Dines, Montagna, and Ruggiero 2015), the lived experiences, materialities, and micro-topographies of such sites have yet to be fully explored.

Table 7.2. Dead and Missing by Major Refugee Route, 2015–2017

	2015	2016	2017
Greece	799	441	46
Italy	2,913	4,578	2,856
Spain	59	77	217

Data source: UNHCR 2018.

Table 7.3. Sea Arrivals in Greece by Key Island Location, 2015–2016

	2015	2016
Lesvos	506,919	94,854
Chios	120,556	39,550
Samos	73,134	13,255
Leros	31,618	8,723
Kos	58,503	5,101

Data source: UNHCR 2018.

In the summer of 2015, I and Katerina Stefatos (Stefatos, Papadopoulos, and Haralambous 2015) visited the Moria camp on Lesvos. This is one of the refugee hot spots that has attracted global media attention. Lesvos, less than ten miles from the Turkish coast, witnessed more than half a million sea arrivals in 2015. This is not the first time the island has had to accommodate a massive number of refugees. Both prior to and following the 1923 Greek-Turkish population exchange, thousands of Greek refugees from Asia Minor relocated to the island. The echoes of this legacy are discernible in the ways that locals deal with the current refugee crisis.

To manage the influx on Lesvos, local police and other authorities have employed a separation system for the locations of the refugee camps and their inhabitants, based on country of origin. Kara Tepe, three miles from the island's port town, hosts Syrians granted refugee status. Moria is the home of the "others," who are seen as Europe's undesirable migrants: Iraqis, Afghans, Somalis, and Eritreans. Moria military base is in an olive grove. A wire fence surrounds a documentation unit partitioning Moria between registered and unregistered people, colloquially called "Moria In" and "Moria Out." The camp is also divided into Arabic-speaking (west) and non-Arabic-speaking (east) sections. At the time of our visit to the camp (August 2015), there were about 600 people in the Moria In unit. On the periphery of the camp (Moria Out), 2,000 people waited to be called in and documented. Many lived in tents in groups of five or six, most of them families with young children or young couples. Food and water were scarce. The camp was sweltering, as the area lies exposed to the sun for most of the day, exacerbating the results of poor hygiene conditions and shared and self-maintained toilets.

As we were preparing to leave the camp, exhausted and almost dehydrated after spending only a few hours at the site, a young Somali who had thus far been preoccupied with making his phone work, turned to us and asked in English, "What place is this?" We said, "This is Moria." He looked at us, disoriented, and thanked us. A few seconds later, he asked again, "What place is this? Is this island?" "This is Lesvos," we answered, realizing that he did not know which part of Greece or Europe he had landed in.

"What place is this?" is a fundamental question that highlights the fragmented personal geographies of displacement, but it also brings forward the function, type, and features of the refugee camp as a unique spatial entity or a "space of exception" (Agamben 2005; Dorsey and Díaz-Barriga, this volume).

This is also a question that challenges and exposes our shortcomings as researchers and "observers." What kind of place is the Moria camp, and how are we to understand the refugee hot spots as new spatial categories? What are the legal and institutional frameworks and conditions that govern and regulate them? How do we map such spaces and render them visible? How do we trace and record their ephemeral materialities and their boundaries? These are critical questions, especially considering the urgency and contingency associated with these sites. Both activists and researchers have started looking at the micro-scale of these places (Kourelis 2016; Hamilakis 2016; MapFugees Project 2016), but there is still a lot to be done. Dunn and Cons (2014, 106) in a comparative analysis of border sites and refugee camps respond to the need to map such "sensitive spaces" with the concept of "aleatory sovereignty" and suggest "the centrality of contingency, context, and ethnographic engagement to any such project of analysis."

The Moria camp has turned out to be a landmark of these new geographies and materialities of displacement, division, and migration deterrence (figure 7.3). In their daily congestion, their infrastructure failures (Green 2017), and the tragic deaths associated with them, camps such as Moria represent Europe's policy shortcomings as a "ruin-in-the making" (Hamilakis 2016). The camp's military organization of space—its combination of nested, enclosed, and accessible sections, the fences, and the gates—manifests and reproduces spatialities of operational segregation, exclusion, and incarceration. Similarly, the few miles separating Moria from the Kara Tepe open-air camp spatializes a hierarchical classification and division between "refugees" and "economic migrants." This separation is required for the categorization of the "worthy" and the "unworthy" to enable the implementation of the current European policies (see Dinzey-Flores, this volume, on separating the haves and the have-nots).

The walls and fences of the Moria camp are not border walls; in some ways, they fulfill the function of segregation walls found in contemporary cities (McAtackney, this volume). They separate the haves from the have-nots and act as containers for those who have already crossed the border. The national border in the Aegean seems to be penetrable, navigable, even invisible, promising proximity in contrast to the solidity of a built barrier, but this perceived ease of movement is illusory. The absence of built walls at the border is linked to the presence of walls elsewhere and to the rapid development of a supportive border infrastructure of surveillance, detention, and deportation, which has arisen precisely in response to the lack of physical walls and barriers. The border

Figure 7.3. The main gate of Moria camp, Lesvos. Photo by Dimitris C. Papadopoulos, August 2015.

fence on the Greek-Turkish land border, which Greece constructed in 2012, caused a shift of migrant flows to the Aegean. Consequently, Greece dealt with the increased flows in the Aegean with increased border security, surveillance, and infrastructure. Greece is having to manage the Aegean influx as well as the refugees that are stranded within its territory and in response has created a number of new hot spots to facilitate the processing and documentation of arrivals. In reality, these hot spots have turned into pre-deportation or indefinite detention centers for migrants and asylum seekers.

Although not boundary markers themselves, the hot spots can be seen as part of the regional networked and enhanced border security infrastructure, which includes databases, operational centers, and sea patrols. They are also to be viewed as part of a continuous operational border seascape defined by both soft and rigid border policies and conditions. One thing that the "soft" border often masks is the violence it produces. A less rigid border does not mean an unhindered crossing. On the contrary, the Aegean crossing is dangerous and deadly. Refugees on overcrowded dinghies have to deal with faulty safety and navigation controls, poor weather conditions, and reported pushbacks by sea border patrols. From January 2015 to September 2016, 1,224 deaths, including many children, were reported along the eastern Mediterranean route. The deaths in the Aegean and in the Mediterranean painfully demonstrate the violence and biopolitical power of the "wall-less" soft border, which in reality works as an extension of the walled borders and security mechanisms of Fortress Europe.

In discussing the critical and traumatic issue of missing migrants on Lesvos, Iosif Kovras and Simon Robins (2016) use the concept of "death as border" to illustrate the effect of border-crossing deaths, most important in relation to the invisibility of the dead bodies as worthy of a process of mourning and the challenges that family members face in trying to identify and properly grieve their loved ones. The words of an NGO activist interviewed by Kovras and Robins (2016, 41) are telling:

> The dead [migrants] are the most appalling spectacle I have ever seen, because I [have] visualized the death and what it means not to be able to cross the border. So, the theoretical framework about walls, securitization, acquires a new dimension when you see decomposed bodies. Even more tragic is the fact that you [could] not bury them as they deserved to be buried and that no one could identify them.

The death-as-border condition highlights the often-overlooked long-term effects of border security policies and the hidden infrastructures that have turned the Aegean into an invisible wall separating families, even in death. It sheds light on the unseen slow violence and psychological impact of loss and separation at the key sites where the nation-state implements border security measures, such as refugee camps (see Bishara, this volume). The operation, openness, visibility, and purpose of these sites and structures of (im)mobility are contested. There are several issues concerning the type and character as well as the legal or administrative jurisdiction over the refugee camps and hot spots. Their status—whether ephemeral or semipermanent, isolated and unseen by the public or open to efforts of support and solidarity—embodies the spatial tensions and relations between the state, local stakeholders, and the refugees themselves.

The micro-topography of sites such as the Moria camp does not merely reflect an implementation of exceptional measures in response to an unprecedented crisis. It rather dictates certain modes of presence, visibility, and legitimacy. Such border sites aim to secure the European territory from the "intrusive" or "contaminating" "other," who is imagined as a possible threat, and to keep the

Figure 7.4. Moria camp, Lesvos. Photo by Dimitris C. Papadopoulos, August 2015.

presence of this imagined "other" contained within controlled conditions and environments. Although not always manifested as physical walls, these sites and structures display the wall effect of defensive or preemptive isolation and segregation. Seen as part of the extended regional network of border security, they morph into built walls and fences, sea patrols, and/or military checkpoints. Their "thickening" (Rosas 2006b) intensity adapts to refugee routes, policy and security priorities, and landscape morphologies. Their rigidness follows the ebbs and flows of human mobility, and their violence is unmasked when triggered by local crises and incidents.

In October 2016, a fire almost completely destroyed the Moria camp (figure 7.4). In November 2016, another fire killed a woman and a child, and in the first months of 2017 three men died after reportedly inhaling fumes from a heater. Local authorities rebuilt part of the camp after this damage. Meanwhile, refugees, including families, continue to share tents in the harsh winter and the broiling summer. Yet the question of "What place is this?" remains largely unanswered.

The Walled-In Lakes: Landscape, Separation, and Boundary Work

On the northwest side of the Greek border, not far from the Balkan refugee route, the region of the Prespa lakes has witnessed a different kind of displacement and a spatial regime of division and fragmentation. At first gaze, not much in these scenic landscapes shared by Greece, Albania, and North Macedonia suggests a story of conflict or separation. Yet from the first moment of drawing the border in 1913, the inaccessibility of the region has been continuously used in parallel with human interventions to produce a sense of separation and amplify a walling-in effect. The landscape itself has been the wall, and it was perceived as such as early as 1852 when landscape painter Edward Lear (1852, 61) described a "bright lake, walled in by high, snowy mountains."

Like the borders on the Aegean, borders in Prespa are not always visible. As Eleni Myrivili (2003, 26) observes in her ethnography of the border in Prespa, "Only if you cross the boundary, the policing of the border is revealed: the border becomes apparent through the repercussions of your act of transgression." I was largely unaware of the materiality of the border in Prespa when I first started fieldwork there, but I soon realized its layered and multidimensional presence through certain interactions. In the summer of 2007, Petros, a thirty-five-year-old border police officer, gave me a tour of the Greek-Albanian border in the mountains above the Prespa lakes (Papadopoulos 2016). In a wide plateau giving access to Cerje, the nearest Albanian village, Petros pointed to a whitewashed concrete pyramid planted in the ground. On two sides, there were two letters carved: "E" and "A." The third side was marked with a letter and a number: "I10." A series of these concrete pillars, located at intervals of a few hundred meters, marks the borderline across the mountain; the boundary even continues on the surface of the lake, where it takes the form of a buoy marking the triple national border of Greece, Albania, and North Macedonia. Petros explained that although occasionally used by the border police, this infrastructure of boundary pillars and military outposts or watchtowers has been largely abandoned following the partial demilitarization of this part of the Greek-Albanian border after the collapse of the communist regime in Albania.

In this border walk, the boundary was revealed as a solid, material thing and, at the same time, as a ruin in the making. The carefully measured distances between the pillars demonstrated the labor and design invested in the construction of the border. Colonel Frank L. Giles, a member of one of the original

Figure 7.5a–b. Boundary pillar (*a*) and abandoned military post (*b*) on the Greek-Albanian border. Photos by Dimitris C. Papadopoulos, 2015.

demarcation survey teams in the region, described this labor as "boundary-work" (Giles 1930). At the same time, the lack of care and maintenance of the border and its half-ruined supportive infrastructure is testimony to the ability of borders to slowly but steadily dissolve when not maintained (see McWilliams, this volume). Walking and driving across the border was a powerful reminder that historical and political fluctuations are made material in the fluctuations of the border's visibility (Papadopoulos 2016).

This border infrastructure has not only been exposed to the corrosive force of time but it has also been haunted by the historical shifts and conflicts or political anxieties and priorities of different eras (figures 7.5a–b). In mid-2013, a local Greek border police officer and two Albanian drug smugglers were killed in a shootout (Vithoulkas 2013). Many commentators and police officers saw this and other border incidents as a result of a shift of priorities and resources from the understaffed local border police to immigration prevention on the Greek-Turkish border.

Almost thirty years after the act of drawing the nation-state boundaries in Prespa, the border became a site of conflict, destruction, and displacement. The Greek Civil War ended dramatically in 1949 with the defeat of the communists in the mountains around the Prespa lakes. The devastating impact of the war was reflected in the 1951 census, which recorded fewer than 3,000 people in the region compared to the 1940 census, which documented more than 10,000 people. The landscape was dramatically transformed. Most villages were either sparsely populated or entirely deserted; houses, schools, and roads had been damaged by bombing; and fields were left uncultivated and overgrown. The civil war established a condition of destruction, abandonment, and ruination that still defines the region to a large extent (Papadopoulos 2016).

During the war, the guerrilla forces used the national border, first on the Greek-Yugoslav side and ultimately on the Greek-Albanian side, as a tactical device for retreat and regrouping purposes. Thousands of Slavic-speaking ethnic minority villagers, both fighters and civilians, followed the final retreat of the Democratic Army in 1949 into Albania (Danforth and Van Boeschoten 2012). For most of the people who abandoned their villages, including many children, this would be a permanent displacement. Living in Eastern Europe as political refugees, deprived of their Greek citizenship, and excluded, with a few exceptions for short visits, from the right to return to their homelands, most of them found the border that they had once walked indefinitely shut to them. The national border, strategically porous during the civil war, was now rigid, securitized, punitively divisive, and unforgiving for the ones displaced. But even those who stayed or were able to return to their village had to deal with the alienating experience of coming back to a place they could barely recognize. This sense of alienation was a consistent pattern in my interviews with locals:

On December 11, I left prison and came to Prespa. I came here but had no one . . . no mother, no father. The whole village was deserted. We gathered about twenty individuals. We were going to the neighboring village to sleep over. No one was allowed to stay here at night. (Stavros)

When I first came here I was scared. . . . All [of the] people were in army suits . . . returning from prisons, exiles, former captives. They were looking ugly to me, [and] I could not recognize them, even my own people. I had a cousin—we grew up together—dressed in uniform, he was unshaven, he hugged me. Who are you[?] I asked him. (Christos)

I stayed in Poland for sixteen years. From '49 to '65. When we got back, we once got to see our village. . . . There was nothing but ruins . . . only the church was recognizable. We had nowhere to go [and] we didn't even have a boat. They wiped out everything. (Sophia)

Although the destruction of the war altered the landscape in dramatic and, in some cases, irreversible ways, the postwar void in this border region was strategically convenient for the government. The state employed a series of quarantine and surveillance measures in the border area—instrumentalizing the spatial vacuum created by the war—that were not lifted until the late 1980s. Declaring the area a military zone, the government merged the populations of villages, established checkpoints, required special permits for locals traveling to nearby towns or villages, and provided land and other incentives to attract settlers from central Greece.

Apart from this selective resettlement of villages, there was a lack of state provision or planning to revitalize the region. The slow ruination was not inevitable, but rather was intentional or calculated. By the 1950s, most of these deserted villages were accessible only by boat since the government had failed to maintain the infrastructure or construct new networks.[2] This post–civil war state-regulated condition of securitization at the border thus limited access and increased abandonment, dotting the landscape with ruined fields. The ruins of collapsed houses, schools, and churches in Prespa are slowly blending into the area's landscape and ecology. Three of the villages that were abandoned after the war now lie at the core of the national park designated in 1973. These "ecologies of ruin" (Papadopoulos 2016), now recategorized within the domain of "nature," were made possible by the absence of human activity in a militarized border zone of control and surveillance. They echo and amplify the postwar void of demographic shock, displacement, and discontinuation of economic life.

For at least four decades following the civil war, the state treated the region as a part of its military defense to repel the "communist threat" from the north. The external national borders with Albania and Yugoslavia were reinforced and heavily guarded. However, there was not a physical wall marking the border. Greece used the landscape—insular in its geomorphology, sparsely populated, and militarized—as division and separation infrastructure. Wall-less but still preventive and potentially violent, the border morphed across fifteen miles from a liquid state on the surface of the trinational Prespa lake to wire fences and checkpoints, and from abandoned fields and deserted villages to boundary pillars on mountaintops. The absence of a continuous, physical wall did not ease the sense of division and fragmentation. On the contrary, the military and surveillance infrastructure and the voids in between together formed an invisible yet impenetrable "wall," a peculiar no-man's-land dissected into a series of internal security and administrative boundaries, environmental preservation zones, and pockets of limited human activity.

In the twenty-first century, borders, routes, and networks, especially in the Western Balkans, have been increasingly highlighted as post-conflict sites of peace, cross-border collaboration, and European integration. The twin Prespa lakes have emerged as an iconic landscape in the changing context of this post-conflict, cross-border peace-building project.

The end of the conflicts in the former Yugoslavia and the expansion of European Union structures in southeastern Europe have created a completely new political environment that offers new possibilities compared to previously impenetrable national borders. International organizations, financial institutions, and NGOs have funded several programs to establish zones and protected areas of rich biodiversity and cultural heritage. These designated conservation areas have emerged as symbolic loci of reconciliation and transnational cooperation, as islands of celebrated heritage or valued nature in an archipelago of conflict debris.

Some initiatives have taken this remapping project one step further by connecting these conservation areas through green corridors and networks of cooperation. The Balkan Green Belt, part of the European Green Belt stretching from Northern to Southern Europe along the traces of the Iron Curtain, aims to establish an extended nature conservation corridor through "countries once hostile to one another" as a "shining example" of achievable reconciliation (Euronatur 2016). The region of the Prespa lakes is part of this envisioned Balkan Green Belt and home of the first transboundary park in the Balkans. The park was established in 2000 with the support and collaboration of multiple regional actors and international organizations, such as the Mediterranean Wetlands Initiative, Euronatur, the Swiss Federal Institute for Environmental Science and Technology, the International Union for Conservation of Nature, the World Bank, the United Nations Environment Programme, the United Nations Development Programme, and the World Wildlife Fund. Such initiatives remap the Western Balkans in ways that cancel, circumvent, or render obsolete physical or metaphorical walls. In this sense, initiatives like the Prespa transboundary park or the Balkan Green Belt are projects of both unbordering and rebordering. Not only do they signify but they also actually produce a new spatial reality on the ground in which the Iron Curtain gives way to a continuum of porous borders, green corridors, and islands, imagined and designed beyond national territories.

Of course, the narrative of cross-border peace building and cooperation in the Balkans is spatially and temporally specific and has been abruptly interrupted by wall-building responses to the recent migration flows. Current tensions and border spasms seem to be at odds with the cross-border integration initiatives. This dissonance echoes past tensions and conflicts during which the border had a more solid presence manifested through physical walls and infrastructures—to which it seems to be returning in the current moment. The transboundary Prespa park is a telling case that demonstrates the capacity of national borders for temporal fluctuations and material morphing.

Boundary Work: Rebordering, Rewalling, Remapping

The tensions, conflicts, and political conditions that have defined the form and function of the border on the island of Lesvos and in the Prespa lakes region are different in significant ways. There are, however, analogies to be drawn and patterns that emerge when it comes to the capacity of the Greek border to function as a diverse but continuous terrain of deterrence and separation in response to crises and political priorities.

It is clear that the bordering practices in both cases have used the synergy between the diverse morphology of the landscapes and built structures and designed interventions. In this sense, the weaponization of the Aegean as a seascape of deterrence is an extension of the border work done by the ten-mile fence on the mainland Greek-Turkish border. Likewise, the construction of new walls and fences all the way from Greece to Hungary is part of the massive securitization project in the Mediterranean, which Saskia Sassen (2006) has described as constructing "a sort of Berlin wall across the Mediterranean." Despite the undeniable visual and symbolic power of the border-as-wall metaphor (Brown 2010; Dorsey and Díaz-Barriga 2010; Jones 2012 and this volume; McGuire and McAtackney, this volume; Marcuse 1994), the border dynamic is far more complex, historically evolving, and inherently unstable (McGuire, this volume).

A nuanced approach to understanding walls and borders would lead us to think about the forms, qualities, and functions of both external and internal boundaries as rather fluid and responsive, especially in relation to their (1) solidity or materiality, (2) historicity and temporality, and (3) expansiveness and internalization.

First, not all walls are solid or impenetrable, and unbuilt elements, such as landscape features, can operate in the same way as physical barriers. The reinforcement and regulation of borders involves "softer" or less visible forms, including monitoring and surveillance infrastructure, drones (Fotiadis 2015), software, and databases (see Dorsey and Díaz-Barriga, this volume). Acknowledging the various hard and soft border qualities is not meant to make a distinction between "real" impenetrable barriers and less effective boundaries but rather to highlight alternative, less visible or tangible, yet often equally powerful or violent forms of division and separation. The violence that borders produce is not caused by their thickness, visibility, or wall-like qualities but is often generated in the absence of these qualities. For all the walls of Fortress Europe to be rendered visible, we should look beyond the physical boundaries to the effects and repercussions of the acts of transgression: refugee hot spots, detention centers, pushbacks on the sea, and/or involuntary relocations. We should also not underestimate the performative power of walls as statements, which are effective even before an actual wall is built or even if a wall is not built at all (see the conclusion of this volume). The concept of Fortress Europe has a certain impact in filtering perceptions and regulating human behavior even before it materializes on the ground.

Second, it is important to historicize the border in all its transformations and reincarnations. The European borders that refugees have to cross have been reinforced with physical walls and, in some cases, internally shifted in just a matter of a few years or even months. These rapid shifts or transformations quite often echo past anxieties and responses to similarly perceived threats or crises and in some cases even reactivate dormant apparatuses of security and surveillance. The Greek borders provide an imaginary site for the shifting fears, anxieties, and desires not only of the Greek nation-state but—in the case of the refugee crisis— of Europe as well. The complete border shutdown along the Balkan route puts on hold visions of borderless cooperation and echoes instead the ghostly presence of the Iron Curtain or the Second World War. West-Pavlov (2011) argues that World War II's Atlantic Wall bunkers are haunted by the cultural anxiety of immigrant "invasions" at the limits of contemporary Europe. Similarly, the ruins of the Greek Civil War or the Iron Curtain, including abandoned military barracks, checkpoints, and even concentration camps (Hardach 2015), are reanimated through the urgencies, fears, and anxieties—real or perceived—that the refugee crisis has produced. In this sense, walls and boundaries should be viewed as multitemporal projects, always in the making or unmaking (McGuire, this volume). Instead of static borders, we should be talking about processes of bordering, rebordering, and unbordering.

Finally, another key quality of how borders operate is their elasticity. Borders not only endure but also breathe and grow into new spatial forms and relations. The remains, networks, and infrastructures of the Greek border, from Lesvos to Prespa, seem to act as "pulsating ruins" that are both expanding and contracting (Gordillo 2013). As Navaro-Yashin (2009) argues in the case of Cyprus, borders can be seen as both rooted and rhizomatic. The material rootedness of a border anchors its authority on the ground, while at the same time less visible shifts and slow transformations are in play. In the Aegean, the "invisible" sea border extends through a network of nested military, surveillance, and administrative units, such as the hot spots. In a similar way, the post–civil war northern border gradually accumulated a series of internalized boundaries that defined security zones, environmental preservation areas, and access or mobility restrictions. These internalized bounded spaces are meant to restrict, contain, filter, and classify politically dangerous subjects or ethnically and racially defined "others." Whether implemented by the nation-state targeting unwanted minorities and potential internal threats in villages, or dictated by European policies creating hierarchies between migrants and refugees, these internal walls, fences, and checkpoints function as strategies of othering the bodies of both the living and the dead. They wall in the perceived "others," making them unable to move freely and placing them in limbo.

If borders are both hard and soft, walled and wall-less, materially rooted and fluid, physically condensed and sporadic, how should we study and analyze them? If they materialize not just in the form of monumental barriers but also as checkpoints, hot spots, detention centers, border patrols, drones, and surveillance software, how can we map them and render them visible?

I return to the term "boundary-work," used by Frank Giles (1930) as a way of thinking about the labor of bordering and rebordering as an ongoing project. Boundary work draws from what has been defined as an "anthropology of borderlands" (Alvarez 1995) and from analytical approaches to the border as "technique" and "process." A similar concept of border work has been used by Malm and Green (2013) and Reeves (2014). My use of "boundary work" here has a dual function. On one hand, boundary work aims to destabilize established notions of the border as form, scale, and temporality. At the same time, I use it in a constructive way to try to underline the labor required to "anchor" the border on the ground and to imagine new ways of writing about, narrating, and mapping borders and their stories. If borders are multitemporal projects of contingent and dispersed phenomena that mobilize a multitude of networks and assemblages on different scales, how do we show the painstaking and methodical work invested in drawing, constructing, and maintaining them? And how do we narrate and visualize their spatial and material histories? As Reeves (2016, 179) points out: "Getting borders to cohere as material-territorial things demands constant work of construction and repair." If Frank Giles's boundary work involved theodolites, boundary pillars, and the enforcement of the will of the early twentieth-century Western powers against the knowledge and priorities of local villagers, contemporary boundary work in the Aegean or across the Balkan route involves Frontex ships, drones, thermal cameras, tear gas, riot police, detention centers, pushbacks, and deportations.

Boundary work of course is not limited to the national territory. As Saskia Sassen (2005, 523) reminds us, bordering capabilities "entail a partial denationalising of what has been constructed historically as national and hence an unsettling of the meaning of geographic borders." The European response to the refugee crisis is a major project of rebordering, reimagining, and reclassifying (Green 2013) that is still unfolding and that should be seen within long historical trajectories, across different geographic scales, and through specific and decisive border making or unmaking moments.

A multiscalar, multitemporal boundary work, as a form of research work, is not meant as a separation from the immediacy of the border as the "field." On the contrary, it requires revisiting the border in all its sites, materialities, and less visible formations with the scrutiny, but not imperial arrogance, of Frank Giles's survey team. It also requires sharing the boundary work with those most affected by borders: the ones trying to cross them and the ones living near them. Some successful solidarity initiatives, such as the MapFugees Project (2016), have shown that border crossers and border dwellers can be empowered by collaborative, bottom-up border mapping.

The cases discussed in this chapter certainly have geographical and historical specificities that are not necessarily transferable or translatable to other contexts. They do share, however, certain key features with cases in other parts of the world, as discussed in this volume. Putting emphasis on processes and trajectories, boundary work opens up ground for comparative work. We have a lot to gain from comparative border studies from the Balkans to the US-México borderlands (Dear, and Dorsey and Díaz-Barriga, both this volume) and from wider historical perspectives that trace different moments of border "mutations" (McGuire and Jones, both this volume). At a moment in which Europe is responding to a major humanitarian crisis—wrongly perceived as a border security crisis—by raising new physical and invisible walls, we need to interrogate the effectiveness of walls and borders in ways that capture a sense of urgency while also maintaining a sense of historical depth.

Notes

I would like to thank Randall McGuire and Laura McAtackney for organizing the timely and inspiring advanced seminar "A World of Walls" at the School for Advanced Research in Santa Fe, New Mexico, in April 2016, and for their patience and guidance in preparing this publication and in improving this chapter. I would also like to thank all the participants of the seminar for helping me rethink and refine some of the ideas included here. Finally, I am grateful, once again, to Katerina Stefatos for discussing parts of the text and for her enduring trust and patience.

1. The terms "wall" and "fence" do not merely indicate a difference of typology. They are politically charged and used to legitimize or trivialize policies of division and segregation. For the semantic problems and political uses of the terms, see Parry 2003; McGuire and McAtackney, this volume.

2. Despite differences in scale and geopolitical context, the Greek government's project of evacuation and ruination bears some similarities to the "spacio-cidal" practices described by Sari Hanafi (2012). Amahl Bishara (2015 and this volume) describes the instrumentalization of infrastructure and mobility as resistance in Palestine.

CHAPTER EIGHT

Whose Borderland? What Evidence?

Divergent Interests and the Impact
of the US-México Border Wall

MICHAEL DEAR

Much of the US-México borderland now resembles a zone of military occupation. The presence of the US Department of Homeland Security (DHS) is
announced most directly in fences and walls, surveillance towers, official
ports-of-entry, and border patrol stations. However, other infrastructures of
occupation are manifest in dams, stadium lighting, diverted drainage channels,
landfills, aerial surveillance, custom-built access roads, staging areas, parking
facilities, internal checkpoints, endless vehicular patrols, armed foot patrols,
large-scale earth removals, warehousing, acres of trash, drones, and the ubiquitous signage of prohibition. Border residents in Arizona refer to this occupied
zone as a "police state."

The border is a place where the burdens of US national security, drug traf-
ficking, and immigration enforcement policies converge and are experienced.
The issue may be characterized as involving distributed benefits and concentrated costs, in the sense that an entire nation gains from the burdens borne by
a subset of its citizens. From the viewpoint of those who are obliged to shoulder
these burdens, such responsibility holds limited appeal especially when the task
threatens the integrity and well-being of the impacted communities and when
federal aid to beleaguered border communities mostly takes the form of funding
for law enforcement, such as personnel, armaments, and detention centers. This
divergence between national and local interests is at the heart of the tensions in
the borderlands today, because the well-being and viability of border communities are jeopardized by federal priorities concerning security, drugs, and immigration. For its part, the federal government in México pays scarce attention

to its northern border unless and until the nation's trade and commerce are interrupted (e.g., through congestion delays at the border crossings). On both sides, the fate of the borderland communities hardly registers as a concern.

In this chapter, I examine the nature and consequences of the fault line separating national and local perspectives on the US-México border wall. Federal practice in the United States is concerned to ensure operational control over the nation's borders based solely on metrics of risk analysis and program performance (see Dorsey and Díaz-Barriga, this volume). Such unidimensionality ignores the subjective imagined community of US-México border residents, who place greater emphasis on their shared cross-border identity and joint well-being. By conjoining these national and local dimensions into the same discursive space, I uncover a more comprehensive basis for evaluating the border wall that is less obsessed by the exigencies of the present crisis and more cognizant of protecting the borderland's long history of cross-border connectivity.

The Borderlands before Borders

A century and a half ago, there was no international boundary between the United States of America and the Estados Unidos Mexicanos. The Mexican republic extended northward to include parts of present-day California, Nevada, Utah, and Colorado and even as far as the Oregon border. The Republic of Tejas (Texas) was battling for independence from México, partly because Tejanos were keen to maintain slavery, a practice that Mexicans abhorred.

In the centuries before the United States and México existed, the vast continent of North and Central America was occupied by empires of indigenous peoples, and north-south connections were the principal axes for trade, migration, conflict, and society. Indeed, strong connections existed since prehistoric times across what was to become the US-México border (Dear 2015, chap. 2). In Mesoamerica, great cities extended throughout Yucatan and central and southern México into Central America. Nothing in the territories now occupied by the United States matched the splendor of, for instance, the Aztec Empire. Nevertheless, the Southwest Puebloan cultures (primarily Anasazi, Hohokam, and Mogollon) developed sophisticated settlement systems that reached a pinnacle of cultural brilliance in the late ninth and early tenth centuries CE. These southwestern cultures were connected by trade to Mesoamerica via the Chichimeca region in the Sierra Madre. The whole continent was an integrated landscape in motion.

The Spanish swept through México in 1521 and stayed for 300 years. They governed with an iron military fist and a velvet religious glove, spreading their conquest via presidio (fort), mission, and mine. However, the conquerors had difficulty pacifying the northern regions of Nueva España, often facing resistance and revolt that obliged them to adopt a more pragmatic approach to government. From a base in El Paso del Norte (present-day Ciudad Juárez), the conquest probed north toward the Puebloan domains. By the late 1700s, Spanish missions had penetrated deeply into Alta California, and Spain had established a program of town building, which provided the foundation for settlements in today's borderlands. The conquerors constructed a discontinuous string of presidios extending along the Río Bravo almost to the Gulf of California; the path they followed was close to what would eventually become the US-México border (Reséndez 2016, 198–99; Weber 1992, chap. 8). Yet there was little east-west connection among the trading zones of Tejas, Nuevo México, and Alta and Baja California; the direction of connectivity along the frontier spaces was firmly north-south.

México's Independence, War, and Revolution

As soon as México gained independence from Spain in 1821, efforts were made to incorporate the northern territories more closely into the new republic. However, these attempts were quickly compromised as the fledgling nation opened up to outside influences. Foreign trade with the United States, Britain, and France—which had been illegal (although tolerated) during Spanish rule—was legalized. Anglo migration into Tejas was encouraged by Mexican president Guadalupe Victoria. Despite México's best intentions, its northern territories stubbornly looked to the United States for opportunity.

A mere twenty-five years after independence, México was at war with the United States. The conflict was ostensibly about securing the boundary of the recently annexed state of Texas, but it was clear from the outset that US president James K. Polk's ambition was to realize America's "Manifest Destiny," that is, to extend its territory to the Pacific Ocean. After two years of war, on February 2, 1848, the Treaty of Guadalupe Hidalgo was signed. México gained peace and

Figure 8.1. First boundary monument erected after the 1848 Treaty of Guadalupe Hidalgo, at the Pacific Ocean near Tijuana. This photograph was taken at the end of the nineteenth century after the original marble monument was renovated, fenced to prevent vandalism, and renumbered as monument 258. Source: Blanco 1901.

$15 million, but lost half of its territory. The United States had achieved the largest land grab in its history through a war that many (including Ulysses S. Grant) regarded as dishonorable.

After 1848, both nations rushed to secure their new territorial limits by building twin towns along the new boundary line (figure 8.1). For example, Eagle Pass and Piedras Negras were both founded in 1850 at a river crossing near Fort Duncan, Texas. Nuevo Laredo was established on the Mexican side opposite Laredo, Texas, by people who preferred to live under the Mexican flag. Cultural and ethnic mixing swiftly became facts of life along the changing frontier as "scores of Mexican-Texans went from [being] Spanish subjects, to Mexican citizens, to Texans, and wound up as Americans, in the short span of a lifetime" (Reséndez 2005, 2). A common refrain, then as now, was "We didn't cross the border, the border crossed us."

For most of the remainder of the nineteenth century and into the twentieth, the borderlands were wracked by conflicts. The most immediate issue confronting both countries was the troublesome "Indian problem," notably the spectacular incursions of the raiders of the Comanche Empire deep into the Mexican heartland. Under Article 11 of the treaty, the United States had agreed to curtail raids by indigenous peoples into México from the United States, but it would take decades of murderous conflict to secure this aim.

The US Civil War and the twentieth-century Mexican Revolution consolidated cross-border ties. For instance, during the close blockade of the southern ports in the Civil War, the Rio Grande was left free, and the Confederacy utilized facilities in Brownsville, Texas, and in Matamoros, Tamaulipas, to export immense quantities of cotton and import war munitions and food. During the Mexican Revolution, the war sometimes spilled over into the United States, as when Pancho Villa led a raid into Columbus, New Mexico, and was subsequently pursued deep into Mexican territory by US general John Pershing. When conflicts occurred in Mexican towns, refugees commonly sought shelter by crossing into calmer territories north of the border.

The Mexican Revolution was the last great military upheaval experienced by the borderlands. Afterward, peace and prosperity took hold, and cross-border migration from south to north grew. Worried about the loss of its labor force, México took steps to staunch the outflow of migrants; faced with a chaotic inflow of newcomers, the United States responded by creating the federal Border Patrol in 1926. This was a defining moment. Henceforward, the space between México and the United States ceased to be a relatively open frontier and instead became a distinct line of separation enforced by a police authority constituted solely for this purpose (see Dorsey and Díaz-Barriga, and Jones, both this volume). For the remainder of the twentieth century, the boundary between the two countries became the locus of muted binational discord.

Twentieth-Century Modernization and Integration

In 1942, provoked by a shortage of labor induced by World War II, the US Bracero Program began issuing identity cards to Mexican citizens seeking work in the United States. This integration of labor markets in the two nations started slowly, but so great was the demand for work that the rate of undocumented crossings from México increased. In response, a chain link fence was erected for five miles on either side of the All-American Canal in California near Calexico, México, in 1945. (The fence used materials that had been recycled from a former World War II internment camp.) By the time the Bracero Program was terminated in 1964, more than 4 million braceros had participated, and border towns were subsequently overwhelmed by repatriated workers. In response, the Mexican government launched the Border Industrialization Program in 1965, aimed at providing employment for returning workers. Out of this, the maquiladora (assembly plant) industry was born.

Located just across the US border in México, where labor costs are lower, maquilas import raw materials and components from the United States, assemble them into finished products (such as televisions), and then return the finished goods to the United States for distribution and sale. There has been a symbiotic relation between assembly plants on the Mexican side and supplier/distribution facilities in the United States. By 1979 maquila production accounted for one-quarter of Mexican manufacturing exports; twenty years later, maquilas employed more than a million Mexican workers. Two-thirds of all maquilas were established initially in just three border towns (Tijuana, Mexicali, and Ciudad Juárez), although smaller twin towns later joined the boom.

Because of the increasing demand for Mexican workers in the United States and severe downturns in the Mexican economy, the volume of undocumented crossings from México reached new heights in the late twentieth century. In the mid-1990s, the United States responded by building border fences opposite the cities where most crossings were occurring: Tijuana, Nogales, and Ciudad Juárez (figure 8.2). (This time, the fences were constructed from steel plates that had originally served as temporary landing strips for aircraft during the war in Vietnam.) Beyond these urban fortifications, the boundary line remained largely unfenced, and undocumented migrants turned to more remote desert and mountain regions to cross over (see Papadopoulos, this volume). Not surprisingly, the number of deaths from drowning, heatstroke, and hypothermia increased.

Binational economic integration intensified after the signing of the North American Free Trade Agreement (NAFTA) in 1994. The treaty's effects were geographically uneven, but México and Canada quickly consolidated their status as the leading trading partners of the United States. By the turn of the twenty-first century, the six border states of México (Baja California, Sonora, Chihuahua, Coahuila, Nuevo León, and Tamaulipas) contained 18 million people, or 16 percent of México's total population. The four US border states (California, Arizona, New Mexico, and Texas) were home to 67 million people, or 21 percent of the

Figure 8.2. Border fencing from the mid-1990s Operation Gatekeeper era near Campo, California. Photo © Michael Dear, 2002.

US population. On both sides, border states were among the fastest-growing regions in each country; the twin towns of the mid-nineteenth century had mutated into twenty-first-century transborder metropolises. As of this writing, goods and services worth $1.3 billion cross the US-México border every day.

Building the Wall

After the 9/11 attacks, the administration of President George W. Bush created the Department of Homeland Security, which is charged with ensuring operational control over the nation's borders. The centerpiece of DHS operations was the 2005 Secure Border Initiative (SBI), which engaged the Coast Guard, the Border Patrol (USBP), and Immigration and Customs Enforcement (ICE); this group of agencies is now collectively known as Customs and Border Protection. The DHS actions also incorporated certain functions of agencies with no direct responsibility for immigration, such as growing the caseloads of the Department of Justice and suspending environmental protection laws to expedite the construction of fortifications. In addition, the DHS outsourced many of its obligations to states and municipalities, thereby co-opting local law enforcement into national security protocols. ICE contracted with private corporations, such as Boeing and the Corrections Corporation of America (now called CoreCivic), for the construction of physical and virtual fences, private detention facilities, deportations, and security training and services (Brill 2016).

After his 2008 election, President Barack Obama continued the SBI policies of his predecessor. First, a goal of "prevention through deterrence" calculated that a concentration of resources (in wall construction, policing, and surveillance) would deter unauthorized crossers. A second goal, "enforcement with consequences," aimed to discourage border transgressions by imposing tougher penalties. By 2012, the Obama administration was spending nearly $18 billion annually on a suite of "enforcement first" strategies, making that the nation's premier immigration policy.

SBI Outcomes

In 2006, just as the SBI was getting under way, RAND security expert Jack Riley testified before the US House of Representatives that the country had "woefully underinvested" in developing a comprehensive border security strategy. The nation was undertaking numerous security programs, yet "the impacts and cost effectiveness of virtually all of these initiatives are poorly understood" (Riley 2014, 2). Eight years later, by which time SBI interventions were fully operational, Riley lamented that his assessment remained essentially unchanged. While the federal government collects information on many immigration measures, no agency explicitly measures the most pertinent indicators, namely, the volume of undocumented border crossings and the extent to which the border is "secure" (Willis et al. 2010). Risk analysis experts have developed sophisticated conceptual models and credible evaluation metrics for which there are no available empirical data. Consequently, analysts are obliged to fall back on inadequate surrogate measures, which cannot provide definitive results or unambiguous policy direction, and to rely heavily on expert panels as necessary adjuncts in their research protocols. Their work is further compromised when publications in scientific journals cannot report findings that are based on classified information (e.g., Levine and Waters 2013).

Given the sprawling, multifaceted nature of the DHS enterprise plus the absence of appropriate information on program performance, a comprehensive accounting of SBI program outcomes is unlikely ever to be forthcoming. Using

Figure 8.3. The post-9/11 Department of Homeland Security fence at San Luis, Arizona. The locked box contains boundary monument 201. Photo © Michael Dear, 2008.

the best available evidence derived from a wide variety of sources, I constructed an aggregate accounting of the principal SBI programs over its first decade. The following is a short summary of the main indicators pertinent to this chapter; I have italicized the terms for ease of identification (see Dear 2015, chaps. 7 and 11).

By January 2013, DHS contractors had installed a total of 651 miles of *fencing* along the border: 352 miles to stop pedestrians and 299 miles to block vehicles (figure 8.3). This total was only 2 miles short of the distance identified by the USBP as "appropriate" for barrier construction (some land on the border is simply too steep, and fencing water boundaries is impractical). During the most frenzied period of construction (2006–2009), the extent of fencing grew from 150 to 600 miles.

In order to complete the fortifications, congressional *appropriations* (including funds for surveillance technologies) increased from $25 million in 1996 to $298 million in 2006 and peaked at $1.5 billion in 2007. After that, expenditures on these "tactical infrastructure appropriations" steadily dropped: to $324 million in 2013.

The *number of border patrol agents* along the line more than doubled after 2000, to more than 20,000, with growth concentrated in Tucson and El Paso, the most active sectors of undocumented crossings.

The number of migrant *apprehensions* dropped to almost 421,000 in 2013, the lowest level since the early 1970s. Almost two-thirds of these apprehensions were made by the USBP in the border zone and the remainder by ICE officials acting in the US interior.

In the five years up to 2014, there were 2 million deportations from the United States, the highest level ever recorded. In 2013 alone, a historic high of 438,000 people were removed. Two-thirds of all deportations originated from the border region and the rest from the interior. The Obama administration explained that its tough policy on deportations was a necessary prelude to a more humane approach, but when President Obama later stepped in to slow deportation rates by executive order for certain categories of undocumented people, lawsuits by several states derailed the order's implementation.

Nationwide, the number of apprehensions fell, and total deportations reached record levels. The outflows of Mexicans from the United States began to exceed inflows. Overall, the total unauthorized migrant population living in the United States fell from an estimated 12.4 million in 2007 to 11.1 million in 2011. This statistic may be regarded as the best available single indicator of the impact of the SBI intervention. But what caused its decline?

The prevention-through-deterrence calculus that gave rise to the wall (in its many forms) is likely to have contributed, but very early in its operations the DHS adjusted public expectations by issuing a clarification that its goal in constructing the wall was not to stop migrants but merely to slow them down so that they could be apprehended by conventional forces. The enforcement-with-consequences components in the DHS portfolio—more agents on the ground, increased ICE raids in the workplace, proliferation of interior checkpoints, draconian prosecution and deportation rates, and so on—have been identified as causal factors in the drop in apprehensions. However, exogenous factors unrelated to SBI programs also played a role. Primary among these were the decline in US job opportunities due to the economic recession as well as improvements in the Mexican economy, which reduced the incentive to migrate and thus the number of Mexicans who intended to cross. Other contributing factors were the spiraling costs of assisted border passages, the rising deaths and injuries experienced by border crossers, and their increased exposure to personal violence, such as kidnapping for ransom.

What no one is able to demonstrate conclusively is the contribution of any specific SBI program toward the decline of the undocumented population in the United States since 2007 (Rosenblum and Hipsman 2016; Seghetti 2014).

Collateral Damage: The Border-Industrial Complex

Beyond the performance statistics, the SBI actions created a vast border security apparatus that is called the "border-industrial complex" (BIC). Its emergence could hardly have been a surprise, since vast quantities of money were being directed toward security industries, with a distinct preference for private-sector contractors. Only later would complaints surface about BIC overreach and abuse as testament to the collateral damage caused by the infrastructures of occupation as they penetrated ever more deeply into the lives of ordinary citizens. And only much later did opposition to DHS and BIC practices result in corrective interventions.

The USBP has authority to operate within a 100-mile zone inside the nation's borders, including its water boundaries—a territory encompassing two-thirds of the US population. Its agents possess stop-and-search capacities that exceed those of local law enforcement. Journalist Todd Miller (2014, 211) claims that the entire country has been transformed into a "virtual border zone" under the authority of a "Border Patrol nation." According to Miller, the border has the largest concentration of surveillance technologies, and there is nowhere in the United States where people are as clearly divided between the police and the policed. One example of the expanding mandate of the USBP is the leasing of its Predator drones to other domestic agencies, including the FBI, the National Guard, and the US Forest Service. In 2009, USBP drones were used by other agencies 30 times; by 2012, rentals had risen to 250.

An increased belligerence toward law-abiding citizens is evident in border policing. In one notorious 2008 incident, Vermont senator Patrick Leahy was stopped at a USBP checkpoint 125 miles south of the US-Canada border. Ordered to get out of the car, the senator asked the agent whose authority he was acting under. The agent pointed to his gun and told the senator that it was all the authority he needed. This story is important not only because of the agent's explicit threat, but also because the checkpoint was so far inside US territory.

The USBP is often accused of using excessive force; some situations have resulted in death. A culture of impunity is also part of what US citizens rebuke. In 2014, new guidelines were issued to ensure greater restraint by USBP agents. ICE officials have also been accused of exceeding their authority. In 2013, revised guidelines were issued governing their conduct during raids on private homes in search of undocumented migrants.

As the numbers of migrant apprehensions increased, ICE's detention system expanded into a far-flung network consisting of more than 500 county jails, for-profit prisons, and federal jails, where detainees are held prior to being assessed for deportation (figure 8.4). According to Tom Barry (2011, 6–7), these centers are a new mode of incarceration: "the speculative public-private prison, publicly owned by local governments, privately operated by corporations, publicly financed by tax-exempt bonds, and located in depressed communities." Immigrant advocates hurl their harshest complaints against these privatized, for-profit jails under contract with ICE. They are often underregulated and unaccountable, where detainees are sequestered in unsafe conditions without legal representation or adequate medical care—and often transferred unnecessarily within the detention system, making it more difficult for them to maintain contact with legal counsel and their families. Excessive use of solitary confinement in detention centers is an especially contested practice subject to ongoing challenges.

Finally, in a great irony, migrants held in detention centers often work in kitchens and laundry rooms, for which they usually get paid one dollar per day. Such coercive use of detained migrant labor makes the federal government—which prohibits hiring undocumented workers—the largest single employer of undocumented migrants in the country.

The most dramatic response to SBI failure was the termination of its Secure Communities program, a centerpiece of both the Bush and Obama administrations. Marketed as a program to identify and deport serious criminals among the undocumented population, the program was perverted in two ways: it suffered from bait-and-switch tactics (i.e., the program was justified one way, but then implemented in a different way) and from mission drift (a conscious deviation from the original program intentions). Approximately three-quarters

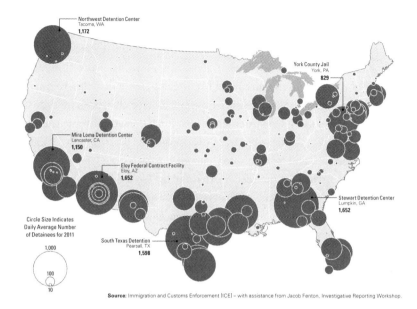

Figure 8.4. Locations of private detention centers in the United States, 2011. Artwork by Dreamline Cartography. © Michael Dear, 2013.

of those deported under Secure Communities had no criminal record, merely convictions related to minor offenses. In 2015, the DHS terminated the program, conceding that it had failed to meet its stated goal of making communities more secure.

The business of security shows no sign of withering away, and walls remain a popular topic of political grandstanding. In the three and a half decades since the 1986 Immigration Reform and Control Act was passed, the United States has spent more than $187 billion on immigration control and border security. The ill-fated 2013 US Senate plan for immigration reform outlined a budget of $40 billion, which included another 700 miles of walls and a doubling of the number of USBP agents (to 40,000). The trade publication *Homeland Security Today* described the bill as a treasure trove for contractors in the border security industry (Miller 2013). The bill failed, but it seems unlikely that BIC appetites will become sated anytime soon; there are simply too many corporations and businesses that stand to gain from its continuation.

Borderland Voices

Since its creation in 1848, the borderline between the United States and México has been subject to constant renegotiation and adjustment as a consequence of disputes at both international and local scales (see Jones, this volume, for borderlines versus walls). Geopolitical imperatives have often been subordinated to exigencies of place and environment, of pragmatism and convenience, and of memory and tradition. The ascendancy of oppositional practices has historically provided substance and form to autonomous, localized spaces, including what I refer to as a "third nation" between México and the United States. A third nation describes an identity constituted by shared affiliations and territorial attachment among borderland peoples, which become manifest through myriad practices pertaining to work, family, leisure, law, commerce, and culture. (For some of the broader theoretical and conceptual issues in current borderland studies, see Blatter 2001; Herzog 2014; Konrad 2015.)

Few borderlanders of the in-between spaces refer to a third nation in everyday conversation, yet they readily adopt alternative expressions descriptive of emerging hybrid identities, such as "transborder" citizen. They recognize and value the cross-border connection, referring to their twin cities as *ciudades hermanas* (sister cities) or *ciudades amistosas* (friendly cities). They understand that their lives are rooted on both sides of the border, and some profess to forget which side of the line they are on. In my experience, the single most common signifier of third-nation status is the self-proclaimed belief of people that they have more in common with one another than with citizens of their adjacent nation-states. Many borderlanders lament that cross-border ties are being threatened by the new fortifications.

The Idea of a Third Nation

In formal terms, we speak of a "nation" when referring to a group of people whose members voluntarily identify with others on the basis of shared history, geography, ethnicity, cultural tradition, language, and alliances against external threat. The sentiment uniting a nation's affiliates is commonly called "nationalism." Many tenets underlying nationalism are nebulous and transitory—which is why nations are sometimes referred to as "imagined communities"—but there can be no doubt about their power and consequence. When people acquire the sovereign right to govern a territory, and that right is recognized by others, the territory is deemed to be a nation-state.

A "third nation" is a community of interest carved out of the territories between two (or more) existing nation-states. It occupies an in-between or supranational space, transcending the boundary that divides its constitutive nation-states and creating from them a hybrid identity distinct from the host countries. The third nation at the US-México border has several historical and contemporary precedents, including the Tohono O'odham Nation, which today is bisected by the boundary line between Arizona and Sonora and which possesses an enduring sense of identity, autonomous tribal institutions and laws, and a formal territorial organization.

Although the US-México third nation is not a nation-state, the strategies involved in promoting third nationalism may congeal into a political movement aimed at third nationhood, that is, a quest for territorial autonomy characteristic of a nation-state. Nationhood strategies vary greatly over time and space, and they may advance through positive or negative actions. For instance, constructive cross-border cooperation may be promoted by trade or by the desire to overcome a shared exogenous threat, but perverse forms of integration can result through international criminal networks or the penetration of repressive regimes into adjacent territories.

The idea of an integrated political space with mixed sovereignties between México and the United States has gained some credence in recent decades. In 1988, international relations scholar Robert Pastor recognized the emergence of new forms of culture, new attitudes, and new markets along the border and noted that people there were "more like each other than either is like its nation" (Pastor and Castañeda 1988, 298). Mexican academic and former statesman Jorge Castañeda agreed that the idea of a "third state" was gaining currency and that notions of a "new border nation" were consistent with what he had actually witnessed on the ground. But, he added, Mexicans generally did not share a "third-nation view," and convergence (of whatever form) lay far in the future (Pastor and Castañeda 1988, 303–4).

After NAFTA was signed in 1994, views of borderland integration garnered new support. Discussing emerging North American identities, Robert Earle and John Wirth (1995, 9) characterized the borderlands as "transborder areas [that] are the testing grounds of socio-economic integration in North America." Jorge Bustamante (1995, 193) used the term "MexAmerica" to describe "a region of interchangeable cultures, ethnicities, and languages, distinct from both nations." However, Bustamante reasserted Mexican and US sovereignty: "We can do quite well as the two separate peoples and nations that we are." Later, almost two decades after NAFTA, Robert Pastor (2011, 69) took another look at the borderlands and grasped the significance of both territory and perspective in borderland identity: "The closer you live to the borders, the more you see them connecting the people on both sides. The further you live from the borders, the more you see them as separating the countries." In short, people who know the border recognize the special qualities that go into making community on both sides.

Attitudes and Aspirations

In May 2016, a border poll conducted by Cronkite News, Univision News, and the *Dallas Morning News* surveyed almost 1,500 residents in seven pairs of twin cities in the United States and México from California/Baja California to Texas/Tamaulipas, providing a timely sketch of attitudes among border residents and their degree of integration (Bilker 2016; the quotations in the following paragraphs are from the narrative and video clips available at the web link).

Survey respondents overwhelmingly preferred more bridges instead of fences. Opposition to building more walls was intense: 72 percent of people on the US side and 86 percent in México were opposed. Roughly three-quarters of those surveyed in each country considered the wall unimportant when compared with other issues, such as education, jobs, and crime.

The poll reinforced the notion that the border is increasingly becoming "one giant economically integrated, bicultural society." Only fifteen years earlier in a similar poll, border residents viewed themselves as more distant neighbors, as separate communities marching to their own beat. Today, three-quarters of those polled on both sides recognize their economic codependency with the other side. Overwhelmingly, they say they like their neighbors across the line, and they cross frequently to visit family, shop, work, get a haircut or dental care, and attend school.

Most respondents valued their shared communities, which had been forged by a common history, blood ties, and livelihood. In interviews separate from the survey, the degree of self-awareness among border dwellers was striking. Daisy Garcia in San Diego said: "I feel I'm connected to my roots . . . to where we come from." US representative Beto O'Rourke (D–El Paso) went further: "It says something really beautiful that the border, two countries, two languages, two cultures, at this point become essentially one people." An active engagement across cultures also was pointed out by Philip Skinner, the mayor of Columbus, New Mexico: "One of the things we celebrate is the bicultural aspect of living on the border."

Seventy to eighty percent of those questioned in both countries felt that their cities depended either "somewhat" or "very much" on their twin city across the border. One Arizona man offered: "Our lifeline is across the border, Mexico. . . . Without Mexicans, we don't exist. Our life is sucked away." Just as dramatically, Cesar Martinez of Nuevo Laredo, Tamaulipas, made this statement: "If [they] build a wall, we will be alone."

Cross-border unity is fueled in part by the perceived indifference or even hostility displayed in the two federal capitals—Washington, DC, and México DF—and border dwellers expressed frustration that issues important to them were not discussed at the federal level in either country. Sixty-two percent of Mexican respondents and nearly half of the US respondents felt that the federal government did not understand border perspectives. As a consequence, politicians in DC and DF fail to grasp the importance of cross-border connections and mistakenly believe that walls provide secure borders.

By and large, people who live on the border hate border walls, and they do not make the elementary mistake of equating a wall with border security. Certainly, border residents on both sides prefer more security, not less (though for different reasons). Victor Galvan, originally from Ciudad Juárez and now living in El Paso, said in an interview that he was not opposed to more Border Patrol officers, or the presence in México of US military to help in the drug war, or better training for police officers. But walls, he was against: "A wall is a symbol of discrimination, racism, segregation, not a solution for security, or for reducing violence" (see McGuire and McAtackney, and Jones, both this volume). Christopher Wilson, deputy director of the Woodrow Wilson Center's Mexico Institute, agreed with Galvan's distinction: "The clear rejection of building a new border wall is not a rejection of border security or the notion of having walls; it's something else." People on both sides want better public security, "but they don't want a wall. That's because they want to be more connected with their neighbors."

The Cronkite survey confirms that cross-border lives are inextricably linked and that residents are fully aware of their codependency. Such observations are consistent with the results of my borderland research over the past two decades.

Based on my conversations on both sides of the line over that period, I have assembled a set of community development goals defined by border dwellers themselves. In a nutshell, they want their lives back; they want their communities cleaned up; they want money diverted from building more walls into upgrading border crossings; and they want power to manage their own destinies without interference from outsiders. Any comprehensive assessment of past and future SBI/BIC interventions should incorporate third-nation concerns, so it is worth itemizing them in detail (Dear 2015, chap. 11).

REPAIR THE DAMAGE

1. *Take down the wall.* The single most important symbolic action would be to take down the wall, at least in those zones where surveillance and security are adequate through other means. There is no wall or fence near monument number 1 at El Paso/Ciudad Juárez, where electronic surveillance is effective. Fences and walls will never achieve complete coverage along the line simply because the terrain is too inhospitable to permit construction everywhere, nor would they ever totally stop undocumented migration.

2. *End the occupation.* Border communities deeply resent the presence of the multiplicity of law enforcement agencies that permeate their lives (see Bishara, this volume, on the West Bank). Undoing the occupation would require scaling back on overreach by the Department of Homeland Security, Border Patrol, Immigration and Customs Enforcement, the border-industrial complex, and local police departments conscripted into immigration enforcement. Disruptive practices at interior checkpoints should be minimized, and community access should be restored to informal crossings and border meeting places.

3. *Restore the land.* Environmental damage that scars the entire third nation in and near the occupied zones should be remedied by the responsible agencies, including the wall builders. Federal, state, local, and binational authorities should provide proper compensation for the damage that has been dumped in borderlanders' backyards.

PROMOTE ECONOMIC DEVELOPMENT AND COMMUNITY INTEGRATION

4. *Invest in economic growth.* The prosperity and well-being of communities on both sides are vital to our binational economies. The fortifications along the line disrupt cross-border connections contrary to centuries of established interaction, and they cause protracted delays at border crossings that hinder prosperity and social interaction.

5. *Encourage local cultural dynamism.* A cultural renaissance took hold decades ago in Tijuana and has since spread to other border cities. Today, the Tijuana culture scene is an integral part of the city's postviolence recovery. A transnational community of border artists is changing the region. Local architects, city planners, politicians, and developers are collaborating across the borderline to grow creative neighborhoods and attract cultural pioneers to reinvent border city spaces.

ENGAGE THE GRASSROOTS AND SPREAD AWARENESS

6. *Restore self-determination to borderlanders.* Third-nation dwellers want what most people want: respect, autonomy, access to their family and friends, peace, and the opportunity to work and make something of their lives. Left to their own devices, local mayors, chambers of commerce, entrepreneurs, cultural groups, nonprofits, families, and individuals will continue to develop myriad cross-border alliances to mutual benefit.

7. *Promote the third nation.* Everyone in both countries should understand the immense importance and achievements of border communities' contributions to national security, economic prosperity, health care, education, and cultural identity.

I do not purport to speak for borderlanders, any advocacy group, or a political party. My seven-point synopsis is intended to demonstrate the enormity of the gap separating the unidimensional, security-obsessed world of wall builders from the profusion of material and cognitive intelligence characterizing the tens of millions of people residing in border communities and states. The synopsis could also be read as a manifesto confirming third-nation identity, legitimacy, rights, and place in the world, or as a blueprint for those in both nations concerned about framing coexistence in a postborder world, including a pathway to greater national security.

A View from the Third Nation

From a federal perspective, the border is the nation's *edge*, and its integrity must be secured; for people who live there, the border is the *center*, and its integrity too should be protected. Both the national and the local have standing in debates over border security, even though their legal obligations and remedies differ greatly. Thus, any evidence-based assessment of national security proposals in the borderlands should engage not only measures of infrastructure cost and benefit but also the material and cognitive dimensions of third-nation attitudes and aspirations.

Examining the border wall purely as an artifact of national security, no one can conclusively demonstrate that the wall itself is causally related to the decline in numbers of the undocumented population in the United States, nor that the wall acts to deter potential migrants, nor that it has caused the decline in rates of border apprehensions. Each of these trends is more likely attributable to a wider set of forces (such as record-level deportation rates) or to factors unrelated to SBI actions (e.g., improvements in México's economy). I can see no justification for building more walls as instruments of border security. The marginal benefits that might accrue from additional walls would hardly justify the billions of dollars that they would cost.

More than a decade of experience with the border wall has shown that appraisals of future security infrastructure should take account of the collateral side effects of security practices. These include the penetration of immigration-related policing deep into the US interior, overreach and abuse by USBP and ICE authorities, and the inhumane and punitive practices at many migrant detention centers (Dorsey and Díaz-Barriga, this volume). These affect not only migrants and refugees but also residents in the impacted border zone and the national population at large. The border-industrial complex has emerged as a sprawling congeries of infrastructure construction agencies, equipment suppliers, and purveyors of diverse security services. Many contractors are private companies primarily motivated by profit making and shareholder interests, and they are less transparent in their day-to-day operations or publicly accountable in their operations.

The value of a third-nation perspective is that it heightens awareness of the degree of integration between peoples on either side of the border. Other terminologies, such as "twin cities" or "transborder metropolis," convey the material connectivity across the line, but the "third nation" appellation embodies the added weight of the subjective and experiential integration, attachment, loyalty, traditions, and shared identity across the line.

The obligations of hosting the federal security apparatus fall squarely on borderland communities, which have no choice in the matter. Residents are required to absorb the acute economic, social, and environmental disruptions of the occupation, usually without compensation or representation in security-related decisions. The consequent losses take diverse forms and are manifest at multiple geographical scales, from the daily indignity of scrutiny at internal checkpoints, through the loss of family property, to the border-length suspension of environmental protection laws. Sometimes, the cost of occupation is death by gunfire.

In 2012 a Mexican teenager named José Antonio Elena Rodríguez was walking at night along the border fence in Nogales, Sonora, when he was shot eight times in the back and twice in the head by a USBP officer firing across the line from Nogales, Arizona. The boy died, and a civil prosecution of the assailant was pursued before the US Court of Appeals in Arizona by the boy's mother with the assistance of the American Civil Liberties Union. A key point in the prosecution's case was that the protections of the US Constitution apply across the fence into México, and those protections should include the victim because the two Nogales towns are an integrated single community. (They are commonly referred to collectively as Ambos Nogales, or Both Nogales.) The remarkable conclusion to an amicus curiae brief prepared for the appeals court reads:

> In considering this case, *amici* urge the Court to recognize that Ambos Nogales—though it extends into two countries—is a single community of families, workers, and businesses. When a person who lives here walks beside the border, he walks beside a fence that is a mundane and unremarkable fixture in his world. He walks past shops that cater to tourists; he walks where his neighbors come to work. He walks through the middle of

his community. (United States Court of Appeals for the Ninth Circuit 2016, 22–23)

On the concrete base of the steel border wall near the shooting, anguished graffiti make the same point more forcefully: "Somos un Pueblo sin Fronteras | ¡Justicia para José Antonio!" (We are a community without borders | Justice for José Antonio!).

The border wall is an unprecedented aberration in the continent's history. Nothing like it has ever existed in the territory that became the US-México international boundary; it usurps connections and collaborations that extend back into prehistoric times. Today, the wall disrupts binational trade worth more than $500 billion annually and causes material and mental hardship in the everyday lives of more than 10 million US and Mexican citizens who reside in the six major borderland twin cities (Bersin and Huston 2016). Their claims should be factored into any decisions regarding national prosperity, border security, and effective democracy. In the meantime, the third nation endures.

Note

This chapter draws heavily upon materials from Dear 2015, where more comprehensive citations and sourcing can be found. I am very grateful for the hospitality and support offered by the School for Advanced Research in Santa Fe and to Laura McAtackney and Randy McGuire, whose efforts made our Advanced Seminar residency possible. Grateful thanks to the seminar participants, who brought such a wide variety of experience and insight to our conversations, and to Andrew Burridge for his perfect timing in alerting me to some very pertinent source materials.

Part III

Supporting Walls

CHAPTER NINE

Algorithms, German Shepherds, and LexisNexis

Reticulating the Digital Security State
in the Constitution-Free Zone

MARGARET E. DORSEY AND MIGUEL DÍAZ-BARRIGA

The editors of this volume, Laura McAtackney and Randall McGuire, asked us to participate in a conversation about walls and their materialization, including their significations, while also paying attention to the "constant presence of backup" that walls require, "including armed agents, ground vehicles, helicopters, surveillance devices, drones, and airplanes that fulfill the threat of violence embodied in the physical wall." This chapter peers into the interface of walls and their backup, drawing attention to their meanings for politics, citizenship, and state reformulation. We advocate for an anthropology of the state that considers how the crossing of fortifications (walls, blimps, checkpoints, guards, dogs) with technology (algorithms, data aggregators, software suites) curtails the rights of citizens. We start with border residents' confusion about the wall and its technology, which in South Texas extends seventy-five miles north of the US-México border, to reframe this conversation in terms of moving from the specificity of the material wall (see Dear, this volume) to a security grid that enmeshes populations within the United States.

The Security Grid

The border wall and its backup—armed agents, ground vehicles, helicopters, surveillance towers, drones, airplanes—are intrinsic to realizing the threat of violence ostensibly aimed at border crossers. Visualize the US-México border wall from a different perspective. It is not uniform: it is an assemblage of Vietnam landing mats, concrete facades, bollards, Normandy barriers, and so on that draws from the detritus of "American imperialism" (Hattam 2016). It is not whole, but it is sometimes solid: in places, miles of rusted metal bollard polls stand atop eighteen feet of austere, white concrete. It abruptly stops for ten feet and then begins again. Imagine that it is not the hodgepodge that it is, but instead take a clean cropped and framed snapshot of it. From that perspective, vertical parallel lines run into the air: infinity realized. Imagine another cropped and framed photo of the border wall's gates: horizontal lines cutting straight across the vertical lines, creating clean cells. Boxes, boxes, and more boxes.[1] These cells resemble the most undemocratic and unfree spaces: prisons and their mind-numbingly simple and replaceable rows of cells. In our vision, the border wall symbolizes and materializes the devolution of rights normally attendant with US citizenship.

In "The Constitution Free Zone in the United States: Law and Life in a State of Carcelment" (Dorsey and Díaz-Barriga 2015), we argue that South Texas is and that South Texans live in a legal and actual prison. We describe how, within a hundred-mile zone of any international boundary, the US Border Patrol exercises extraconstitutional powers in establishing checkpoints and conducting searches based on "de-escalated" Fourth Amendment rights (Wilson 2002, 127). According to the American Civil Liberties Union, the Border Patrol routinely searches individuals and vehicles in ways that violate constitutional rights—rendering the region a "Constitution free zone" (American Civil Liberties Union 2018). For residents of South Texas, the materialization of this rights-free zone begins at the border wall and ends at the interior checkpoints of Falfurrias and Sarita, approximately seventy-five miles north of the actual international boundary line. (See the interior checkpoint depicted in figure 9.1. Note the German shepherd that the Customs and Border Protection agent handles. The CBP agents are wearing bulletproof vests. Note the camera-like device above the stop sign.)

While the checkpoints and the walls mark the boundaries of rightslessness, we focus on the immaterial backup not listed by McAtackney and McGuire, such as algorithms and database structures, which also "fulfill the threat of violence embodied in the physical wall."[2] Even though many do not know about such databases, when residents and visitors to the borderlands drive north and, more recently, south, they cannot avoid noticing these structures' embodiment in an ever-expanding array of halogen lamps, cameras, and sensors that flash as drivers pass or wait in line (figures 9.2a–c). Border security technology, the border wall, and the social relations produced by and through interaction with

Figure 9.1. Falfurrias, Texas, checkpoint. Photo by Margaret E. Dorsey and Miguel Díaz-Barriga, 2016.

them confuse South Texans. Traveling north, residents of South Texas must pass through interior checkpoints at Falfurrias and Sarita (figure 9.3). No one is quite sure what information these camera arrays capture, how these data are analyzed, and who owns the data. At the southern border of the security net, border residents are unsure if they can or should go near the border wall. They also do not know if they can pass the border wall into the space between the wall and the international boundary, the Rio Grande/Río Bravo.[3]

Materializations of border (in)security—walls, CBP agents, camera arrays, interior checkpoints—create what we consider a "strategic ambiguity" among border residents about their rights as citizens (Díaz-Barriga and Dorsey 2020). Confusion about border walls and cameras is not simply about (mis)understanding rights but is rather a symptom of the reticulation of citizens into security grids. As we describe below, the DHS and CBP have contracted with commercial data aggregators in an engagement with predictive law enforcement (trying to identify threats before they happen). These commercial aggregators collect information that is personally identifiable, and federal privacy laws do

Figures 9.2a–c. Camera arrays at a checkpoint. Photos by Margaret E. Dorsey and Miguel Díaz-Barriga, 2016.

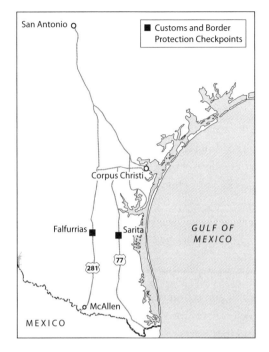

Figure 9.3. To leave South Texas, border residents must travel through interior Customs and Border Protection checkpoints. Highways 281 and 77 are the major routes used by border residents to reach San Antonio and other cities in Texas. Source: US General Accounting Office (http://www.gao.gov/new.items/d05435.pdf) via Wikimedia Commons.

not hinder their gathering efforts. We use the term "security reticulation" to index how border security programs create nets that enmesh citizens and ensnare their rights (e.g., privacy) both on the ground and in cyberspace. The combination of strategic ambiguity, the lack of clarity about citizens' rights, and a profusion of heavily armed personnel encourages residents not to question the devolution of their rights or the larger function of border securitization as it manifests in daily life.

Scanning Subjects and Automated Racial Profiling: What's Happening in Texas

Within the anthropology of security, there is a growing call for ethnographic research on the technologies of border security, which transform borders from walls and fortifications into technological frontiers. Murphy and Maguire (2015, 173), for example, have conducted ethnographic fieldwork in European airports both to analyze state engagement with predictive governance and to explore the "kinds of relationality" that "these technologies engender and promulgate." They conceptualize this turn to automation in border security, vis-à-vis Foucault, as a question of how to maintain security without physical walls (see Virilio 1997). Murphy and Maguire are careful to note that their focus is on airport technologies and not heavily fortified borders. For those of us who study increasingly heavily fortified borders and interior checkpoints, their research can serve as a starting point for mapping the physicality of walls and checkpoints onto the broader application of security technologies, which now dominate border security initiatives. Our research therefore explores the kinds of relationality generated when border walls, checkpoints, and camera arrays interface with algorithms and database structures.

We piece together the security net of South Texas based on our living in South Texas, studying the construction of the border wall, passing through interior checkpoints approximately 200 times, and formally (recorded semistructured interviews and focus groups) and informally talking with residents about their experiences at border walls and checkpoints over the span of eight years (2008–2014, 2015–2017). We have attended congressional hearings on border security, watched podcasts of hearings, read transcripts of congressional testimony, and waded through heavily redacted documents obtained under the Freedom of Information Act and the research of agencies that contract with CBP and state and local law enforcement. In Texas, the state police force is called the Department of Public Safety (DPS), and it coordinates border security with CBP. Depending on the county and city in which you live, or are passing through, sheriffs and local police can also act as immigration agents. Any one of these agents roaming the streets and highways of South Texas might be equipped with handheld or mobile ALPR (automated license plate reader) scanners, a fingerprint reader, and a laptop or tablet that runs on software connected to larger networks and databases. Thousands of law enforcement agents patrol South Texas using that hardware.

ALPR scanners operate at the fixed checkpoints, in some border security/law enforcement vehicles, and on the signs that flash your speed.[4] Like most border residents, we do not know when they are turned off, when they work, or exactly how they communicate with each other. When turned on and working, ALPRs can capture the text from a license plate of a car traveling up to 150 miles per hour by employing optical character recognition (OCR). This technology works through an infrared light housed in each camera, which scans the images of license plates and then translates those images into computerized text in the span of milliseconds (Leonardo Company 2019). In addition, ALPR scanners arrive equipped with "software for data collection and hot list management" that "runs on a standing remote PC and can support several networked AD3-FH units [a form of ALPR]" (Leonardo Company 2019). This software includes TECS, the Automated Targeting System, and the Statistical Analysis System, which run through databases that include suspicious activity reports (SARs) and the Terrorist Screening Database.[5]

A goal of the DHS following 9/11 has been to integrate its software package and expand its access to databases from both the government and the private sector. In 2012, CBP incorporated many of the older software suites into a software package called Analytical Framework for Intelligence (AFI). CBP's descriptions of AFI emphasize its ability to cross-reference and establish "non-obvious relationships" within the DHS-owned system. The DHS mentions that the system also relies on information collected by commercial data aggregators (Department of Homeland Security 2012, 1). This information includes but is not limited to race, physical characteristics, marital status, Social Security number, vehicle information, social media, travel information, law enforcement records, and familial information. These data are all personally identifiable.

Commercial data aggregators are unbound by federal privacy restrictions, and citizens' information is unprotected by law. By basing risk assessment on the factors listed above, law enforcement's use of AFI simultaneously lends itself to automated profiling (i.e., assessing risk based on race and background factors; Electronic Privacy Information Center 2016) and provides law enforcement with a justification for questioning an individual that evades privacy laws and President Barack Obama's decrees against racial profiling (US Department of Justice 2014).

The DHS's access to personally identifiable information through commercial data aggregators raises privacy concerns (American Civil Liberties Union 2015). The Electronic Privacy Information Center (EPIC) has made numerous FOIA requests to learn about AFI's use of commercial aggregators. EPIC's 2014 request focused on the right of the public to know "which data aggregators are providing information to DHS, what types of information they are providing, and how such information is used." EPIC also requested the DHS's AFI training modules, "documents that discuss potential or actual sources of information not currently in DHS databases" (in other words, data coming from outside sources), and contracts with commercial data aggregators related to AFI (Electronic Privacy

Information Center 2016). The federal government returned heavily redacted documents to EPIC. We inspected these documents and learned that commercial aggregators, which collect personal information, and academic publishing houses fall under the same corporate umbrella.

Getting Personal: Elsevier, LexisNexis, and the Security State

In reviewing documents related to AFI, we learned that it links to troves of data, ranging from impersonal academic work to intimate health-care records. We found a contract (GS-02F-0048m) from 2015 with Reed Elsevier Inc.[6] Reed Elsevier, which after a merger in 2015 is now RELX Group, is a multinational based in London that has four market segments. One of its market segments includes the dissemination and control of scholarly output; for example, subsidiaries of RELX Group are Elsevier and LexisNexis. Branches of this company control our ability to access our own articles (for instance, through LexisNexis), and these and other branches of that same company share information about us with the government. Another subsidiary of LexisNexis that we use for research is Accurint. LexisNexis Accurint claims that it has access to 65 billion public records and that its software can verify identities, detect fraud, and conduct investigations. AFI links CBP to Accurint's vast data set, which includes personally identifiable information related to health care, disease, border security, and other "risks."[7]

Commercial aggregators, such as Accurint, pose a challenge to civil society because the government's ability to access data housed in corporate aggregators operates under a shroud of secrecy and in murky legal landscapes, particularly as privacy rights increasingly intersect with the profit motive. Immigration and Customs Enforcement (ICE), for example, unveiled a plan to purchase data gathered by ALPRs that is stored and mined by corporate aggregators (the program is aptly titled Access to License Plate Reader Commercial Data Service). The scope of this data collection is enormous, some 2 billion data points growing at a rate of 70 million scans per month (Friedersdorf 2016). This program will augment ICE's extensive ALPR data collection throughout the security grid (including but not limited to international and interior checkpoints, border walls, in towns at security towers, and wherever a law enforcement vehicle might be roving with one), giving the agency the ability to track people's travel throughout the United States. The legality of ICE accessing ALPR data on citizens not suspected of crimes, and the ability of private corporations to collect ALPR data in a targeted manner that could include racial profiling, raise legal issues around privacy rights that are yet to be resolved. Indeed, the ACLU (American Civil Liberties Union 2015) has raised concerns about ICE's privacy provisions and argues that commercial aggregators providing information to government agencies should also be held to federal privacy laws. ICE's ALPR program illustrates a technologically driven state of exception where legal precedent is, in effect, attempting to catch up with advances in data gathering and mining.

The power of the security grid over the rights (or rightslessness) of US citizens from a privacy standpoint manifests in access to these data across domains that have become more efficient and flexible. The apparatus for mining data is shifting in radical and significant ways for individuals using computational devices. The architecture of database systems is transforming from using SQL (Structured Query Language) to NoSQL databases.

In a nutshell, traditional databases relied on structured queries across set fields of data. Structured Query Language expresses these operations. Now, operators use a much more fluid NoSQL database in which the data are "not stored in neatly bound boxes but can be easily examined at different granularities; for example, rather than retrieving the profile photos of a certain set of users, you can use an algorithm to search eye color" (McQuillan 2015, 567). As McQuillan (2015, 567) illuminates, this unconstraint means that there is "a free field for the projection of the imagination." Given that law enforcement agents have access to vast troves of data, for example, through AFI software with data packaged by Accurint, they do in fact have that free field.[8]

Fusion Centers in Murky Legal Landscapes

The AFI query tool works not only with DHS records and data from commercial aggregators but also in tandem with fusion centers. The seventy-one fusion centers dotted across the United States collect a wide range of data on individuals, including social media and records from SARs. Due to the ways in which they use software and commercial aggregators, fusion centers generate and emerge from a "state of exception," to use Agamben's (2005) term.

Fusion centers evade federal laws by operating at the state level, even though the DHS is their main source of funding. Fusion centers exploit legal loopholes in order to collect, store, and mine records of individuals who are not suspected of criminal activity. A fusion center's "terrorism liaison all hazards analyst" worked for a local police department, for example, monitoring activists from the Occupy Phoenix movement. The analyst recorded the activists' Social Security numbers, arrest records, Department of Motor Vehicle information, financial data, and social media usage. The fusion center analyst ultimately distributed reports containing these data to law enforcement agencies (Hodai 2013). The DHS funded that position (for more on fusion centers, see Díaz-Barriga and Dorsey 2020).

Because fusion centers act as state-level entities, they are unconstrained by federal privacy laws, more specifically the Privacy Act of 1974, which exclusively applies to federal agencies. State police administer most fusion centers, although DHS analysts, local police, and emergency personnel participate in their operation. Algorithms, database structures, and fusion centers amplify the surveillance capabilities and the role of state and local law enforcement in federal issues. The Texas DPS cooperates with CBP and takes border security as one of its main tasks. The goal of the DPS is to create a surveillance network along the Texas-México border that will protect Texas from drug smugglers, terrorists, and human traffickers. The Texas DPS's surveillance capabilities replicate the technology (sensors, video, ALPRs) and practices (checkpoints) that CBP administers. The murky legal landscape encourages interagency cooperation, including corporate partnerships. The interconnections come full circle as the DPS and CBP feed data into fusion centers, and CBP data analysts work at those centers. Since the creation of the Texas Border Security Operations Center (BSOC), automated systems now dispatch DPS agents and the Texas Rangers to areas where sensors and video have signaled crimes in progress.[9]

In our neighborhood in Mission, Texas, we regularly observe DPS agents stationed on the street and pulling drivers over. This heightened presence of DPS is part of an $800 million initiative that will eventually bring an additional 250 DPS agents to the border (Benning 2016), where agents can pull over residents for minor infractions, such as making a U-turn. Agents then can scan the driver's fingerprints into the system, making their information part of the security grid and potentially assessing them as security risks through commercial data aggregators.

The Border Wall, Technology, and Force

The border wall—the southern boundary point of the security grid—also has emerged from a state of exception.[10] The 2005 Real ID Act and the 2006 Secure Fence Act granted the DHS the power to waive laws in order to construct the border wall where it deemed it necessary for national security. Based on this legal state of exception—waiving the law in order to uphold the law—the DHS built the wall quickly since neither citizens nor organizations had the ability to challenge its construction in court.[11] In South Texas, the DHS's ability to waive the laws has been especially significant. The DHS built the wall in some places up to two miles north of the actual boundary, the Rio Grande/Río Bravo, placing it on levees, private property, nature preserves, and a university campus. The wall has materialized from a state of exception and operates through strategic ambiguity (or confusion) about US citizens' rights when they are near the wall or its attendant gaps and gates.

We have listened to numerous stories about confusion relating to the border wall while leading tours of the wall and in casual conversation with residents about our research. The following story, while unique to the narrator's experience, reflects that of many residents who walk or drive near the border wall.[12] A twenty-something local Latinx resident took some friends to photograph the wall and reported:

The second [border wall] location I went to was located behind a flea market close to the [international] bridge and behind a Whataburger. I got there at around 3:00 [p.m.], and this time I was able to get closer [to the wall]. There was still a Border Patrol truck, but there was sunlight and more people around. As I made my way up a little hill to get close to the wall, another truck showed up and stopped us. He asked what we were doing, and I explained that I was taking photos. He was very nice about it. He asked us to be careful and told us that as long as we did not cross the fence, we would be okay. Right as we got to the fence, another Border Patrol truck showed up, and he [the agent] asked us what we were doing and made us go back down [the hill]. He told us that it was dangerous to be that close [to the wall].

As we walked back down, yet another [Border Patrol] truck showed up, and he [the agent driving the truck] just nodded. When we left and [were] out on the road, a[nother] Border Patrol [truck] followed us.

On her first attempt to approach the border wall, she was immediately turned away. In her second attempt, a Border Patrol agent told our acquaintance that she could approach the wall but could not pass south of it. Our acquaintance did not challenge the CBP agent about her right to stand on the southern side of the wall even though that side of the wall is inside the United States. She remained on its northern side. When she moved toward the wall again, another CBP agent approached in his vehicle and told her that she was in danger even though there was no apparent threat. The CBP agent advised her to leave the area around the wall, and while she was doing so another agent saw her but chose not to engage. Finally, another CBP agent followed her as she drove away. This experience highlights the confusion created by CBP about the wall and the area near it (Dear, this volume). What is clear is that CBP did not want her near the wall.

While there are no legal rulings limiting US citizens' rights to stand near or south of the wall, CBP often treats the area as off-limits. In spaces around the border wall, CBP challenges the rights of US citizens—in this case, through questioning, ordering, and following. It is worth noting that CBP agents have killed people near the border wall.

The Border Patrol's deployment of strategic ambiguity to mislead US citizens is not a novel occurrence encountered by visitors to the border wall in South Texas, by citizens driving to San Antonio, or by those passing through an interior checkpoint south of Falfurrias wondering about the lights and cameras. It reflects the culture of the agency. The head of CBP's internal affairs, James F. Tomsheck, stated that CBP leadership has "a well-established history of intentional misinformation." Speaking about official reports and meetings on CBP shootings, some of them near the border wall, he stated: "Having sat through these meetings for years, after every one of these shootings, there's an effort to spin and distort the facts and obscure a clear understanding of what actually occurred." In eight years, CBP agents killed thirteen US citizens, and "at least three involved unarmed teenagers who were shot in the back" (Luce 2016). CBP agents faced "few if any repercussions, even in cases in which the justification for the shooting seems dubious" (Luce 2016). When reading such reports, one wonders from whom does the threat emanate.

The strategic ambiguity surrounding the border wall for border residents (can one go near it, pass through it, or photograph it?) stands in sharp contrast to the clarity with which CBP views the border wall as a "force multiplier." The wall serves as a "persistent impedance" that "buy[s] time" because it delays people and allows technology to trigger agents to deploy to certain areas: technology and the wall work in tandem. These quoted terms are used in the following CBP explanation of this relationship between technology, the wall, and force (US Customs and Border Protection 2016):[13]

Tactical infrastructure supports CBP's ability to respond in several ways. Fence, for example, is a fixed resource that provides a constant and continuous effect. I wish to be very clear—fence alone does not and cannot provide effective control of the border. It does, however, deter and delay illicit cross-border incursions. This continuous and constant ability to deter or delay is what we refer to as "persistent impedance." There are areas of the border where we have concluded that we must have persistent impedance in order to achieve operational control, because we must at least delay attempted illicit incursions. These delays buy time for our agents to respond. This is critical in areas near cities, for example, where illicit border crossers can easily blend into the population before we interdict them.

Although some refer to technology as a "virtual fence," technology does not have the persistent impedance capability of a real fence. It does, however, provide timely and accurate information that physical infrastructure could not. Technology is a powerful force multiplier because it has tremendous capability to provide the situational awareness that is a precursor to operational control.

CBP's rendering of technology as an interface that takes advantage of "persistent impedance" is stated here in a matter-of-fact manner that is stunning in its simplicity. Indeed, perhaps overstating the obvious, technology does not physically impede, and a wall does not (at least for now) provide technical information. This statement, we think, should be read as reflecting the extent to which the wall and technology intensify the security grid.

Security reticulation, as we have described, not only operates at the international boundary but extends throughout South Texas, from the Rio Grande/Río Bravo to the internal checkpoints seventy-five miles north. For CBP, undocumented Mexican and Central American families, smugglers, and "terrorists" too easily "blend" into Mexican American border neighborhoods. CBP's logic categorizes the local US population as suspect and in need of surveillance (see Bishara, this volume, on the West Bank). It is perhaps unsurprising then that the construction of the border wall has occurred alongside a buildup of Border Patrol and DPS agents, who roam not only near the wall but throughout South Texas's neighborhoods. CBP and the DPS search the security grid's baseball stadiums, neighborhood parks, and scenic wetlands for suspects in the process of "blending." The aesthetics of the wall itself, designed with rusty poles and metal cells, monumentalizes a radical politics of exclusion aimed at US citizens.

Conclusion

When seeing the US-México border wall, we should also contemplate NoSQL queries, algorithms, ALPRs, and facial recognition software interfacing with corporate and security needs. Next time you search LexisNexis or run a data set through Accurint, visualize German shepherds, camera arrays, and interior checkpoints as part of that encounter. And finally, ponder our limited knowledge about how the data gathered about us are collected, stored, and used as we open our browsers at home and as we take to the "open" road in our cars. In this chapter, we have argued that the border wall is more than an object that impedes migrants' mobility. Rather, the wall materializes a virtual security grid that binds border residents into a series of encounters and relationships that undermine their rights as US citizens. In this process, fusion centers are key nodes as they provide the infrastructure, personnel, and legal flexibility that allow for the materialization of the virtual security grids manifest at checkpoints and walls.

The violence that the border wall embodies is implicit not only in the militarized personnel that patrol around it (Jones, this volume) but also in the algorithms, database structures, and strategic ambiguity that support it. Given that border residents live in a Constitution-free zone, it is unsurprising that they are confused about their rights around and past the wall, at checkpoints, and while faced with arrays of sensors and cameras (Dorsey and Díaz-Barriga 2015; American Civil Liberties Union 2018). For actors on the ground, murky legal landscapes, opacity, and insecure security seem to be the new norm. Border walls and checkpoints are mere manifestations of the reticulation of the digital security state. As the physical barriers recede into virtual walls, we must ask: how deep will the security state sink? How far will the net extend?

Notes

1. We can in some ways interpret the wall as minimalism, a recombination through design that is democratic and liberating. See, for example, Hattam (2016, 37) on the imperial aesthetic of the border wall's materialization and its attendant politics, which "like Legos, the Eames House of Cards, and other domestic counterparts, invite recombination through design."

2. Security hardware and software at interior checkpoints have expanded exponentially. For example, in 2013, the array of surveillance equipment at northbound inland checkpoints included two automated license plate readers (ALPRs), six video cameras, two high-intensity lights, and two LED (light-emitting diode) arrays. In 2019, we counted—and we were unable to count everything—fifty camera-like machines pointing at us and our car. Some flashed red lights at us and took pictures.

3. By emphasizing the confusion created by current securitization techniques, including using the Constitution-free zone and waiving laws in order to fortify border security, we are not saying that local residents do not have agency or that they are not fighting back. Border lawyers, activists, and artists, in fact, push back by drawing attention to the border wall and the concentration of law enforcement in the region (http://www.celestedeluna.com; Siefert 2016). Many residents also resist through weapons of the weak, using strategies such as flipping off (or giving the middle finger to) the cameras at interior checkpoints.

4. We know this because we read "ALPR" on one of the cameras that we photographed while we were waiting in an interior checkpoint line.

5. TECS is an updated and modified version of the former Treasury Enforcement Communications System, according to the DHS. TECS is the automated database system that assists CBP in targeting individuals for secondary inspection, questioning, or detention. Data collected through SAR reports appear unbounded, and these reports have been taken to extreme levels. One report involves an elderly man who forgot his cell phone at a food court. Law enforcement agents from many ranks and even meter readers and firefighters can submit SARs on US citizens.

6. EPIC continues its legal tussle with the DHS over this FOIA request, and the DHS has released numerous documents that are highly redacted.

7. Accurint has "a combination of over 33 billion records from over 8,800 different data sources. Data sources are updated daily, weekly, monthly, and annually, depending on the particular data source." https://secure.accurint.com/bps/368/html/leg/faq_general.html, accessed September 27, 2019.

8. While it is difficult to obtain data from the DHS about Accurint, epidemiologists have noted its power for tracking and contacting research subjects, including gathering data on illnesses, cause of death, addresses, and identity verification (see Pack et al. 2013).

9. The DPS describes the BSOC in the following terms: "The Border Security Operations Center (BSOC) is headquartered in Austin and serves as the focal point for the six Joint Operations and Intelligence Centers (JOICs) located along the Texas/Mexico border. Responsibilities include analyzing intelligence and

collecting border security information, while collaborating with state, local, and federal law enforcement partners to conduct intelligence-directed border enforcement operations and ensure information exchange between agencies. BSOC is tasked with the timely dissemination of intelligence through a variety of mediums to law enforcement and governmental partners, including the in-depth weekly Border Operations Sector Assessment of the Texas/Mexico border. BSOC operates the State of Texas' technology initiatives to combat criminal and border exploitation while supporting tactical initiatives, such as the Special Operations Group" (Texas Department of Public Safety n.d.).

10. A number of scholars have noted the role of states of exception at border walls. For example, Reece Jones (2009) describes the role of legal states of exception for the India-Bangladesh border wall, and Clarno (2013) does so for the Israel-Palestine wall.

11. The wall was built through the US Congress waiving the law. Legal precedent, according to privacy advocates, has not caught up with technological advances that enable corporations and the government to store vast amounts of personal data. Checkpoints are founded on the easing of Fourth Amendment rights, which seems to allow for the use of a wide variety of cameras and sensors at interior checkpoints. Indeed, when we first passed through the checkpoints in 2008 as part of this research project, there were neither cameras nor light arrays. The border wall and checkpoints are, of course, part of a larger history of how the United States has targeted immigrants. See Inda (2005) for a discussion of this larger history.

12. See Díaz-Barriga and Dorsey (2011) for further discussion of border residents' concerns about approaching the border wall. Also see Dorsey and Díaz-Barriga (2010) for a description of how the border region is conceptualized as a war zone even though it is one of the safest regions in the United States. Rosas (2006b, 2012) theorizes that border militarization has generated a "treacherous geography" that "thickens" the border as a zone of violence.

13. Since President Trump has taken office, many documents have been removed from government websites. While the cited document no longer exists at the link provided in the reference list, the quoted argument about technology and the wall is commonplace. We have kept the original citation and web link to highlight the US government's removal of documents.

CHAPTER TEN

The Material and Symbolic Power of Border Walls

REECE JONES

I first began to wonder about the peculiar nature of borders almost twenty years ago while driving with my brother and a friend along a road at the edge of the Sahara Desert between the Moroccan cities of Ouarzazate and Errachidia. We had rented a car in Marrakesh and recklessly driven over the Atlas Mountains during a snowstorm in December, but the expense and danger were worth it once we reached the Saharan side. The road stretched for miles with the yellow sands of the Sahara in the distance to the south and the jagged Atlas Mountains to the north. We only encountered a handful of other vehicles on the road. The extent of the emptiness heightened our senses, and our eyes picked out distant goats on the mountains and camels in the desert.

We were still a few hours from Errachidia when a structure of some sort became visible along the road ahead. As we drove closer, we grew concerned because it appeared to be a boundary marker or security checkpoint. It had turrets like a castle and had minarets painted on it. There were openings on each side that might hold guards or security officers. We wondered whether we had made a wrong turn and were actually at the nearby border with Algeria, which was fighting an insurgency in the area. After a few moments of uncertainty, our worries about armed guards at a security checkpoint proved unfounded. It was a decorative marker, not a functional border, and it stretched less than fifty feet into the desert. Since we were alone there, we stopped to take a look.

Except for the road and the marker, there were no other human-made objects visible in any direction. The landscape was continuous, but the marker divided it and established a boundary between two different administrative divisions in Morocco. My eyes followed the direction of the wall out into the desert, and I could imagine where the line was. But that is the thing: the line was imaginary and only as real as the marker and my imagination made it. The incongruity of the boundary marker in the empty desert made obvious the difference between the physical landscape and the maps and political systems we use to organize, administer, and control it. The marker only made sense because I already knew that territories and borders exist on maps. At the time, I was struck by the curious nature of this particular marker in the desert, but its implications for all borders were not clear to me until years later. We only stayed a minute or two, but the experience left me with lingering questions about lines on maps and borders on the ground.

Most people are familiar with maps that depict the earth divided up into countries, even if they cannot name or identify more than a few. These maps simplify the 7 billion people in the world into easy to understand categories where everyone belongs. Although most people have only visited a handful of countries, it is taken for granted that these categories are real, are meaningful, and broadly represent a historical connection between a people and a place. Italy is where Italians live, and it is completely separate from France where the French live. Children are often taught they are members of one group that is unique and distinct from all the others on the map. They learn the history of their people and land, which is distinct from the histories of other cultures around the world. The people who live in each country are thought of as a single homogeneous group that shares a culture, a history, and a way of life.

Today, a growing number of the lines on maps are also inscribed on the earth with walls, guards, military technologies, and sophisticated surveillance systems (Brown 2010; Dear 2013; Di Cintio 2012; Jones 2012; Stephenson and Zanotti 2013; Till et al. 2013; Vallet 2014). For example, since 2006, the United States has built almost 700 miles of walls and fences on its almost 2,000-mile border with México (Dear, this volume). Donald Trump, a real estate tycoon, upended the 2015–2016 Republican presidential nomination contest by campaigning on a hard line against immigration and arguing for completely sealing the border. In his announcement speech in June 2015, he said, "When Mexico sends its people, they're not sending their best. They're not sending you. They're not sending you. They're sending people that have lots of problems, and they're bringing those problems with us [*sic*]. They're bringing drugs. They're bringing crime. They're rapists. And some, I assume, are good people" (*Washington Post* 2015). To the surprise of many, the anti-migrant rhetoric did not sink his campaign but rather vaulted him to the presidency of the United States.

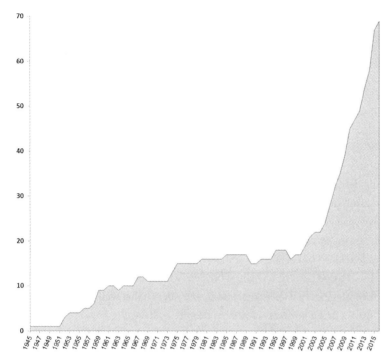

Figure 10.1. Border wall construction, 1945–2015. Created by Elisabeth Vallet, Zoe Barry, and Josselyn Guillarmou.

It is not just in the United States that border walls have become popular political symbols. In 2015 alone, Austria, Bulgaria, Estonia, Hungary, Kenya, Saudi Arabia, and Tunisia all announced or began the construction of barriers on their frontiers (see Brian and Laczko 2014). At the end of World War II, there were only five border walls around the world. According to Elisabeth Vallet (2019) of the University of Quebec at Montreal, in 2017 there were almost seventy walls, three-quarters of them built in the previous twenty years (figure 10.1).

International borders, of course, are not the only lines on maps that shape our lives. From the moment we are born to the moment we die, we live in a multitude of overlapping bounded spaces that affect every aspect of our existence (Popescu 2011; Diener and Hagen 2012). These lines include state boundaries, county boundaries, city boundaries, city council districts, police precincts, fire station districts, school districts, electricity grids, trash collection areas, neighborhood boards, gated communities (Dinzey-Flores, this volume), and private properties. The list could go on and on. Although many of these lines are invisible and permeable, they affect our way of life in terms of the quality of the school we go to, the taxes we pay, the benefits we receive, the rights we are guaranteed, and the opportunities we have. We rarely think about how completely our lives are bounded by lines on maps and by borders on the ground.

In this chapter I question the connections among lines on maps, categories in our minds, and the surface of the earth. When we see something on a map, we often trust that it exists in the world because maps are thought of as unbiased representations of facts (Harley 2002; Wood 1992). Walls materialize this idea by visually demonstrating the existence of a border. However, maps are always a representation of a much larger object and therefore inevitably include erasures and omissions because the mapmaker has decided what to include and how to depict it. In the second half of the chapter I engage with the construction of walls and fences on borders.

The global trend toward hardened borders with walls and other security infrastructure suggests that there must be clear evidence that walls are an effective strategy for securing borders. However, despite walls' widespread use, there is relatively little evidence of their effectiveness, particularly at long and remote borders. While walls are effective at visually demonstrating authority over land and at slowing the movement of some border crossers, they are ineffective against a military threat or, for the most part, smugglers. Given their general ineffectiveness at controlling movement across borders, in the concluding section I suggest that border walls primarily have symbolic value (McAtackney and McGuire, this volume). They bring into being the authority of the state, they demonstrate the resolve of politicians to do something about perceived external threats, and they contribute to a growing homeland security industry that relies on narratives of security and insecurity to continue to expand the construction of surveillance infrastructure (Dorsey and Díaz-Barriga, this volume). Walls materialize the imagined lines on maps and instantiate claims to sovereignty and authority over space.

Maps and Borders

The Moroccan boundary markers are examples of the complicated ways that our minds categorize information on maps and then apply that knowledge to the world. Contemporary maps are powerful because they are ubiquitous and seem innocuous. The idea that they depict our world in an objective way hides the important role they play in shaping our understanding of the world around us (Harley 2002; Winichakul 1994; Wood 1992). A map does not simply represent a preexisting reality. Instead, it represents a human idea: it is a depiction of a desire of what is meant to be but often is not achieved. It is a jumble of lines, symbols, and blank spaces that convey some sort of information. There is a real world, but a map is a piece of paper with ink on it or, increasingly, a collection of differently colored pixels on a screen.

Although maps are a partial and incomplete depiction of some aspect of the world, our minds perceive maps in a very different way. Maps appeal to a powerful need in our brains for information to be categorized and organized (Brubaker et al. 2004; Lakoff 1987; Lakoff and Johnson 1999). Our mind takes the information collected on the map and converts it into the world, at least in our minds. Cognitive scientists have found that our brains have difficulty comprehending large amounts of data, and so our minds quickly look for patterns in order to organize the information into a system of categories that makes sense (Lakoff and Johnson 1999). It is not that these various categories are completely made up, but rather that the boundaries they impose are not necessarily the boundaries of the world (Abbott 1995).

This is what maps do to the landscapes around us. They take the diverse and complex world and organize it into a clear system so we can make sense of it. Then our brain interprets the categories of the map as the categories of the world. However, since the world is represented at a smaller scale on a map, something has to be taken out; otherwise, the map would have to be the same size as the world and would be of no use at all. This means that maps are not a mimetic representation of the world, but rather an approximation of the world. Every map includes a series of decisions, omissions, and erasures, which always result in a biased and partial representation of the earth (Harley 2002).

With most human-made objects, we immediately understand that someone created them for particular purposes. Typically, the higher the quality, the more we associate a name or brand with it. Maps are different (Wood 1992). The most effective maps are the ones in which the mapmaker fades from view. Although every map is made from someone's perspective, a perfectly made map seems to be an unbiased representation of the earth, a simple collection of facts. Only a handful of people have actually peered down at the world from space, but maps allow everyone to imagine spatial relationships from that perspective, rather than from our grounded place on the earth.

The modern system of bordered states is closely linked to the emergence of modern cartography. Prior to the sixteenth century, it was difficult for rulers to visualize their lands as bounded territories with borders because accurate maps of large areas did not exist (Winichakul 1994). States existed prior to this period, and they had the edges of the land under their control, but these frontiers were not as clearly established and marked as they are today. The frontiers were about actual control on the ground rather than a political agreement of control between neighboring states. A few ancient walls, such as the various Chinese walls to protect resources from Mongol raids and Hadrian's Wall in northern England, were built, but they were not on agreed-upon borders (Lovell 2006; Rojas 2010; Waldron 1990; McGuire, this volume). Instead, they were often last-ditch efforts to prevent the incursion of a more mobile external threat.

Early European states established the first modern borders in the late seventeenth century. Modern borders are mutually agreed-upon lines between sovereign states that are marked on maps and on the ground (Diener and Hagen 2012). As accurate maps of the land of Europe became available and as the devastating aftermath of the inconclusive Thirty Years' War (1618–1648) made clear that territorial expansion through war was difficult, some European states turned to negotiations to settle who governed where (Wilson 2009). The kingdoms of Spain and France used maps to draw a boundary in the Pyrenees in 1659, and over the ensuing centuries states in Europe slowly came to agreements on the territorial extent of their authority (Sahlins 1989). This process was complicated in Europe by the long history of conflict and shifting frontiers, which meant that some regions, like Alsace-Lorraine along the modern-day French-German border, had been claimed by different rulers at different points in time.

The idea of marking political boundaries on maps was used much more efficiently to make agreements between European states as they colonized the rest of the world. The colonists often had minimal knowledge of the local landscape in the regions they wanted to colonize, but they possessed maps that depicted the outlines of the territories along with major rivers and mountains. They used these maps to draw lines around the areas where each colonial power would agree to focus its resource-extraction regime, while allowing other states free rein in other locations.

The first example of this sort of agreement is the Treaty of Tordesillas between the kings of Spain and Portugal, which was brokered by Pope Alexander VI in 1494 after the discovery of the Americas by Europeans. The audacious agreement divided the world in half, granting Spain the right to lands to the west of the meridian 370 leagues from the Cape Verde islands and giving Portugal everything to the east. The idea was to give Spain the new lands it had discovered in the Americas while Portugal wanted to protect its profitable trade routes to Africa and Asia. However, at the time of the agreement, their knowledge of the world was so limited that they did not have the capability to measure the location of the meridian in the ocean, and they did not realize that a large chunk of South America was west of the line, which is why Brazil eventually became a Portuguese colony.

Over the ensuing centuries, other similar agreements between colonial states were reached, culminating with the 1884–1885 Conference of Berlin, which came to be known as the "scramble" for Africa or the "partition" of Africa. With a huge map of Africa on the wall, representatives of most of the European powers worked to draw lines on the map to delimit the zones of influence of each state across the continent. France maintained influence over North Africa as well as much of West Africa. Germany was awarded what is today Namibia and Tanzania. Portugal took Angola and Mozambique. Britain maintained zones of influence across the continent, including present-day Egypt, Ghana, Kenya, Nigeria, South Africa, and Uganda. For the most part, those lines, which paid no attention to the local conditions, histories, peoples, or politics, remain the borders of African states today even after independence (Herbst 1989).

There are not any natural political boundaries on the earth. Instead, all borders have to be inscribed on the earth in order to bring them into being, to symbolize the claim of authority over a place, and to signify the extent of that claim (Eilenberg 2014; Johnson et al. 2011; Lentz 2014). Borders are material expressions of power (Ferdoush 2018; Paasi 2012). They are the location where an individual or group of people claims a resource and then excludes other people from access to that resource through territoriality (Diener and Hagen 2012; Popescu 2011). Sack (1986, 19) defines territoriality as "the attempt by an individual or group to affect, influence or control people, phenomena and relationships by delimiting and asserting control over a geographical area."

Since most modern borders were first inscribed on a map, the actual location of a border on the ground was often surveyed and marked much later. Although

France and Spain agreed on their border in the Pyrenees in 1659, they did not get around to marking it on the ground until the Treaty of Bayonne in 1868 (Sahlins 1989). The US-México border was finalized through the Treaty of Guadalupe Hidalgo in 1848 and the Gadsden Purchase in 1853–1854, but it was not surveyed and demarcated with boundary stones until the 1890s (Dear 2015 and this volume). The situation at each border differs, but for many the idea in the popular imagination of a hard line guarded by troops and forged through centuries of conflict with neighboring states is not accurate. Instead, in the twentieth century many borders were marked by occasional boundary markers, if at all, and guarded by a small border force that served as a presence in the area but did not have operational control over vast stretches of land.

As borders between states were institutionalized, states rarely fortified the lines on the ground with walls or fences. This is the case for several reasons. First, since most borders were agreed upon between the two states, each country worried less about the possibility of invasion, which had necessitated older walls like the Chinese ones. Second, many of the border locations were at the distant edges of the political space of the state, remote by design. Often the states had minimal knowledge of these places, and they were not densely populated. Third, building walls over long distances is prohibitively expensive. Since the borders were not seen as a threat, they were remote, and it is expensive to build walls, few states engaged in substantial border fortification in peace times.

The Turn to Walls

There were some hardened borders during the middle of the twentieth century, for example the Iron Curtain in Europe (McWilliams 2013 and this volume) and contested borders between states still at war, such as the demilitarized zone between North and South Korea (McGuire, this volume) and the Line of Control between India and Pakistan in Kashmir, but these were exceptions to the rule of lightly guarded borderlines. When the Cold War ended and the Berlin Wall fell, there was even a moment when a borderless world seemed possible as globalization connected the earth economically, socially, and politically. This has happened, but only partially. Businesspeople, consumer goods, and investments cross borders very easily. Corporations are able to operate in dozens of countries, and they rely on new communication and transportation technologies to utilize differences in wages globally to improve profits. However, for most people, particularly the poor and the racialized "other," the world is the most bordered it has ever been (Jones 2016; McGuire and McAtackney, this volume). This has occurred because the purpose of political borders has changed in the era of globalization. After the creation of the United Nations, which requires in its charter that all member states respect the sovereignty and territorial integrity of all other members, borders were transformed into lines that separate different systems of legal, economic, and political practices. Expensive border fences and walls are not necessary for these purposes: they are not impediments to the missiles or fighter jets of an invading army nor are they any better than a map at representing the edges of different legal or political systems.

Since the 1980s, the model of security at crossing points but largely open borders in the vast stretches in between has given way to increasingly hardened and fenced borders at many locations around the world. While walls are not necessary to mark a territorial claim or stop an invading army, they are relatively effective for other purposes, such as slowing the movement of migrants and making a political claim. In the twenty-first century, these other functions of borders have become more significant, and consequently a number of states around the world have turned to walls (Vallet 2014).

Although new border walls are justified in a multitude of different ways in different countries, most of the reasoning can be boiled down to a fear of "others" crossing the border and changing the cultural, political, or economic situation in a particular place. Trump's language about México not sending its best epitomizes this sentiment, but it is evident in many countries around the world. French politician Marine Le Pen compared the current migration into Europe from Africa and the Middle East to the "barbarian" invasions of the Middle Ages. In India, the fear of demographic and religious change brought by Bangladeshi migrants has fueled the construction of fences on the border (Jones 2012).

Similar fears pervade the discourse about walls around the world from South Africa to Israel, from Bulgaria to Spain (Vallet 2014). One common characteristic is that many of the walls are built on borders where there is a sharp wealth gap across them. In 2012, the gross domestic product per capita of countries building walls was more than $14,000 while on the other side it was $2,900 (Rosière and Jones 2012). Similarly, many of the locations of contemporary border walls are not places where the two neighboring states were at war with each other or engaged in a territorial dispute. Instead, these locations are characterized by civilian movements across the border: workers moving from a poorer country to a more prosperous country in search of better wages and opportunity. In many places, however, the perceived fear of terrorists crossing the border with the flows of workers was often cited to increase the urgency to build the border wall and to increase security in border spaces (Jones 2012).

The attacks of September 11, 2001, in the United States and the ensuing "war on terror" played a significant role in changing the national narrative about border walls. Although the underlying factors of wealth inequality and population movements were already in place in the 1980s and 1990s, the idea of building a massive border wall retained a negative stigma. The stigma was tied to the representation of the Berlin Wall during the Cold War in which the wall symbolized both the oppression of the totalitarian East German state and communism generally (McWilliams, this volume). Presidents of the United States used it as a backdrop for political speeches, and Ronald Reagan implored Mikhail Gorbachev to "tear down this wall" in 1987. Consequently, when it did fall in 1989, it became very difficult for democratic states to build walls. It was just not something democracies did. However, after 9/11, the narrative shifted, and it became imperative that states did everything they could to protect their populations from the threat of terrorism. Hardening borders became a key part of this process as airport security screening was expanded and new security measures at borders were considered. Walls went from something that democracies did not do to something that was an obligation to protect the population in the years after the attack.

Walls and fences are particularly effective mechanisms for communicating a political claim at a specific location, but the evidence is mixed as to whether walls work for security purposes (Pallister-Wilkins 2016). They materialize the edges of the imagined territory from a map and demarcate where a claim is made on the ground. While it is easy to stumble onto an unmarked territory or property, with the construction of a wall the boundary is unmistakable in the landscape. However, walls are often meant to do much more than simply communicate a claim. The stated purpose of most border walls built since the 1990s is to prevent unauthorized movement by closing long stretches of the border. The dramatic increase in the number of walls globally—from around fifteen in the late 1990s to almost seventy today—illustrates this transformation (figure 10.1).

What Work Do Walls Do?

Some walls can be extremely effective at preventing movement. Modern prison walls, for example, demonstrate that compact walls with a large contingent of guards can create almost complete control over access to a particular area. Short, high, well-guarded walls around medieval cities were also difficult to breach. At the US-México border, the effectiveness of a wall backed up with a heavy presence of guards was tested in the 1990s with Operations Hold the Line and Gatekeeper (Andreas 2009; Dunn 2001, 2009; Nevins 2010). Prior to these undertakings, the US Border Patrol had primarily relied on a strategy that allowed migrants to cross the border before attempting to locate them on the US side (Heyman 1999, 2008; Hernandez 2010). Operations Hold the Line and Gatekeeper used short sections of fence and large deployments of Border Patrol agents on the borderline to deter crossings in El Paso, Texas, and south of San Diego, California (Haddal 2010; Garcia 2015). In the immediate areas of the operations, they were successful. Crossings and apprehensions dropped to zero, and movement through those short sections of the border, both roughly ten miles, was largely stopped. However, these undertakings had no impact on the total number of people crossing the border since migrants and smugglers simply relocated to other sections of the border outside those two areas.

The results of these operations were an early indication of the impact most border walls would have on migration flows as dozens more walls were built (Miller 2014; Rosière and Jones 2011). There is little doubt that fences and walls make crossings in the immediate area of their construction more difficult and that they funnel migrants to other, often more dangerous locations without walls and with less security infrastructure. The redirecting of migrants is evident at the US-México border. Crossings in California declined precipitously in the early 2000s as enforcement increased, and at the same time, crossings in Arizona soared as did deaths due to the harsh terrain (Anderson and Parks 2008; De León 2015). Similarly, as easier crossings have closed at the edges of the European Union, migrants have been funneled to ever more dangerous locations through Libya and across the Mediterranean (Spijkerboer 2007; Weber and Pickering 2011). The International Organization for Migration suggests: "The relatively low number of migrant deaths before 1990 may be related to the fact that it used to be much easier to reach Europe by regular means, even in the absence of official government authorization to immigrate" (Brian and Laczko 2014, 88).

Although deaths have increased, many migrants still cross borders, even the most heavily fortified like the US-México boundary and the Mediterranean borders of the European Union (Papadopoulos, this volume). This is true for several reasons. First, although the scale of border wall construction over the past few years is unprecedented, most borders are still nowhere near completely fenced and sealed. For example, the US-México border has 670 miles of fencing and walls on the almost 2,000-mile border, which leaves two-thirds of the border unfenced. Second, as the length of border walls grows, it becomes much more difficult to adequately patrol the entirety of a nation's boundary. Even prison walls are only as effective as the guards who ensure that they are not breached. Unlike prison perimeters, borders can be thousands of miles long, which makes them difficult to monitor properly. The United States employs more than 20,000 Border Patrol agents, but even if they were all on duty at the same time, each would need to guard a 1,700-foot section of the border. Without a guard watching it, a wall is only a slight impediment to someone who wants to cross. Most of the US fence can be climbed in less than fifteen seconds (McGuire and Van Dyke 2017). As the former secretary of the US Department of Homeland Security, Janet Napolitano (2016), puts it, "Show me a ten-foot fence and I will show you an eleven-foot ladder."

Another factor that undermines the effectiveness of border walls is that few borders are meant to completely seal off movement between the two sides. Although there is a tendency to think about borders as technologies of closure that prevent movement between different places, most borders serve more nuanced purposes (Cons 2016). Borders work as membranes simultaneously limiting some movement, while encouraging and facilitating others. While there are a few exceptions—there is very little movement across the demilitarized zone between North and South Korea, particularly since the closure of the Kaesong industrial region in 2016—most states desire cross-border trade. They want to regulate flows by allowing capital, consumer goods, and the wealthy to pass through while preventing the movement of poor people and those who are perceived to be threats (Abraham and van Schendel 2005). Consequently, the enormous numbers of people, cars, trucks, and shipping containers that cross borders every day create many opportunities to slip through or around even a heavily guarded border wall. The traffic at crossing points allows those with money to use a fake document or bribe a guard in order to cross the border. Additionally, only a very small percentage of shipping containers are searched at borders, allowing people and smuggled goods another avenue to get across.

The 2015 escape of the drug cartel leader Joaquín "El Chapo" Guzmán from a Mexican prison highlights another vulnerability of border walls: tunnels. Since 1990, the US Border Patrol has found 150 tunnels beneath the US-México border (Sorrensen 2014). Since 2006, Israel has found thirty-two tunnels under its border fence with Gaza, and it is constructing an underground wall that will extend more than ten meters below the surface to combat tunnel construction (Kershner 2016). The challenge with tunnels is that they are difficult to identify from the surface and can exist for years without being detected by the authorities.

One of the unexpected results of the construction of walls and fences and the expansion of security practices at borders is that the fortifications often benefit smugglers and cartels. By preventing easy crossings, these security technologies force most people to rely on smugglers' tunnels and bribery networks. Although government officials are often quick to blame smugglers or human traffickers for deaths at borders, the reality is that the hardening of the border is the factor that strengthens the position of the traffickers and forces migrants to rely on their services.

The necessity of monitoring border walls points to one of the fundamental truths about them: historically, most have failed (Sterling 2009). The most famous sections of the Great Wall of China were overrun within a few decades of their construction. Subsequent emperors saw them as embarrassing blunders (Lovell 2006). When Germany invaded France in World War II, it simply went around the Maginot Line. The Berlin Wall fell within thirty years of its construction (McWilliams, this volume). Fencing and walls are expensive and not particularly effective at preventing movement across a border.

Conclusion: Material and Symbolic Power

Despite serious questions about the effectiveness of border walls, countries around the world are rushing to build more. Part of the reason is the industrial sector that has emerged around border security. Border infrastructure is expensive to build and maintain, which creates lucrative contracts for military suppliers and construction companies (Lipton 2013; Visiongain 2013). Israel's wall in the West Bank cost more than $1 million per mile to construct (Bishara, this volume). Building the existing 670 miles of fencing and vehicle barriers on the US-México border cost $3.9 million per mile in 2007 and $6.5 million per mile in 2008 (Jones 2012; US Government Accountability Office 2011). At the 2008 price, fortifying the remaining 1,300 miles of the US-México border would cost more than $8.4 billion. After the election of Donald Trump to the US presidency, the stock prices of Betafence, Magal Security, and other firms that build border walls surged to all-time highs.

While walls do not have a substantial impact on the flows of people or goods across borders at a large scale, they do have significant material and symbolic impacts at individual borders. The first material impact of border walls and the expanded security practices that surround them has been a dramatic increase in deaths at borders globally. The International Organization for Migration reported that more than 40,000 people died attempting to cross a border from 2006 to 2015. At the edges of the European Union before the borders were walled and securitized, there were only a handful of deaths per year in the 1990s. In 2016, there were more than 8,000 deaths, mostly because overcrowded and unseaworthy ships sank in the Mediterranean Sea (International Organization for Migration 2019; Papadopoulos, this volume). Despite the hardening of borders and the increase in deaths, the walls have not completely shut off movement to the European Union, and in 2015 a record number of migrants arrived. Germany alone received 2.1 million people that year (Fuchs 2016).

A second material impact of the construction of border walls is a transformation of the environment in border spaces. Walls disrupt the visual space of the landscape, and they also affect the movement of animals and the fluvial geomorphology of the border zone (Linnell et al. 2016). Matt Soniak (2016) writes about the US-México border: "By militarizing the border—building walls and fences, Border Patrol outposts, spotlights and service roads and clearing vegetation—we sever the connections that wildlife relies on. We cut animals off from habitats, resources, and breeding partners and block migration routes, just as climate change and habitat loss makes every bit of land ever more important." In addition to fragmenting habitats, damaging sensitive landscapes, and disrupting migrations, border walls also funnel water away from traditional floodplains or dam its movement. At the US-México border in Arizona, there has been significant flooding caused by the wall at Organ Pipe National Monument and at the Nogales border crossing point (US National Park Service 2008).

Beyond these physical changes, the broader significance of border walls is symbolic. They materialize a series of political claims about the state, the nation, and the homeland that consolidate the group building the wall and its political discourse inside particular states. Modern cartography transformed how maps represent the world and made it possible to imagine the earth as bounded territorial units. Our minds grasp the categories and lines on the map and instinctively use those to understand the world out there. Once you have seen a political map with borders—as we all have—it is hard not to think of the world as a patchwork of distinct countries. Border walls continue the process of imposing these imagined lines on the ground, literally bringing into being the idea of territory and homeland by creating the edges of these spaces.

Borders are important sites for the performance of territorial control, separation between polities, identity, insecurity, and resistance (Amilhat Szary 2012; Jones 2012; Walia 2013). High-tech surveillance and boots on the ground may be more effective at preventing people from crossing a border, but a wall can be used as a political prop. While most of the issues that surround borders are complex, it is easy to say "build a wall," a phrase that fits nicely into the short attention span of politics at the present moment. A wall provides imposingly tangible evidence that something is being done to address fears in the community about jobs, unwanted cultural beliefs and practices, or the threat of terrorism. Whether a border wall actually contributes to solving any of these issues is beside the point; it symbolizes action. The power of walls on borders is that they materialize the connections among maps, our knowledge of the world, and physical features in the landscape. Walls create a powerful symbol of the right of a political community to exclude "others" by preventing their movement.

CHAPTER ELEVEN

Conclusion

The Repercussions of Walls and Their Future

LAURA MCATACKNEY AND RANDALL H. MCGUIRE

> *Yes, segregate.*
> *Create a slum for me.*
> *Build walls.*
> *Render us apart.*
> *Hide.*
> —Kevin J. Taylor (2016)

In a few words, Kevin Taylor's poem "The New Apartheid" captures the global trend in wall building that the contributors in this book seek to understand. Around the world, people are building barriers to solve a range of problems. Yet despite the variety of ills that walls claim to confront—including providing safety and security—there is great consistency in whom they wall in and whom they wall out. Increasingly in our world, walls define in a brutally material way the haves and the have-nots or those who belong and those who do not belong. They separate people of different races, nationalities, religions, classes, and ethnicities. They segregate white from black, rich from poor, and citizen from noncitizen. Walls create slums for the poor and provide comfortable shelter for the privileged to hide behind. The wall always has two sides, and which side of the wall you originate from defines how easily you can cross to the other side. As the authors in this volume demonstrate, wall building occurs on many scales: between individuals, within cities, and along national borders.

This volume has brought together case studies from a wide variety of per-spectives, geographical locations, and scales of construction and has initiated a cross-disciplinary discussion on key issues of contemporary wall construc-tion. The contributors reveal how walls invite precise reflections on the material practices of erecting and maintaining boundaries, as well as the struggles against them and the destruction of them. By integrating temporal and spatial perspectives, we have explored how contemporary walls succeed or fail at resolving the problems they were meant to address, and we have asked the pertinent question: what are the repercussions of an increasingly materially segregated world? Even though the authors have considered different scales of analysis, have studied diverse regions, and originate from various disciplines, we agree on eight foundational insights about modern walls (see the final section of this chapter).

Scales of Analysis, Temporality, and Spatiality

In our examination, we have broadened the field of inquiry from walls being constructed at national borders to focus on the process of walling in and walling out as these phenomena occur on numerous levels. We have focused on local walls, national walls, and supporting walls to organize our discussions. The reality of wall building is extremely complex and involves the need to consider issues of scale, spatiality, and temporality. Despite presenting as static and monumental, walls are dynamic and retain the potential to change in form and meaning and so retain the potential to transgress scales and categories. However, we have found that walls almost always address two intersecting social differences. Wall builders commonly recognize the social distinction of class and advertise barriers' ability to keep the socially undesirable poor away from the arena of the rich. The social distinction that wall builders rarely speak of, but that transcends all levels, is race. At every scale, most modern walls materialize at the intersection of race and class.

LOCAL WALLS

Builders usually construct local walls to address socioeconomic difference, putting them up around urban and suburban neighborhoods to wall out the economically disadvantaged "other" or sometimes to wall them in. Gated communities in Puerto Rico show how walls can be used to both wall in and wall out and therefore solidify inequality in multiple and complex ways. Race and class intersect and materialize in two different forms of walled neighborhoods: one that walls the lower classes into their housing projects and the other that walls them out of affluent gated communities (Dinzey-Flores 2013 and this volume).

In Lima, Peru, gated communities have become the norm with more than 3,000 walls, fences, and other types of physical structures controlling access to public streets (Boano and Desmaison 2016). The most infamous of these is the "wall of shame" that separates the wealthy barrio of Las Casuarinas from the slum of Pamplona Alta. This concrete wall stands three meters tall and is crowned with rolls of barbed wire.

Some walls are thought of as modern anomalies, throwbacks to unresolved historical disputes that keep diametrically opposed groups—often based on ethnicity, race, or religion—apart on the local level. In Belfast, Northern Ireland, walls carve up areas of social housing into "Catholic" and "Protestant" areas and in doing so ignore those who do not wish to be categorized or do not belong to either side (McAtackney 2011 and this volume). In the Palestinian context, walls do not signify complete division, yet they doubly divide the significant numbers of Palestinians in Israel and the increasing numbers of Israeli settlers in the West Bank (Bishara 2013 and this volume). In theory, these local walls separate different people and polities, but in practice, they twist through neighborhoods and disrupt everyday life.

NATIONAL WALLS

The proliferation of walls and other material barriers at national borders in the early twenty-first century has historical precedent. In ancient times, Eurasian states built long walls on their borders as part of military defenses meant to keep "barbarians" out (McGuire, this volume). In contrast, the materialization in Cold War Europe of the Iron Curtain, which cut through Berlin, served to wall in people (the East) rather than wall out intruders (the West) (McWilliams 2013 and this volume).

We are seeing a massive expansion of national border barriers built to wall out not invading armies but rather stigmatized, unruly individuals (Dear and Jones, both this volume). These walls show the neoliberal freedoms of movement, trade, and ideas to be deliberately partial—available only to the select few. These walls increasingly materialize the inequalities between the Global North and the Global South and between developed nations and developing nations. The aim of national walls to discriminate is most evident, but also contested, at the highly developed third-nation borderland of the United States and México. In contrast, the border between the Global North of Europe and the Global

South of the African continent and the Middle East fluctuates in form and scale, pushing potential transgressors into more and more perilous journeys if they wish to cross over (Papadopoulos, this volume). Such borders manifest the in-equalities of the contemporary world in which the "right" race, religion, citizen-ship, or socioeconomic group determines social belonging (Jones, this volume).

National walls have received significant mass media attention and popular commentary (Rice-Oxley 2013; Tomlinson 2015). Adding nuance to the hysteria of much of the coverage by mass media, especially the tabloids—which often present walls as necessary to "hold back the tide of migrants" (e.g., Tomlinson 2015)—scholars interpret the proliferation of national walls as a manifestation of governments' and other entities' desire for social control and as their attempt to assert national sovereignty in an increasingly globalized and transnational world (see Jones 2016). Certainly, walls can map onto and reinforce borders, but they also take many other forms and appear in a variety of contexts. The political walls that governments build to control and separate peoples are solid, seemingly immovable constructions, yet their forms and meanings change (Pa-padopoulos and McWilliams, both this volume). They can be added to or have holes drilled into them. They can dampen protest or be transgressed. Over time, they can shape landscapes and the interactions of communities, but they also can become obsolete: their defensive functions lost and their forms preserved for heritage and tourism (McGuire, this volume). Eventually, almost all walls come down.

By focusing on the many forms of walls, rather than on the ambiguity of the border, this volume offers a materialist emphasis that goes beyond the well-worn terrain of geopolitical analysis. Borders are imaginary lines in the sand that demarcate one territory from another; they cannot vary without state-level legal changes. Ink on a map cannot effectively create sovereign space until states materialize those lines on the ground.

SUPPORTING WALLS

Walls require a massive investment and infrastructure to build, to maintain, and to support. The use of advances in technology has led to the rise of the border-industrial complex (Dorsey and Díaz-Barriga 2010; Dear, this volume) that profits from the walls. The border-industrial complex has become a powerful lobby devoted to maintaining, remodeling, and building new walls. Increasingly, engagements with national border walls reveal that states use them for nefarious surveillance purposes (Dorsey and Díaz-Barriga, this volume).

By moving beyond exploring walls as individual, material manifestations located in particular places, several contributors in this volume have acknowledged the infrastructure and conceptual landscapes that weaponize contemporary walls. This includes the use of the US-México border as a means to an end—be that creating convict labor (Dear, this volume) or surveying the citizen body (Dorsey and Díaz-Barriga, this volume). Walls provide the backdrop and infrastructure for discreet cameras and other electronic devices that record movement. They facilitate government overreach by feeding into the online surveillance of the millions of US citizens who live, travel, and work within the broadly defined border zone. Contemporary wall building is a truly global phenomenon, a multibillion-dollar industry, and an expression of neoliberalism that facilitates the movement of some and curtails the choices of others.

What We Think about When We Think about Walls

In 2016, the authors in this volume met in a workshop hosted by SAR in Santa Fe. During those five days we discussed, dissected, and explored our very different approaches and thoughts on walls. Our interactions exposed many points of contention but also a significant number of points of agreement. All the participants in Santa Fe focused on the materiality of walls. The walls we study are highly visible, massive structures that exist as obstacles and to control movement. We agreed that the solid physicality of walls has tangible effects on how people can bodily negotiate and experience their surroundings, especially if they are not permitted to pass through heavily regulated checkpoints. Builders construct walls where people once could move freely in order to limit agency. Walls direct movement to official boundary crossings for those permitted to cross or to perilous landscapes and seascapes for those who must do so illicitly.

The contributors express many different perspectives and critiques on walls, but they also share at least eight foundational ideas: (1) wall building is not new, but modern walls differ in significant ways from earlier walls; (2) modern walls define belonging and not belonging by materializing the intersections of race, class, citizenship, religion, and gender; (3) the material forms of walls shape how those who live beside them interact with them, and their design indicates whom they wall in and whom they wall out; (4) monumental walls embody identities and carry enormous symbolic loads; (5) walls create and serve new kinds of technology and industry; (6) builders create walls to obstruct and exclude the "other," but those excluded can manipulate walls in ways that compromise and challenge the builders' intent; (7) walls will not solve the problems of our neoliberal world; and (8) twenty-first-century walls will eventually crumble and fall.

1.   Wall building is not new. People have built walls for millennia for a host of reasons, including control, safety, and defense. Examining the history of wall building (McGuire, this volume) reveals how walls have participated in and have been altered by cultural and technological change in ways that are deeply embedded in their materiality but also can be separate from it. In some ways, contemporary wall building has clear historical precedents, but it also differs in terms of intention and the ability to change due to the ambiguity of simultaneously walling out while claiming to protect and wall in. Modern walls are paradoxical in a way that previous walls were not. Twenty-first-century walls exist in a world that claims to tear down barriers and break down differences.

Neoliberalism has increased the cross-border flows of goods, capital, culture, ideas, and people to unprecedented levels while simultaneously initiating a new enclosure movement (i.e., by creeping privatization of public lands) thereby increasing flow in one sense while simultaneously increasing walled exclusivity in terms of access and ownership. Builders construct walls to allow the movement of those whom neoliberalism benefits while simultaneously compromising the movement of those deemed unruly and undesirable. On all scales, they build walls to separate those who belong from those who do not.

Historic walls always have a contemporary meaning and use. These meanings may be the same as when the walls were built, or they may have changed. Antiquated walls that survive past their original use often transition from their first function to become deactivated heritage sites. People may consider some long-term dividing walls as anachronisms or anomalies, throwbacks to unresolved historical disputes that kept diametrically opposed groups apart, but such walls always have contemporary uses and meanings that can evolve even if their material form remains the same.

2. Modern walls are presented as the answer to emerging problems of the neoliberal world by materializing belonging and not belonging. However, national border walls now target nonstate, transnational actors rather than international enemies, reacting to a world where nation-states no longer exclusively define global political relations (Brown 2010; Jones 2012). Local walls in many cities around the globe create enclaves to exclude criminals, the poor, and the culturally different and to separate warring religious/ethnic neighborhoods. Walls are built at the intersections of race, class, citizenship, religion, and gender. They separate the Global North from the Global South, black from white, believers from unbelievers, and rich from poor.

3. The material forms of walls shape how those who live beside them experience the world, including in the West Bank (Bishara, this volume) and Belfast (McAtackney, this volume). This is true for many of the case studies of local walls in this volume, even if they take forms not always expected by the builders who constructed them. Some authors have indicated that walls can be experienced differently depending on which side of the wall you find yourself (McWilliams, this volume), and other authors have shown that walls can be placed to force desperate people to attempt even more dangerous terrain to bypass them (Papadopoulos, this volume). The subtle details in the design of walls can indicate whether you are being walled in or walled out (Dinzey-Flores, this volume).

4. Scholars have argued that monumental walls can endure and materialize clashes between identity and nations (Dey 2011, 1–2). We found that the form of endurance must be considered alongside the concept of change when thinking about the role and sustainability of contemporary wall building. Walls can stand for extensive periods of time, and their meanings can change dramatically even when their material form does not (McGuire, this volume). Conversely even when walls "fall" in the popular imagination, their material form can continue and their impact can still be felt. For celebrated examples, such as the Berlin Wall, this transition can result in their preservation as heritage rather than their destruction as unviable functional structures (McWilliams, this volume). The walls we study appear powerful because they symbolize

authority in addition to being immense, situated physical entities. Their scale, form, and situation make them symbolic as well as functional but herein also is their weakness. When people defile or break through them (Bishara, this volume), they damage not just the material but also the power, legitimacy, and authority of those who constructed them.

5. Walls do not stand alone; rather, they create, conceal, and serve new kinds of technology and industry. Transgressors may easily cross if the walls lack backup from armed agents, dogs, ground vehicles, helicopters, drones, airplanes, and/or surveillance devices. This backup executes the threat of violence embodied in the material barrier (Dear, this volume). As transgressors develop new ways to cross walls, builders use new designs, innovative technologies, and a range of auxiliaries to restore the efficacy of the barriers. Walls may be decoys for implanting many forms of ephemeral electronic surveillance that compromise people's rights by stealth even when they leave the border zone (Dorsey and Díaz-Barriga, this volume). The border-industrial complex at the national level and the security companies that protect local walls make profits in this exchange and ambiguity.

6. Walls create an obstacle, but they exist in temporal and social contexts that challenge their existence: they can face the weight of long-standing histories of interaction, crossings, and feelings of community that defy the walls' attempts to materially separate (Dear, this volume). The global scope of wall building implies that they are a modern necessity and that their tangible effects at the local level will answer preexisting and emerging problems connected to movement and inclusion. Eventually, as Jones (this volume) has argued, they will not fulfill these roles. Conversely, walls enable agency that the builders did not imagine and can communicate meanings that they did not intend. Walls provide a materialized focal point and an evolving challenge: crossers continually create new ways to transgress or bypass walls, and the walls become canvases to protest their own existence (Dear, this volume; McGuire 2013). These interactions with walls can subvert and even undermine the builder's intentions. Walls can become focal points of transgression and protest (Bishara, this volume) because they are inherently mutable and ambiguous in their uses and meanings. They exist simultaneously as "face" and "barrier" (Baker 1993) in that they control movement but

also communicate dynamic and uncontrollable meanings that differ depending on which side of the wall you stand (McWilliams, this volume). This ambiguity and inability to fulfill the aims they claim result in walls falling in many contexts and scales.

7. The contributors of this volume argue that walls are facile and false solutions to the problems created by a neoliberal world. Walls attempt to solve problems that are unsolvable under current Global North models of governance by insulating the privileged from the consequences of neoliberalism. Ultimately, vastly more people lose from the neoliberal model than gain from it. The sheer masses of people whose lives are determined and limited by the neoliberal promise will ensure that its ultimate materialization—ideological walls—will remain the focus of attempts to defeat it. The massive movement of people from the Global South to the Global North, the poverty in modern cities, and racism and ethnic/religious conflicts all spring from the neoliberal ideology. Walls cannot fulfill their promise of protecting the Global North—and its enclaves in the Global South—from the perilous position neoliberalism forces onto the "other." Walls currently do not protect the children of the Global South from violence, put food on the table in public housing and shantytowns, or resolve long-standing animosities between racial, religious, and ethnic groups, and they will also not closet the Global North from the repercussions of neoliberalism. Time will reveal the futility of twenty-first-century walls and lead to their fall.

8. Ultimately, all walls fail in attempting to control movement and will fall. Due to the ambiguity of their form, walls retain the potential to be both positive and negative, and this will ensure that they stand—for now—and that they will continue to be built. However, when their intention is to stop movement and control access based on race and class, their lived reality tips toward the negative for the majority who are walled out. Walls invite transgression and defiance that compromise their ability to fulfill their role: to control the flow of movement of those deemed undesirable. In this context, the transgression of walls becomes more powerful because of the symbolic loads they bear: the monumentality of walls directly relates to their symbolic weight (Jones, this volume). As happened in Berlin in 1989, the transgressors can rise and tear the walls down.

This volume has presented a variety of case studies across several scales that highlight the negative impacts of walls from micro- to macro-levels. Walls are a global phenomenon, and in the twenty-first century many people perceive them as the ultimate answer to both acknowledged and implicit fears and threats. They rise where populations meet and where the powerful feel threatened. They manifest division and fear and materialize the promise of neoliberalism to wall out the racialized "other" and wall in the Global North's elite. They fundamentally control movement in a way that is not bilateral and that is determined by neoliberal indicators of belonging (wealth, the "right" passport, elite connections). Walls materialize inequality, but those they wall out have agency. The current global proliferation of walls provides focal points for resistance and defiance. Transgressors subvert walls by making them canvases for protest graffiti and art, and sometimes the transgressors violently attack and tear down the walls.

The contributors to this volume emphasize the need to consider walls over the long term and engage with the impacts of temporal change. Walls have a life cycle, and history is made when they are constructed, when they are substantially altered (in form or meaning), and when they eventually crumble. The builder does not always conceive or control what that change will be. Ultimately, this ambiguity is the biggest risk in walls' construction, and it will lead to their failure alongside the neoliberal ideology that supports them.

Abbott, Andrew. 1995. "Things of Boundaries." *Social Research* 62: 857–82.

Abraham, Itty, and Willem van Schendel. 2005. *Illicit Flows and Criminal Things: States, Borders, and the Other Side of Globalization*. Bloomington: Indiana University Press.

Addameer. 2017. *Imprisonment of Children*. http://www.addameer.org/the_prisoners/children.

Agamben, Giorgio. 2005. *State of Exception*. Chicago: University of Chicago Press.

Al-Azza, Mohammad, dir. 2016. *We Have a Dream to Live Safe*. Lajee Center. https://www.youtube.com/watch?v=mUi3bxsCwUE.

Alazzeh, Ala. 2014. "Locating Nonviolence: The People, the Past, and Resistance in Palestinian Political Activism." PhD diss., Rice University, https://scholarship.rice.edu/handle/1911/76336.

———. 2015. "Seeking Popular Participation: Nostalgia for the First Intifada in the West Bank." *Settler Colonial Studies* 5 (3): 251–67.

Alves, J. A. 2014. "From Necropolis to Blackpolis: Necropolitical Governance and Black Spatial Praxis in São Paulo, Brazil." *Antipode* 46 (2): 323–39.

American Civil Liberties Union. 2015. "DHS Wants Contract for Access to Database of Innocent Drivers' Locations." https://www.aclu.org/blog/dhs-wants-contract-access-database-innocent-drivers-locations.

———. 2018. "The Constitution in the 100-Mile Border Zone." https://www.aclu.org/other/constitution-100-mile-border-zone.

Amilhat Szary, Anne-Laure. 2012. "Walls and Border Art: The Politics of Art Display." *Journal of Borderland Studies* 27: 213–28.

Amnesty International. 2014. *Trigger-Happy: Israel's Use of Excessive Force in the West Bank*. London: Amnesty International.

anarhistickisajamknjiga. 2014. "8th Balkan Anarchist Bookfair: Over the Walls of Nationalism." https://bask2014.wordpress.com/2014/07/11/8th-balkan-anarchist-bookfair-over-the-walls-of-nationalism.

Anderson, Benedict. 2006. *Imagined Communities: Reflections on the Origins and Spread of Nationalism*. London: Verso.

Anderson, Bruce, and Bruce Parks. 2008. "Symposium on Border Crossing Deaths: Introduction." *Journal of Forensic Sciences* 53: 6–7.

Anderson, Charles. 2017. "State Formation from Below and the Great Revolt in Palestine." *Journal of Palestine Studies* 47 (1): 39–55.

Andreas, Peter. 2009. *Border Games: Policing the US-Mexico Divide*. Ithaca, NY: Cornell University Press.

———. 2015. "International Politics and the Illicit Global Economy." *Perspectives on Politics* 13 (3): 782–88.

Andrews, G. R. 2004. *Afro-Latin America, 1800–2000*. Oxford: Oxford University Press.

———. 2016. *Afro-Latin America: Black Lives, 1600–2000*. Cambridge, MA: Harvard University Press.

Arendt, Hannah. 2005. *The Promise of Politics*. New York: Schocken.

Asher, Catherine B. 2000. "Delhi Walled: Changing Boundaries." In *City Walls: The Urban Enceinte in Global Perspective*, edited by J. D. Tracy, 247–81. Cambridge: Cambridge University Press.

Atlas, R., and W. G. LeBlanc. 1994. "The Impact on Crime of Street Closures and Barricades: A Florida Case Study." *Security Journal* 5: 140–45.

Babín, M. T. 1958. *Panorama de la cultura puertorriqueña*. New York: Las Americas.

Bacha, Julia, dir. 2009. *Budrus*. Just Vision.

Baker, Frederick. 1993. "The Berlin Wall: Production, Preservation and Consumption of a Twentieth Century Monument." *Antiquity* 67: 709–33.

Ballí, Cecilia. 2018. "Two Cities, Two Countries, Common Ground." *New York Times*, February 5. https://www.nytimes.com/2018/02/05/travel/nogales-arizona-mexico-border.html.

Banko, Lauren. 2016. "Citizenship Rights and the Semantics of Colonial Power and Resistance: Haifa, Jaffa, and Nablus, 1931–1933." In *Violence and the City in the Modern Middle East*, edited by Nelida Fuccaro, 75–94. Stanford, CA: Stanford University Press.

Barry, Tom. 2011. *Border Wars*. Cambridge, MA: MIT Press.

Bavinck, Maarten, Lorenzo Pellegrini, and Erik Mostert, eds. 2014. *Conflicts over Natural Resources in the Global South: Conceptual Approaches*. Boca Raton, FL: CRC Press.

BBC News. 2008. "Berlin Wall Slab Sold at Auction." September 20, http://news.bbc.co.uk/2/hi/europe/7626439.stm.

Beiler, Ryan Rodrick. 2014. "Palestinians Mourn Woman Who Died after Inhaling Tear Gas." *+972 magazine*, April 15. https://972mag.com/photos-tear-gas-kills-woman-in-aida-refugee-camp/89713.

———. 2015. "Israeli Army Increasing Use of Live Fire at West Bank Protests." *+972 magazine*, January 19. http://972mag.com/israeli-army-increasing-use-of-live-fire-at-west-bank-protests/101561.

Benning, Tom. 2016. "DPS Not Yet Ready to Stop Rotating Troopers to Border from Other Parts of the State." *Dallas News*, January. http://trailblazersblog.dallas news.com/2016/01/dps-not-yet-ready-to-stop-rotating-troopers-to-border-from-other-parts-of-state.html.

Berda, Yael. 2017. *Living Emergency: Israel's Permit Regime in the Occupied West Bank.* Stanford, CA: Stanford University Press.

Bersin, Alan D., and Michael D. Huston. 2016. "Homeland Security as a Theory of Action: The Impact on U.S.-Mexico Border Management." In *The Anatomy of a Relationship: A Collection of Essays on the Evolution of U.S.-Mexico Cooperation on Border Management,* edited by C. Wilson. Washington, DC: Wilson Center Mexico Institute. https://www.wilsoncenter.org/publication/the-anatomy-relationship-collection-essays-the-evolution-us-mexico-cooperation-border.

Betances, S. 1972. "The Prejudice of Having No Prejudice in Puerto Rico, Part I." *Rican* 2: 41–54.

Bilker, Molly. 2016. "New Poll by Cronkite News, Univision News and the Dallas Morning News Shows Strong Sense of Community on Both Sides of the U.S.-Mexico Border." Cronkite News, July 17. http://cronkitenews.azpbs.org/2016/07/17/border-poll-overview.

Bishara, Amahl. 2010. "Intifadas: First and Second Compared." In *Encyclopedia of the Israeli-Palestinian Conflict,* edited by Cheryl A. Rubenberg, 621–30. Boulder, CO: Lynne Rienner.

———. 2013. *Back Stories: U.S. News Production and Palestinian Politics.* Stanford, CA: Stanford University Press.

———. 2015. "Driving while Palestinian in Israel and the West Bank: The Politics of Disorientation and the Routes of a Subaltern Knowledge." *American Ethnologist* 42 (1): 33–54.

Bishara, Amahl, and Nidal Al-Azraq, dirs. 2010. *Degrees of Incarceration.*

Blakely, Edward, and Mary Gail Snyder. 1997. *Fortress America: Gated Communities in the United States.* Washington, DC: Brookings Institution Press.

Blanco, Jacobo. 1901. *Vistas de los monumentos a lo largo de la línea divisoria entre México y los Estados Unidos de el paso al Pacífico.* N.p.: Polhemus.

Blanco, T. 1942. *Prejuicio racial en Puerto Rico.* San Juan: Biblioteca de Autores Puertorriqueños.

Blatter, Joachim K. 2001. "Debordering the World of States: Towards a Multi-Level System in Europe and a Multi-Polity System in North America? Insights from Border Regions." *European Journal of International Relations* 7 (2): 175–209.

Bloom, Jonathan M. 2000. "Walled Cities in Islamic North Africa and Egypt with Particular Reference to the Fatimids (909–1171)." In *City Walls: The Urban Enceinte in Global Perspective*, edited by J. D. Tracy, 219–46. Cambridge: Cambridge University Press.

Boal, Frederick W. 1994. "Encapsulation: Urban Dimensions of National Conflict." In *Managing Divided Cities*, edited by Seamus Dunn, 30–41. Keele, England: Keele University Press.

———. 2002. "Belfast: Walls Within." *Political Geography* 21: 687–94.

Boano, Camillo, and Belen Desmaison. 2016. "Lima's 'Wall of Shame' and the Gated Communities That Build Poverty into Peru." *Conversation*, February 11. http://theconversation.com/limas-wall-of-shame-and-the-gated-communities-that-build-poverty-into-peru-53356.

Bobo, L., J. R. Kluegel, and R. A. Smith. 1997. "Laissez-Faire Racism: The Crystallization of a Kinder, Gentler, Antiblack Ideology." In *Racial Attitudes in the 1990s: Continuity and Change*, edited by Steven Tuch and Jack Martin, 15–44. Westport, CT: Praeger.

Bonnet, Alistair. 1998. "How the British Working Class Became White: The Symbolic (Re)formation of Racialized Capitalism." *Historical Sociology* 11 (3): 316–40.

Bourdieu, Pierre. 1986. "The Forms of Capital." In *Handbook of Theory and Research for the Sociology of Education*, edited by J. Richardson, 241–58. New York: Greenwood.

Bowman, Glenn. 2013. "A Weeping on the Road to Bethlehem: Contestation over the Uses of Rachel's Tomb." *Religion Compass* 7 (3): 79–92.

Brian, Tara, and Frank Laczko. 2014. *Fatal Journeys: Tracking Lives Lost during Migration*. Geneva: International Organization for Migration.

Brill, Steven. 2016. "Are We Any Safer?" *Atlantic* (September): 61–87.

Brown, Wendy. 2010. *Walled States, Waning Sovereignty*. New York: Zone.

Brownlow, Graham. 2015. "Soft Budget Constraints and Regional Industrial Policy: Reinterpreting the Rise and Fall of DeLorean." *Cambridge Journal of Economics* Working Paper 14-09: 1–32.

Bryan, Dominic, et al. 2010. *Public Display of Flags and Emblems in Northern Ireland, 2006–2009*. Belfast: Institute of Irish Studies.

B'Tselem. 2013a. "B'Tselem Inquiry: No Justification for Shooting and Killing Samir 'Awad, 16." February 21. http://www.btselem.org/firearm/20130221_killing_of_samir_awad_budrus.

———. 2013b. "Five Palestinian Civilians Fatally Shot by Israeli Military in January 2013." January 30. http://www.btselem.org/firearms/201301_fatalities.

———. 2017. "The Separation Barrier." November 11. http://www.btselem.org/ separation_barrier.

Bustamante, Jorge A. 1995. "The Mexico-US Border: A Line of Paradox." In *Identities in North America*, edited by R. E. Earle and J. D. Wirth, 180–94. Stanford, CA: Stanford University Press.

Caldeira, Teresa. 2000. *City of Walls: Crime, Segregation, and Citizenship in São Paulo*. Berkeley: University of California Press.

Campsie, Philippa. 2010. "Concentric Circles." *Decoding Paris*, September 22. https:// decodingparis.wordpress.com/2010/09/22/concentric-circles.

Cebulla, Andrea, and Jim Smyth. 1996. "Disadvantage and New Prosperity in Restructured Belfast." *Capital and Class* 60: 39–59.

Chaichian, Mohammad A. 2014. *Empires and Walls: Globalization, Migration, and Colonial Domination*. Leiden: Brill.

Chalcraft, John. 2016. *Popular Politics in the Making of the Modern Middle East*. Cambridge: Cambridge University Press.

Chomsky, Noam, and Gilbert Achcar. 2015. *Perilous Power: The Middle East and U.S. Foreign Policy Dialogues on Terror*. London: Routledge.

Choon-Piew, Pow. 2009. *Gated Communities in China: Class, Privilege and the Moral Politics of the Good Life*. London: Routledge.

Christopoulos, Dimitris, and George Souvlis. 2016. "Europe's Solidarity Crisis: A Perspective from Greece." *ROAR*, June 8. https://roarmag.org/essays/ europe-refugee-solidarity-crisis-greece.

Clarke, Liam. 2013. "15 Years after Good Friday Agreement and Still No Peace Dividend for Northern Ireland." *Belfast Telegraph*, April 9. https://www.belfast telegraph.co.uk/news/politics/15-years-after-good-friday-agreement-and -still-no-peace-dividend-for-northern-ireland-29182842.html.

Clarno, Andy. 2013. "The Constitution of State/Space and the Limits of 'Autonomy' in South Africa and Palestine/Israel." In *Sociology and Empire: The Imperial Entanglements of a Discipline*, edited by George Steinmetz, 436–64. Durham, NC: Duke University Press.

Collins, John. 2004. *Occupied by Memory: The Intifada Generation and the Palestinian State of Emergency*. New York: New York University Press.

Community Relations Council. 2009. *Towards Sustainable Security: Interface Barriers and the Legacy of Segregation in Belfast*. Belfast: Community Relations Council.

Connah, Graham. 2000. "Contained Communities in Tropical Africa." In *City Walls: The Urban Enceinte in Global Perspective*, edited by J. D. Tracy, 19–45. Cambridge: Cambridge University Press.

Cons, Jason. 2016. *Sensitive Space: Fragmented Territory at the India-Bangladesh Border.* Seattle: University of Washington Press.

Cook, Catherine, Adam Hanieh, and Adah Kay. 2004. *Stolen Youth: The Politics of Israel's Detention of Palestinian Children.* London: Sterling.

Coronado, Irasema. 2014. "Towards the Wall between Nogales, Arizona, and Nogales, Sonora." In *Borders, Fences, and Walls: State of Insecurity?*, edited by Elisabeth Vallet, 247–66. Farnham, England: Ashgate.

Costa Vargas, J. H. 2006. "When a Favela Dared to Become a Gated Condominium: The Politics of Race and Urban Space in Rio de Janeiro." *Latin American Perspectives* 33 (4): 49–81.

Crowley, Tony. 2011. "The Art of Memory: The Murals of Northern Ireland and the Management of History." *Field Day Review* 7: 22–49.

Cupcea, George. 2015. "The Evolution of the Roman Frontier: Concept and Policy." *Journal of Ancient History and Archaeology* 2 (1): 12–22.

Danforth, Loring M., and Riki Van Boeschoten. 2012. *Children of the Greek Civil War: Refugees and the Politics of Memory.* Chicago: University of Chicago Press.

D'Appollonia, Ariane Chebel. 2012. *Frontiers of Fear: Immigration and Insecurity in the United States and Europe.* Ithaca, NY: Cornell University Press.

Darweish, Marwan, and Andrew Rigby. 2015. *Popular Protest in Palestine: The Uncertain Future of Unarmed Resistance.* London: Pluto.

Davidi, Guy, and Emad Burnat, dirs. 2011. *5 Broken Cameras.* Kino Lorber.

Davis, M. 1990. *City of Quartz.* London: Verso.

Dawdy, Shannon. 2006. "The Taphonomy of Disaster and the (Re)formation of New Orleans." *American Anthropologist* 108 (4): 719–30.

———. 2015. *Patina.* Chicago: University of Chicago Press.

Day, Elizabeth. 2010. "The Street Art of JR." *Guardian*, March 7. https://www.theguardian.com/artanddesign/2010/mar/07/street-art-jr-photography.

DCI Palestine. 2013. "Killed—Saleh Amarin (15)." January 18. http://crowdmap.dci-palestine.org/reports/view/22.

De La Croix, Horst. 1972. *Military Considerations in City Planning.* New York: Braziller.

De León, Jason. 2015. *Land of Open Graves: Living and Dying on the Migrant Trail.* Berkeley: University of California Press.

Dear, Michael. 2015. *Why Walls Won't Work: Repairing the US-Mexico Divide.* Rev. ed. Oxford: Oxford University Press.

Demetriou, Olga. 2013. *Capricious Borders: Minority, Population, and Counter-Conduct between Greece and Turkey.* New York: Berghahn.

Department of Homeland Security. 2012. "Privacy Impact Assessment for the Analytical Framework for Intelligence." https://www.dhs.gov/sites/default/files/publications/privacy_pia_cbp_afi_june_2012_0.pdf.

Dey, Hendrik W. 2011. *The Aurelian Wall and the Refashioning of Imperial Rome, AD 271–855*. Cambridge: Cambridge University Press.

Díaz-Barriga, Miguel, and Margaret E. Dorsey. 2011. "Border Walls and Necro-Citizenship: The Normalization of Exclusion and Death on the U.S.-Mexico Border." In *The American Wall: From the Pacific Ocean to the Gulf of Mexico*, edited by Maurice Sherif, 17–23. Austin: University of Texas Press.

———. 2020. *Fencing In Democracy: Border Walls, Necrocitizenship, and the Security State*. Durham, NC: Duke University Press.

Díaz Soler, L. M. 1957. "La esclavitud negra en Puerto Rico." In *Ciclo de conferencias sobre la historia de Puerto Rico*. San Juan: Instituto de Cultura Puertorriqueña.

———. 1974. *Historia de la esclavitud negra en Puerto Rico*. 4th ed. Río Piedras: Editorial Universitaria, Universidad de Puerto Rico.

Di Cintio, Marcello. 2012. *Walls: Travels along the Barricades*. Berkeley, CA: Soft Skull Press.

Diener, Alexander, and Joshua Hagen. 2012. *Borders: A Very Short Introduction*. Oxford: Oxford University Press.

Dillon, D. 1994. "Fortress America." *Planning* 60: 8–12.

Dines, Nick, Nicola Montagna, and Vincenzo Ruggiero. 2015. "Thinking Lampedusa: Border Construction, the Spectacle of Bare Life and the Productivity of Migrants." *Ethnic and Racial Studies* 38 (3): 430–45.

Dinzey-Flores, Z. Z. 2007. "Cache vs. Cas[h]eríos: Puerto Rican Neighborhoods under Siege." In *The Caribbean City*, edited by Rivke Jaffe, 209–26. Kingston, Jamaica: Ian Randle.

———. 2011. "Criminalizing Communities of Poor, Dark Women in the Caribbean: The Fight against Crime through Puerto Rico's Public Housing." *Crime Prevention and Community Safety* 13 (1): 53–73.

———. 2013. *Locked In, Locked Out: Gated Communities in a Puerto Rican City*. Philadelphia: University of Pennsylvania Press.

Donovan, Bill. 2015. "Tear Down the Wall! Or Not: The End of the London Wall." *Easterley—Living and Working in West London*, October 28. http://easterley.blogspot.com/2015/10/tear-down-wall-or-not-end-of-london-wall.html.

Dorsey, Margaret, and Miguel Díaz-Barriga. 2010. "Beyond Surveillance and Moonscapes: An Alternative Imaginary of the U.S.-Mexico Border Wall." *Visual Anthropology* 26 (2): 128–35.

———. 2015. "The Constitution Free Zone in the United States: Law and Life in a State of Carcelment." *Political and Legal Anthropology Review* 38 (2): 204–25.

Doss, Erika. 2010. *Memorial Mania: Public Feeling in America*. Chicago: University of Chicago Press.

Dovidio, J. F., and S. L. Gaertner. 1986. *The Aversive Form of Racism*. Orlando, FL: Academic.

Dunn, Elizabeth Cullen, and Jason Cons. 2014. "Aleatory Sovereignty and the Rule of Sensitive Spaces." *Antipode* 46 (1): 92–109.

Dunn, Timothy. 2001. "Border Militarization via Drug and Immigration Enforcement: Human Rights Implications." *Social Justice* 28: 7–30.

———. 2009. *Blockading the Border and Human Rights: The El Paso Operation That Remade Immigration Enforcement*. Austin: University of Texas Press.

Earle, Robert E., and John D. Wirth, eds. 1995. *Identities in North America*. Stanford, CA: Stanford University Press.

Edwards, Aaron, and Cillian McGrattan. 2010. *The Northern Ireland Conflict: A Beginner's Guide*. New York: Oneworld.

Electronic Privacy Information Center. 2016. "Epic v. CBP (Analytical Framework for Intelligence)." https://epic.org/foia/dhs/cbp/afi.

Elias, Norbert. 1939. *The Civilizing Process*. New York: Pantheon.

Eltis, David. 2000. *The Rise of African Slavery in the Americas*. Cambridge: Cambridge University Press.

Esposito De Vita, Gabriella, Claudi Trillo, and Alona Martinez-Perez. 2016. "Community Planning and Urban Design in Contested Places: Some Insights from Belfast." *Journal of Urban Design* 21 (3): 320–34.

Euronatur. 2016. "Green Belt Europe: From Iron Curtain to Lifeline." https://www.euronatur.org/en/what-we-do/campaigns-and-initiatives/green-belt-europe/?gclid=CjoKCQjw5MLrBRClARIsAPGoWGwzcwAkuNaF2Lx39UELZGSeZsiONheANg2zKQIBNJ9CzPXc8PJIhWsaAnLbEALw_wcB.

Falk, Richard. 2005. "Toward Authoritativeness: The ICJ Ruling on Israel's Security Wall." *American Society of International Law* 99 (1): 42–52.

Farley, Ren, and Judy Mullin. 2014. "Wall Separating Whites from Blacks." *Historic Sites in Detroit's Racial History*. http://detroit1701.org/Black-WhiteWall.htm.

Farmer, Edward L. 2000. "The Hierarchy of Ming City Walls." In *City Walls: The Urban Enceinte in Global Perspective*, edited by J. D. Tracy, 461–87. Cambridge: Cambridge University Press.

Ferdoush, M. A. 2018. "Seeing Borders through a Lens of Structuration: A Theoretical Framework." *Geopolitics* 23 (1): 180–200.

Forty, Adrian. 1999. "Introduction." In *The Art of Forgetting*, edited by Adrian Forty and Susanne Küchler. New York: Berg.

Fotiadis, Apostolos. 2015. *Empori ton sinoron: I nea evropaiki architectoniki epitirisis* [Border dealers: The new European surveillance architecture]. Athens: Potamos.

Foucault, Michel. 1975. *Discipline and Punish: The Birth of the Prison*. New York: Vintage.

———. 2003. *Society Must Be Defended*. New York: Picador.

Fowler, F. J., and T. W. Mangione. 1986. "A Three-Pronged Effort to Reduce Crime and Fear of Crime: The Hartford Experiment." In *Community Crime Prevention: Does It Work?*, edited by D. P. Rosenbaum and M. Cahn. Thousand Oaks, CA: SAGE.

Frankfurter Allgemeine Zeitung. 2014. "Schabowskis Ehefrau: 'Mein Mann wusste, was er sagte.'" November 7. http://www.faz.net/aktuell/politik/25-jahre-deutsche-einheit/mauerfall-schabowski-wusste-um-wirkung-seiner-worte-13253030.html.

Frantz, K. 2000. "Gated Communities in the USA: A New Trend in Urban Development." *Espace, Populations, Sociétés* 18 (1): 101–13.

Frey, Bruno S., Simon Leuchinger, and Alois Stutzer. 2004. "Calculating Tragedy: Assessing the Costs of Terrorism." Working Paper 205, 1–32. University of Zurich: Working Paper Series, Institute for Empirical Research in Economics.

Frey, William H. 1979. "Central City White Flight: Racial and Nonracial Causes." *American Sociological Review* 44: 425–48.

Friedersdorf, Conor. 2016. "An Unprecedented Threat to Privacy." *Atlantic*, January 27. https://www.theatlantic.com/politics/archive/2016/01/vigilant-solutions-surveillance/427047.

Frye, David. 2018. *Walls: A History of Civilization in Blood and Brick*. New York: Simon and Schuster.

Fuchs, Stephen. 2016. "No Surprise, Germany Saw over 2M Migrants in 2015." *German Pulse*, July 18.

Funder, Anna. 2003. *Stasiland: Stories from Behind the Berlin Wall*. London: Granta.

Fusté, J. I. 2010. "Colonial Laboratories, Irreparable Subjects: The Experiment of '(B)ordering' San Juan's Public Housing Residents." *Social Identities* 16 (1): 41–59.

Ganti, Tejaswini. 2014. "Neoliberalism." *Annual Review of Anthropology* 43: 89–104.

Garcia, Michael. 2015. *Barriers along the U.S. Borders: Key Authorities and Requirements*. Washington, DC: Congressional Research Service.

Geoghegan, Peter. 2015. "Will Belfast Ever Have a Berlin Wall Moment and Tear Down Its 'Peace Walls'?" *Guardian*, September 29. https://www.theguardian.com/cities/2015/sep/29/belfast-berlin-wall-moment-permanent-peace-walls.

Giles, Frank L. 1930. "Boundary Work in the Balkans." *Geographical Journal* 75: 300–310.

Glasze, Georg, Chris Webster, and Klaus Franz, eds. 2006. *Private Cities: Global and Local Perspectives*. London: Routledge.

Godreau, I. P. 2015. *Scripts of Blackness: Race, Cultural Nationalism, and US Colonialism in Puerto Rico*. Urbana: University of Illinois Press.

Goldstein, Daniel. 2010. "Toward a Critical Anthropology of Security." *Current Anthropology* 51 (4): 487–517.

González-Ruibal, Alfredo. 2017. "Ruins of the South." In *Contemporary Archaeology and the City: Creativity, Ruination, and Political Action*, edited by Laura McAtackney and Krysta Ryzewski. Oxford: Oxford University Press.

Good Friday (Belfast) Agreement. 1998. *Belfast Agreement*. Belfast: HMSO.

Gordillo, Gaston. 2013. "The Void: Invisible Ruins on the Edges of Empire." In *Imperial Debris: On Ruins and Ruination*, edited by Ann Stoler, 227–51. Durham, NC: Duke University Press.

Gorkin, Michael, and Rafiqa Othman. 1996. *Three Mothers, Three Daughters: Palestinian Women's Stories*. Berkeley: University of California Press.

Gourgouris, Stathis. 2017. "Crisis and the Ill Logic of Fortress Europe." In *Can a Person Be Illegal? Refugees, Migrants and Citizenship in Europe*, edited by M. Rosengren. Uppsala, Sweden: Uppsala Rhetorical Studies.

Green, F. Sarah. 2005. *Notes from the Balkans: Locating Marginality and Ambiguity on the Greek-Albanian Border*. Princeton, NJ: Princeton University Press.

———. 2013. "Borders and the Relocation of Europe." *Annual Review of Anthropology* 42: 345–61.

———. 2017. "When Infrastructures Fail: An Ethnographic Note in the Middle of an Aegean Crisis." In *Infrastructures and Social Complexity: A Companion*, edited by P. Harvey, C. Bruun Jensen, and A. Morita, 271–83. London: Routledge.

Gruen, Claude. 2010. *New Urban Development: Looking Back to See Forward*. New Brunswick, NJ: Rutgers University Press.

Guinier, L., and G. Torres. 2002. "The Ideology of Colorblindness." In *The Miner's Canary: Enlisting Race, Resisting Power, Transforming Democracy*, 38–39. Cambridge, MA: Harvard University Press.

Gusterson, Hugh, and Catherine Besteman. 2009. *The Insecure American: How We Got Here and What Should We Do about It.* Berkeley: University of California Press.

Haddal, Chad. 2010. *Border Security: The Role of the Border Patrol.* Washington, DC: Congressional Research Service.

Hain, Peter. 2017. "Paralysis Has Gripped Northern Ireland, but Politicians Are Just Looking Blithely On." *Guardian*, November 14. https://www.theguardian.com/commentisfree/2017/nov/14/northern-ireland-politicians-sinnfein-dup-stormont-theresa-may.

Hallward, M., and Julie Norman. 2011. *Nonviolent Resistance in the Second Intifada: Activism and Advocacy.* New York: Palgrave Macmillan.

Hamid, Mohsin. 2015. "The Great Divide." *New York Times Magazine*, February 18. http://www.nytimes.com/2015/02/22/magazine/the-great-divide.html?_r=0.

Hamilakis, Yannis. 2016. "The EU's Future Ruins: Moria Refugee Camp in Lesbos." *Nation*, April 15. https://www.thenation.com/article/the-eus-future-ruins-moria-refugee-camp-in-lesbos.

Hammami, Rema. 2010. "Qalandiya: Jerusalem's Tora Bora and the Frontiers of Global Inequality." *Jerusalem Quarterly* 41: 29–51.

Hammami, Rema, and Salim Tamari. 2001. "The Second Uprising: End or New Beginning?" *Journal of Palestine Studies* 30 (2): 5–25.

Hanafi, Sari. 2009. "Spacio-cide: Colonial Politics, Invisibility, and Rezoning in Palestinian Territory." *Contemporary Arab Affairs* 2 (1): 106–21.

———. 2012. "Explaining Spacio-cide in the Palestinian Territory: Colonialisation, Separation and State of Exception." *Current Sociology* 61 (2): 190–205.

Hanafi, Sari, and Linda Tabar. 2005. *The Emergence of Palestinian Globalized Elite: Donors, International Organizations, and Local NGOs.* Jerusalem: Institute of Jerusalem Studies.

Hansen, Thomas Blom, and Finn Stepputat. 2001. "Introduction: States of Imagination." In *States of Imagination: Ethnographic Explorations of the Postcolonial State*, edited by Thomas Blom Hansen and Finn Stepputat, 1–38. Durham, NC: Duke University Press.

Hardach, Sophie. 2015. "The Refugees Housed at Dachau: 'Where Else Should I Live?'" *Guardian*, September 19. https://www.theguardian.com/world/2015/sep/19/the-refugees-who-live-at-dachau.

Harley, John Brian. 2002. *The New Nature of Maps.* Edited by P. Laxton. Baltimore, MD: Johns Hopkins University Press.

Harris, David. 1999. "'Property Values Drop when Blacks Move In, Because . . .': Racial and Socioeconomic Determinants of Neighborhood Desirability." *American Sociological Review* 64: 461–79.

Harris, D. S. 2005. "Little White Houses: Critical Race Theory and the Interpretation of Ordinary Dwellings in the United States, 1945-60." Proceedings from the Warren Center for American Studies Conference on Reinterpreting the History of the Built Environment in North America, August 3, 2. http://warrencenter.fas.harvard.edu/builtenv/Paper%20PDFs/Harris.pdf, accessed October 20, 2011.

———. 2013. *Little White Houses: How the Postwar Home Constructed Race in America*. Minneapolis: University of Minnesota Press.

Harrison, Hope. 2005. "The Berlin Wall: A Symbol of the Cold War?" In *On Both Sides of the Wall: Preserving Monuments and Sites of the Cold War Era*, edited by L. Schmidt and H. von Preuschen. Cottbus, Germany: Westkreuz.

———. 2011. "The Berlin Wall and Its Resurrection as a Site of Memory." *German Politics and Society* 29 (2): 78–106.

Hartigan, J. 1999. *Racial Situations: Class Predicaments of Whiteness in Detroit*. Princeton, NJ: Princeton University Press.

Hass, Amira. 2002. "Israel's Closure Policy: An Ineffective Strategy of Containment and Repression." *Journal of Palestine Studies* 31 (3): 5–20.

Hattam, Victoria. 2016. "Imperial Redesigns: Remembering Vietnam at the US-Mexico Border Wall." *Memory Studies* 9 (1): 27–47.

Hayward, Katy. 2017. "The DUP Was Painted into a Corner by Brexiters' Hyperbole, but a Solution Is Possible." *Guardian*, December 6. https://www.theguardian.com/commentisfree/2017/dec/06/dup-brexiters-northern-ireland-brexit.

Hennessy, Thomas. 2005. *The Origins of the Troubles*. Dublin: Gill and Macmillan.

Herbst, Jeffery. 1989. "The Creation and Maintenance of National Boundaries in Africa." *International Organization* 43: 673–92.

Hernandez, Kelly Lytle. 2010. *Migra! A History of the US Border Patrol*. Berkeley: University of California Press.

———. 2017. *City of Inmates: Conquest, Rebellion, and the Rise of Human Caging in Los Angeles, 1771-1965*. Chapel Hill: University of North Carolina Press.

Hernández, T. K. 2016. "Envisioning the United States in the Latin American Myth of 'Racial Democracy Mestizaje.'" *Latin American and Caribbean Ethnic Studies* 11 (2): 189–205.

Herzog, Lawrence A. 2014. "Globalisation, Place and Twenty-First-Century International Border Regions." *Global Society* 28 (4): 391–97.

Heyman, Josiah. 2008. "Constructing a Virtual Wall: Race and Citizenship in U.S.-Mexico Border Policing." *Journal of the Southwest* 50: 305–34.

Hickman, Mary. 2012. "Constructing 'Suspect' Communities and Britishness: Mapping British Press Coverage of Irish and Muslim Communities, 1974–2007." *European Journal of Communication* 27 (2): 135–51.

Hingley, Richard. 2012. *Hadrian's Wall: A Life*. Oxford: Oxford University Press.

Hodai, Beau. 2013. "The Homeland Security Apparatus: Fusion Centers, Data Mining, and Private Sector Partners." *PRWatch*, May 22. http://www.prwatch.org/news/2013/05/12122/homeland-security-apparatus-fusion-centers-data-mining-and-private-sector-partner.

Hoetink, H. 1967. *The Two Variants in Caribbean Race Relations*. New York: Oxford University Press.

Hogan, Liam, Laura McAtackney, and Matthew Reilly. 2016. "The Irish in the Anglo-Caribbean: Servants or Slaves?" *History Ireland* 24 (2): 18–22.

Horning, Audrey. 2013. *Ireland in the Virginian Sea: Colonialism in the British Atlantic*. Chapel Hill: University of North Carolina Press.

Human Rights Watch. 2016. "Turkey: Open Borders to Syrians Fleeing ISIS." April 14. https://www.hrw.org/news/2016/04/14/turkey-open-borders-syrians-fleeing-isis.

Inda, Jonathan X. 2005. *Targeting Immigrants: Government, Technology, and Ethics*. London: Wiley-Blackwell.

International Organization for Migration. 2019. "Missing Migrants: Tracking Deaths along Migratory Routes." IOM. https://missingmigrants.iom.int.

Ioannides, Mara W. Cohen, and Dimitri Ioannides. 2002. "Global Jewish Tourism: Pilgrimages and Remembrance." In *Tourism, Religion and Spiritual Journeys*, edited by D. J. Timothy and D. H. Olsen, 157–75. New York: Routledge.

Jarman, Neil, and Chris O'Halloran. 2001. "Recreational Rioting: Young People, Interface Areas and Violence." *Childcare in Practice* 7 (1): 2–16.

Jean-Klein, I. 2000. "Mothercraft, Statecraft, and Subjectivity in the Palestinian Intifada." *American Ethnologist* 27 (1): 100–127.

Jeffrey, Keith. 2011. *Ireland and the Great War*. Cambridge: Cambridge University Press.

Johnson, Corey, et al. 2011. "Interventions on Rethinking 'the Border' in Border Studies." *Political Geography* 30: 61–69.

Johnson, Penny, and Eileen Kuttab. 2001. "Where Have All the Women (and Men) Gone? Reflections on Gender and the Second Palestinian Intifada." *Feminist Review* 69 (1): 21–43.

Jones, Jonathan. 2010. "Belfast's Ulster Museum and the Trouble with the Troubles." *Guardian*, May 19. https://www.theguardian.com/artanddesign/jonathanjonesblog/2010/may/19/museums-northern-ireland-troubles.

Jones, Reece. 2009. "Agents of Exception: Border Security and the Marginalization of Muslims in India." *Environment and Planning D: Society and Space* 27: 879–97.

———. 2012. *Border Walls: Security and the War on Terror in the United States, India, and Israel*. London: Zed.

———. 2016. *Violent Borders: Refugees and the Right to Move*. London: Verso.

Jusionyte, Ieva. 2018. "Called to 'Ankle Alley': Tactical Infrastructure, Migrant Injuries, and Emergency Medical Services on the US-Mexico Border." *American Anthropologist* 120: 89–101.

Kershner, Isabel. 2016. "Scanning Borders, Israel Surveys New Reality of Tunnels and Terror." *New York Times*, February 11.

Kim, Suk-Young. 2014. *DMZ Crossing: Performing Emotional Citizenship along the Korean Border*. New York: Columbia University Press.

Klausmeier, Axel, and Leo Schmidt. 2004. *Wall Remnants—Wall Traces: The Comprehensive Guide to the Berlin Wall*. Berlin, Germany: Westkreuz.

Knox, Colin. 2016. "Northern Ireland: Where Is the Peace Dividend?" *Policy and Politics Journal*, July 27. https://policyandpoliticsblog.com/2016/07/27/northern-ireland-where-is-the-peace-dividend.

Konrad, Victor. 2015. "Toward a Theory of Borders in Motion." *Journal of Borderlands Studies* 30 (1): 1–17.

Kotef, Hagar. 2015. *Movement and the Ordering of Freedom: On Liberal Governance of Mobility*. Durham, NC: Duke University Press.

Kourelis, Kostis. 2016. "Archaeology of Care: Refugee Crisis in Greece." *Objects-Buildings-Situations*, March 16. http://kourelis.blogspot.com/2016/03/archaeology-of-care-refugee-crisis-in.html.

———. 2017. "The Greek Landscape as Wall." Paper presented at the 116th American Anthropological Association Annual Meeting, Washington, DC.

Kovras, Iosif, and Simon Robins. 2016. "Death as the Border: Managing Missing Migrants and Unidentified Bodies at the EU's Mediterranean Frontier." *Political Geography* 55: 40–49.

Krämer, Klaus. 2018. "Berlin Wall: Now Down for as Long as It Once Stood." DW.com, May 2. http://www.dw.com/en/berlin-wall-now-down-for-as-long-as-it-once-stood/a-42456108.

Kristof, Nicholas D. 2010. "Waiting for Gandhi." *New York Times*, July 10. http://www.nytimes.com/2010/07/11/opinion/11kristof.html.

Lagerquist, Peter. 2004. "Fencing the Last Sky: Excavating Palestine after Israel's 'Separation Wall.'" *Journal of Palestine Studies* 33 (2): 5–35.

Lakoff, George. 1987. *Women, Fire, and Dangerous Things: What Categories Reveal about the Mind.* Chicago: University of Chicago Press.

Lakoff, George, and Mark Johnson. 1999. *Philosophy in the Flesh: The Embodied Mind and Its Challenge to Western Thought.* New York: Basic.

Larkin, Brian. 2013. "The Politics and Poetics of Infrastructure." *Annual Review of Anthropology* 42: 327–43.

Lear, Edward. 1852. *Journals of a Landscape Painter in Albania, Illyria &c.* London: R. Bentley.

LeBrón, M. 2017. "They Don't Care if We Die: The Violence of Urban Policing in Puerto Rico." *Journal of Urban History.* https://doi.org/10.1177/0096144217705485.

Lennon, John, and Malcolm Foley. 2000. *Dark Tourism: The Attraction of Death and Disaster.* London: Continuum.

Lentz, Christian. 2014. "The King Yields to the Village? A Micropolitics of Statemaking in Northwest Vietnam." *Political Geography* 39: 1–10.

Leonardo Company. 2019. "Elsag Mobile Plate Hunter M6." https://cdn2.hubspot.net/hubfs/2464672/2018%20Brochures/17d130_ELS-ss-ph-m6-100dpi.pdf.

Levine, Evan S., and Julie F. Waters. 2013. "Managing Risk at the Tucson Sector of the U.S. Border Patrol." *Risk Analysis* 33 (7): 1281–92.

Levy, Gideon, and Alex Levac. 2014. "The Most Surreal Place in the Occupied Territories." *Haaretz,* March 30. https://www.haaretz.com/israel-news/.premium-1.582447.

Lewi, Hannah. 2008. "Spectacular Heritage: 'Total Restoration' at the Site of Carcassonne." *Architectural Theory Review* 13 (2): 145–63.

Linnell, John, et al. 2016. "Border Security Fencing and Wildlife: The End of the Transboundary Paradigm in Eurasia?" *PLOS Biology* 14 (6): 1–13.

Lipton, Eric. 2013. "As Wars End, a Rush to Grab Dollars Spent on the Border." *New York Times,* June 7, A1.

Little, Adrian. 2015. "The Complex Temporality of Borders: Contingency and Normativity." *European Journal of Political Theory* 14 (4): 429–47.

Lockman, Zachary, and Joel Beinin, eds. 1989. *Intifada: The Palestinian Uprising against Israeli Occupation.* Boston: South End Press.

Lovell, Julia. 2006. *The Great Wall: China against the World, 1000 BC–2000 AD.* New York: Grove.

Low, Setha. 2003. *Behind the Gates: Life, Security, and the Pursuit of Happiness in Fortress America*. New York: Routledge.

———. 2004. *Behind the Gates: Security and the New American Dream*. New York: Routledge.

Loyd, Jenna, Matt Mitchelson, and Andrew Burridge, eds. 2012. *Beyond Walls and Cages: Prison, Borders, and Global Crisis*. Athens: University of Georgia Press.

Luce, Kristen. 2016. "10 Shots across the Border." *New York Times Magazine*, March 6.

Lynch, K. 1960. *The Image of the City*. Cambridge, MA: MIT Press.

Macdonald, Sharon. 2009. *Difficult Heritage: Negotiating the Nazi Past in Nuremberg and Beyond*. New York: Routledge.

Malm, Lena, and Sarah Green. 2013. *Borderwork: A Visual Journey through Periphery Frontier Regions*. Riga, Latvia: Jasilti.

Manghani, Sunil. 2008. *Image Critique and the Fall of the Berlin Wall*. Bristol, United Kingdom: Intellect.

MapFugees Project. 2016. "Connected Refugees." April 29. https://mapfugees.wordpress.com.

Marcuse, Paul. 1994. "Walls as Metaphors and Reality." In *Managing Divided Cities*, edited by Seamus Dunn, 41–52. Keele, United Kingdom: Keele University Press.

Mark, Joshua J. 2009. "Wall." *Ancient History Encyclopedia*. September 2. http://www.ancient.eu/wall.

Massey, D. S., and N. A. Denton. 1993. *American Apartheid: Segregation and the Making of the Underclass*. Cambridge, MA: Harvard University Press.

Mbembe, Achille. 2003. "Necropolitics." *Public Culture* 15 (1): 11–40.

McAtackney, Laura. 2011. "Peace Maintenance and Political Messages: The Significance of Walls during and after the Northern Irish 'Troubles.'" *Journal of Social Archaeology* 11 (1): 77–98.

———. 2015. "Memorials and Marching: Archaeological Insights into Segregation in Contemporary Northern Ireland." *Historical Archaeology* 49 (3): 110–25.

———. 2017. "Repercussions of Differential Deindustrializaiton in the City: Memory and Identity in Contemporary East Belfast." In *Contemporary Archaeology and the City: Creativity, Ruination, and Political Action*, edited by Laura McAtackney and Krysta Ryzewski, 190–210. Oxford: Oxford University Press.

———. 2018. "Where Are All the Women? Public Memory, Gender, and Memorialisation in Contemporary Belfast." In *Heritage after Conflict: Northern Ireland*, edited by Elizabeth Crooke and Thomas Maguire, 154–73. London: Routledge.

McCormack, J. 2016. "Easter Rising 1916: How Winifred Carney Became James Connolly's Confidante." BBC, March 27. http://www.bbc.com/news/uk-northern-ireland-35849250.

McDonald, Henry. 2017. "Two Men Arrested over Alleged UVF Threats to Catholic Families." *Guardian*, October 9. https://www.theguardian.com/uk-news/2017/oct/09/two-men-arrested-alleged-uvf-threats-catholic-families-northern-ireland.

McDonough, Terrence, Michael Reich, and David M. Kotz, eds. 2010. *Contemporary Capitalism and Its Crises: Social Structure of Accumulation Theory for the 21st Century*. Cambridge: Cambridge University Press.

McDowell, Sara. 2008. "Selling Conflict Heritage through Tourism in Peace-time Northern Ireland: Transforming Conflict or Exacerbating Difference?" *International Journal of Heritage Studies* 14 (5): 405–21.

McGrattan, Cillian. 2009. "'Order out of Chaos': The Politics of Transitional Justice." *Politics* 29 (3): 164–72.

McGuire, Randall H. 2013. "Steel Walls and Picket Fences: Rematerializing the U.S.-Mexican Border in Ambos Nogales." *American Anthropologist* 115 (3): 466–80.

McGuire, Randall H., and Ruth M. Van Dyke. 2017. "Why the 'Big, Beautiful Wall' Is Doomed to Fail." *Sapiens*, March 7. http://www.sapiens.org/culture/big-beautiful-wall-trump.

McMichael, Philip. 2006. "Peasant Prospects in the Neoliberal Age." *New Political Economy* 11 (3): 407–18.

McQuillan, Dan. 2015. "Algorithmic States of Exception." *European Journal of Cultural Studies* 18: 564–76.

McWilliams, Anna. 2013. *An Archeology of the Iron Curtain: Material and Metaphor*. Stockholm, Sweden: Stockholm University Press.

Meari, Lena. 2014. "Sumud: A Palestinian Philosophy of Confrontation in Colonial Prisons." *South Atlantic Quarterly* 113 (3): 547–78.

Mercer, David. 2014. "Hate Crime against Gay People Is on the Rise in Northern Ireland." *Belfast Telegraph*, November 26. http://www.belfasttelegraph.co.uk/news/local-national/northern-ireland/hate-crime-against-gay-people-is-on-the-rise-in-northern-ireland-30774921.html.

Mieder, Wolfgang. 2003. "'Good Fences Make Good Neighbours': History and Significance of an Ambiguous Proverb." *Folklore* 114 (2): 155–79.

Miller, Todd. 2013. "War on the Border." *New York Times*, August 18, SR1.

———. 2014. *Border Patrol Nation: Dispatches from the Front Lines of Border Security*. San Francisco, CA: City Lights.

Mintz, S. W. 1974. *Caribbean Transformations*. Baltimore, MD: Johns Hopkins University Press.

Mohn, Tanya. 2012. "America's Most Exclusive Gated Communities." *Forbes*, July 3. http://www.forbes.com/sites/tanyamohn/2012/07/03/americas-most-exclusive-gated-communities/#53040bad183f.

Monaghan, Rachel, and Peter Shirlow. 2011. "Forward to the Past? Loyalist Paramilitarism in Northern Ireland since 1994." *Studies in Conflict and Terrorism* 33 (8): 649–65.

Morrison, C. 2016. "A Belfast Family Took Part in the Rising and the Somme." BBC, March 22. http://www.bbc.com/news/uk-northern-ireland-35862231.

Mulholland, Marc. 2002. *The Longest War: Northern Ireland's Troubles History*. Oxford: Oxford Paperbooks.

Multimedia Heritage. n.d. *Voices from the North: Gallaher's*. http://www.multimedia heritage.com/projects/gallahers/Gallahersbook.pdf.

Murphy, Andrée. 2015. "Why Is the Debate on Dealing with the Past in Northern Ireland Gender Blind?" EamonnMallie.com, May 13. http://eamonnmallie.com/2015/05/why-is-the-debate-on-dealing-with-the-past-in-northern-gender-blind-by-andree-murphy.

Murphy, Eileen, and Mark Maguire. 2015. "Time and Security: Anthropological Perspectives on Automated Border Control." *Etnofoor* 27 (2): 157–77.

Myrivili, Eleni. 2003. "The Liquid Border: Subjectivity at the Limits of the Nation-State in Southeast Europe." PhD diss., Columbia University.

Nails, Thomas. 2015. *The Figure of the Migrant*. Palo Alto, CA: Stanford University Press.

Napolitano, Janet. 2016. Interview on BBC News, *Hardtalk*, February 25.

Navaro-Yashin, Yael. 2009. "Affective Spaces, Melancholic Objects: Ruination and the Production of Anthropological Knowledge." *Journal of the Royal Anthropological Institute* 15 (1): 1–18.

Nelson, Michael. 2011. "Gated Communities: Class Walls." *History Today* 61 (11). http://www.historytoday.com/michael-nelson/gated-communities-class-walls.

Nevins, Joseph. 2010. *Operation Gatekeeper and Beyond: The War on "Illegals" and the Remaking of the US-Mexico Boundary*. New York: Routledge.

Nieto-Gomez, Rodrigo. 2014. "Walls, Sensors and Drones: Technology and Surveillance on the US-Mexico Border." In *Borders, Fences, and Walls: State of Insecurity?*, edited by E. Vallet, 191–21. Farnham, England: Ashgate.

Nokandeh, Jebrael, et al. 2006. "Linear Barriers of Northern Iran: The Great Wall of Gorgan and the Wall of Tammishe." *Iran* 44: 121–73.

Nora, Pierre. 1989. "Between Memory and History: Les lieux de memoire." *Representations* 26 (Spring): 7–24.

Norman, Julie. 2010. *The Second Palestinian Intifada: Civil Resistance.* New York: Routledge.

OCHA [United Nations Office for the Coordination of Humanitarian Affairs]. 2013. *The Humanitarian Impact of the Barrier.* Jerusalem: OCHA.

Ochs, Juliana. 2011. *Security and Suspicion: An Ethnography of Everyday Life in Israel.* Philadelphia: University of Pennsylvania Press.

Ó Drisceoil, Cóilín, et al. 2014. *The Black Pig's Dyke Regional Project 2014.* Kilkenny, Ireland: Kilkenny Archaeology.

O'Toole, Fintan. 2018. "The Brexit Vision That Reveals England's Perfidy over Ireland." *Guardian*, February 25. https://www.theguardian.com/politics/2018/feb/25/brexit-vision-england-perfidy-over-ireland-good-friday-agreemnt.

Paasi, Anssi. 2012. "Border Studies Reanimated: Going beyond the Territorial-Relational Divide." *Environment and Planning A* 44: 2303–9.

Pack, Quinn R., et al. 2013. "Participation in Cardiac Rehabilitation and Survival after Coronary Artery Bypass Graft Surgery." *Circulation* 128: 590–97.

Pallister-Wilkins, Polly. 2016. "How Walls Do Work: Security Barriers as Devices of Interruption and Data Capture." *Security Dialogue.* doi:10.1177/0967010615615729.

Papadopoulos, Dimitris C. 2010. "Shaping a Lake: Landscape Experience and Mediation in Prespa Park, Greece." PhD diss., Department of Cultural Technology and Communication, University of the Aegean.

———. 2016. "Ecologies of Ruin: (Re)bordering, Ruination, and Internal Colonialism in Greek Macedonia, 1913–2013." *International Journal of Historical Archaeology* 20 (3): 627–40.

Pappé, Ilan. 2017. *The Biggest Prison on Earth: A History of the Occupied Territories.* London: Oneworld.

Parker, Geoffrey. 2000. "The Artillery Fortress as an Engine of European Overseas Expansion, 1480–1750." In *City Walls: The Urban Enceinte in Global Perspective,* edited by J. D. Tracy, 386–416. Cambridge: Cambridge University Press.

Parr, Adrian. 2012. *The Wrath of Capital: Neoliberalism and Climate Change Politics.* New York: Columbia University Press.

Parr, Connal, and Edward Burke. 2017. "Brexit: What Are the Issues Surrounding Northern Ireland's Border and Could It Scupper UK's EU Withdrawal?" *Independent*, December 5. http://www.independent.co.uk/news/uk/politics/

brexit-latest-northern-ireland-border-republic-dup-arlene-foster-theresa-may-david-davis-eu-a8093171.html.

Parry, Nigel. 2003. "Is It a Fence? Is It a Wall? No, It's a Separation Barrier." *Electronic Intifada*, August 1. https://electronicintifada.net/content/it-fence-it-wall-no-its-separation-barrier/4715.

Pastor, Robert A. 2011. *The North American Idea*. New York: Oxford University Press.

Pastor, Robert A., and Jorge G. Castañeda. 1988. *Limits to Friendship: The United States and Mexico*. New York: Knopf.

Paterson, Tony. 2008. "Berlin's Checkpoint Charlie Becomes Tourist Trap." *Telegraph*, August 16. http://www.telegraph.co.uk/news/worldnews/europe/germany/2570286/Berlins-Checkpoint-Charlie-becomes-tourist-trap.html.

———. 2012. "Checkpoint Charlie Divides Berlin." *Independent*, May 20. http://www.independent.co.uk/news/world/europe/checkpoint-charlie-divides-berlin-7768843.html.

Pearce, Fred. 1999. "The African Queen." *New Scientist* 163 (2203): 38–43.

Peirce, Charles. 1985. "Logic as Semiotic: The Theory of Signs." In *Semiotics: An Introductory Anthology*, edited by Robert E. Innis, 1–23. Bloomington: Indiana University Press.

Penrose, Sefryn. 2017. "Creative Destruction and Neoliberal Landscapes: Post-Industrial Archaeologies beyond Ruins." In *Contemporary Archaeology and the City: Creativity, Ruination, and Political Action*, edited by Laura McAtackney and Krysta Ryzewski, 171–89. Oxford: Oxford University Press.

Pepper, Simon. 2000. "Ottoman Military Architecture in the Early Gunpowder Era: A Reassessment." In *City Walls: The Urban Enceinte in Global Perspective*, edited by J. D. Tracy, 282–316. Cambridge: Cambridge University Press.

Peteet, Julie. 1991. *Gender in Crisis: Women and the Palestinian Resistance Movement*. New York: Columbia University Press.

———. 2015. "Camps and Enclaves: Palestine in the Time of Closure." *Journal of Refugee Studies* 28 (3): 1–21.

———. 2017. *Space and Mobility in Palestine*. Bloomington: Indiana University Press.

Pollack, Martha. 2010. *Cities at War in Early Modern Europe*. Cambridge: Cambridge University Press.

Popescu, Gabriel. 2011. *Bordering and Ordering the Twenty-First Century: Understanding Borders*. Lanham, MD: Rowman and Littlefield.

Poppe, Ulrika. 2005. "Life in the Shadow of the Wall." In *On Both Sides of the Wall: Preserving Monuments and Sites of the Cold War Era*, edited by L. Schmidt and H. von Preuschen. Cottbus, Germany: Westkreuz.

Potzsch, H. 2015. "The Emergence of iBorder: Bordering Bodies, Networks, and Machines." *Environment and Planning D: Society and Space* 33 (1): 101–18.

Reeves, Madeleine. 2014. *Border Work: Spatial Lives of the State in Rural Central Asia.* Ithaca, NY: Cornell University Press.

———. 2016. "Time and Contingency in the Anthropology of Borders: On Border as Event in Rural Central Asia." In *Eurasian Borderlands: Spatializing Borders in the Aftermath of State Collapse,* edited by Tone Bringa and Hege Toje, 159–83. New York: Palgrave Macmillan.

Reid, Bryonie. 2005. "'A Profound Edge': Performative Negotiations of Belfast." *Cultural Geographies* 12 (4): 485–506.

Reséndez, Andrés. 2005. *Changing National Identities at the Frontier: Texas and New Mexico, 1800–1850.* Cambridge: Cambridge University Press.

———. 2016. *The Other Slavery: The Uncovered Story of Indian Enslavement in America.* Boston: Houghton Mifflin Harcourt.

Reyerson, Kathryn L. 2000. "Medieval Walled Space: Urban Development vs. Defense." In *City Walls: The Urban Enceinte in Global Perspective,* edited by J. D. Tracy, 88–116. Cambridge: Cambridge University Press.

Rice-Oxley, Mark. 2013. "Why Are We Building New Walls to Divide Us?" *Guardian,* November 19.

Riley, K. Jack. 2014. "Strategic Planning for Border Security." Testimony before the Committee on Science, Space, and Technology, Subcommittee on Research and Technology, Subcommittee on Oversight, US House of Representatives, July 31.

Rivera-Rideau, P. R. 2013. "From Carolina to Loíza: Race, Place and Puerto Rican Racial Democracy." *Identities* 20 (5): 616–32.

Robinson, Julian. 2015. "Peru's Ten-Foot-High Wall of Shame Topped with Razor Wire Which Divides the Rich and Poor to Stop the Less Well-Off Stealing from the Wealthy." *Daily Mail,* December 22. http://www.dailymail.co.uk/news/article-3370316/Peru-s-ten-foot-high-Wall-Shame-topped-razor-wire-divides-rich-poor-stop-stealing-wealthy.html#ixzz53uGBHF00.

Rodell, Magnus. 2007. "Från gotländska bunkrar till bosniska broar." In *Minnesmärken: Att tolka det förflutna och besvärja framtiden,* edited by J. Frykman and B. Ehn. Stockholm, Sweden: Carlsson.

Rodríguez Cruz, J. 1965. "Las relaciones raciales en Puerto Rico." *Revista de Ciencias Sociales* 9 (4): 373–86.

Roediger, D. R. 1999. *The Wages of Whiteness: Race and the Making of the American Working Class.* London: Verso.

———. 2006. *Working toward Whiteness: How America's Immigrants Became White: The Strange Journey from Ellis Island to the Suburbs.* New York: Basic.

Rojas, Carlos. 2010. *The Great Wall: A Cultural History.* Cambridge, MA: Harvard University Press.

Romig, K. 2005. "The Upper Sonoran Lifestyle: Gated Communities in Scottsdale, Arizona." *City and Community* 4 (1): 67–86.

Rosas, Gilberto. 2006a. "The Managed Violences of the Borderlands: Treacherous Geographies, Policeability, and the Politics of Race." *Latino Studies* 4 (4): 401–18.

———. 2006b. "The Thickening Borderlands: Diffused Exceptionality and 'Immigrant' Social Struggles during the 'War on Terror.'" *Cultural Dynamics* 18 (3): 335–49.

———. 2012. *Barrio Libre: Criminalizing States and Delinquent Refusals of the New Frontier.* Durham, NC: Duke University Press.

Rosenblum, Marc, and Faye Hipsman. 2016. *Border Metrics: How to Effectively Measure Border Security and Immigration Control.* Washington, DC: Migration Policy Institute. http://www.migrationpolicy.org/research/border-metrics-how-effectively-measure-border-security-and-immigration-control.

Rosière, Stéphane, and Reece Jones. 2011. "Teichopolitics: Re-considering Globalisation through the Role of Walls and Fences." *Geopolitics* 17: 217–34.

Rottman, Gordon. 2008. *The Berlin Wall and the Intra-German Border, 1961–89.* Oxford, England: Osprey.

Sack, Robert. 1986. *Human Territoriality: Its Theory and Practice.* Cambridge: Cambridge University Press.

Saddiki, Said. 2017. *World of Walls: The Structure, Roles, and Effectiveness of Separation Barriers.* Cambridge: Open Book.

Sahlins, Peter. 1989. *Boundaries: The Making of France and Spain in the Pyrenees.* Berkeley: University of California Press.

Sassen, Saskia. 2005. "When National Territory Is Home to the Global: Old Borders to Novel Borderings." *New Political Economy* 10 (4): 523–41.

———. 2006. "Migration Policy: From Control to Governance." openDemocracy. https://www.opendemocracy.net/en/militarising_borders_3735jsp.

Sawyer, Ralph D. 2011. *Ancient Chinese Warfare.* New York: Basic.

Schmidt, Leo. 2005. "The Berlin Wall: A Landscape of Memory." In *On Both Sides of the Wall: Preserving Monuments and Sites of the Cold War Era*, edited by L. Schmidt and H. von Preuschen. Cottbus, Germany: Westkreuz.

Sears, D. O. 1988. "Symbolic Racism." In *Eliminating Racism*, edited by Phyllis Katz and Dalmas Taylor, 53–84. Boston: Springer.

Seghetti, Lisa. 2014. *Border Security: Immigration Enforcement between Ports of Entry.* Washington, DC: Congressional Research Service. http://trac.syr.edu/ immigration/library/P10204.pdf.

Shalhoub-Kevorkian, Nadera. 2008. "Counter-Spaces as Resistance in Conflict Zones: Palestinian Women Recreating a Home." *Journal of Feminist Family Therapy* 17 (3–4): 109–41.

Shanks, Michael. 2013. "Let Me Tell You about Hadrian's Wall: Heritage Performance Design." Reinwardt Memorial Lecture, Reinwardt Academy, Amsterdam.

Sharoni, Simona. 1995. *Gender and the Israeli-Palestinian Conflict: The Politics of Women's Resistance.* Syracuse, NY: Syracuse University Press.

Shi, Jiuyong. 2004. "Legal Consequences of the Construction of a Wall in the Occupied Palestinian Territory." International Court of Justice. https://www.icj-cij.org/ en/case/131.

Siefert, Michael. 2016. "The Texas Border Surge Is Backfiring." Davis Vanguard, March 23. https://www.davisvanguard.org/2016/03/texas-border-surge-backfiring.

Singleton, Courtney. 2017. "Encountering Home: A Contemporary Archaeology of Homelessness." In *Contemporary Archaeology and the City: Creativity, Ruination, and Political Action*, edited by Laura McAtackney and Krysta Ryzewski, 229–44. Oxford: Oxford University Press.

Singleton, Theresa A. 2015. *Slavery behind the Wall.* Gainesville: University Press of Florida.

Sky News. 2016. "Days of Illegal Migration to EU Over, Says Tusk." March 8. https:// news.sky.com/story/days-of-illegal-migration-to-eu-over-says-tusk-10196547.

Smith, Laurajane. 2006. *Uses of Heritage.* New York: Routledge.

Soniak, Matt. 2016. "Trump's Wall? Also Terrible for Animals, Conservation, and Scientific Collaboration." *Slate*, July 20. https://slate.com/technology/2016/07/ trumps-wall-would-hurt-wildlife-and-halt-science-at-the-border.html.

Sorrensen, Cynthia. 2014. "Making the Subterranean Visible: Security, Tunnels, and the United States–Mexico Border." *Geographical Review* 104: 328–45.

Spijkerboer, Thomas. 2007. "The Human Costs of Border Control." *European Journal of Migration and Law* 9: 127–39.

Spring, Peter. 2015. *Great Walls and Linear Barriers.* Barnsley, England: Pen and Sword.

Stefatos, Katerina, Dimitris C. Papadopoulos, and Chloe Haralambous. 2015. "Notes from the Border: Refugee Lives and Necropolitics in the Aegean,

August–November 2015." *Journal of Modern Greek Studies*, Occasional Paper 8 (November).

Steger, M. B., and R. K. Roy. 2010. *Neoliberalism: A Very Short Introduction*. Oxford: Oxford University Press.

Stein, Mary Beth. 1989. "The Politics of Humor: The Berlin Wall in Jokes and Graffiti." *Western Folklore* 48 (2): 85–108.

Steinhardt, Nancy Shatzmann. 2000. "Representations of Chinese Walled Cities in the Pictorial and Graphic Arts." In *City Walls: The Urban Enceinte in Global Perspective*, edited by J. D. Tracy, 419–60. Cambridge: Cambridge University Press.

Stephenson, Max, and Laura Zanotti, eds. 2013. *Building Walls and Dissolving Borders*. Aldershot, England: Ashgate.

Sterling, Brent. 2009. *Do Good Fences Make Good Neighbors? What History Teaches Us about Strategic Barriers and International Security*. Washington, DC: Georgetown University Press.

Suttles, G. 1972. *The Social Construction of Communities*. Chicago: University of Chicago Press.

Swedenburg, Ted. 1995. *Memories of Revolt: The 1936–1939 Rebellion and the Palestinian National Past*. Minneapolis: University of Minnesota Press.

Tannenbaum, F. 1947. *Slave and Citizen: The Negro in the Americas*. New York: Knopf.

Tate, Winifred. 2015. *Drugs, Thugs, and Diplomats: U.S. Policymaking in Colombia*. Stanford, CA: Stanford University Press.

Taylor, Kevin J. 2016. "The New Apartheid." *Hello Poetry*. https://hellopoetry.com/poem/1681792/the-new-apartheid.

Taylor, R. B. 1988. *Human Territorial Functioning: An Empirical, Evolutionary Perspective on Human and Small Group Territorial Cognitions, Behaviors and Consequences*. Cambridge: Cambridge University Press.

Telles, E. 2014. *Pigmentocracies: Ethnicity, Race, and Color in Latin America*. Chapel Hill: University of North Carolina Press.

Texas Department of Public Safety. n.d. "Specialized Units." https://www.dps.texas.gov/TexasRangers/specialUnits.htm, accessed December 16, 2016.

Tilly, Charles. 2006. *Regimes and Repertoires*. Chicago: University of Chicago Press.

Tomlinson, Simon. 2015. "World of Walls: How 65 Countries Have Erected Fences on Their Borders—Four Times as Many as when the Berlin Wall Was Toppled—as Governments Try to Hold Back the Tide of Migrants." *Mail Online*, August 21. http://www.dailymail.co.uk/news/article-3205724/How-65-countries-erected-security-walls-borders.html.

Tracy, James D., ed. 2000a. *City Walls: The Urban Enceinte in Global Perspective*. Cambridge: Cambridge University Press.

——. 2000b. "To Wall or Not to Wall: Evidence from Medieval Germany." In *City Walls: The Urban Enceinte in Global Perspective*, edited by J. D. Tracy, 71–87. Cambridge: Cambridge University Press.

Tsangadas, Bryon C. P. 1980. *The Fortifications and Defense of Constantinople*. New York: Columbia University Press.

Turner, Jennifer. 2016. *The Prison Boundary: Between Society and Carceral Space*. London: Palgrave Macmillan.

TVXS. 2012. "Parousia tou Papoutsi xekinise h kataskevi tou frachti ston Evro" [Papoutsis, the minister of citizen protection, visits the area as construction work for the border fence on the Evros River starts]. February 6. https://tvxs.gr/news/ellada/paroysia-toy-papoytsi-ksekinise-i-kataskeyi-toy-fraxti-ston-ebro.

UNHCR [United Nations High Commissioner for Refugees]. 2017. "Border Fences and Internal Border Controls in Europe." https://data2.unhcr.org/en/documents/details/55249.

——. 2018. "Refugee Situations: Mediterranean Situation." https://data.unhcr.org/mediterranean.

UNRWA [United Nations Relief and Works Agency]. n.d. "Aida Camp." https://www.unrwa.org/where-we-work/west-bank/aida-camp, accessed February 28, 2017.

US Court of Appeals for the Ninth Circuit. 2016. *Araceli Rodriguez v. Lonnie Swartz*. "Brief for Scholars of U.S.-Mexico Border Issues as Amici Curiae in Support of Plaintiff-Appellee Araceli Rodriguez and Affirmance," no. 15-16410.

US Customs and Border Protection. 2016. "CBP Field Operations Assistant Commissioner and Border Patrol Chief Testify on Plans for Border Security, Highlight Progress to Date." https://www.cbp.gov/about/congressional-resources/testimony/border-security-progress, accessed March 8, 2016.

US Department of Justice. 2014. *Guidance for Federal Law Enforcement Agencies regarding the Use of Race, Ethnicity, Gender, National Origin, Religion, Sexual Orientation, or Gender Identity*. Washington, DC: Department of Homeland Security. https://www.dhs.gov/publication/guidance-federal-law-enforcement-agencies-regarding-use-race-ethnicity-gender-national.

US Government Accountability Office. 2011. *Border Security: DHS Progress and Challenges in Securing the U.S. Southwest and Northern Borders*. Washington, DC: Government Accountability Office.

US National Park Service. 2008. *Effects of the International Boundary Pedestrian Fence in the Vicinity of Lukeville, Arizona, on Drainage Systems and Infrastructure,*

Organ Pipe Cactus National Monument, Arizona. Washington, DC: National Park Service.

Valle, M. M. 2017. "The Discursive Detachment of Race from Gentrification in Cartagena de Indias, Colombia." *Ethnic and Racial Studies* 41 (7): 1–20.

Vallet, Elisabeth, ed. 2014. *Borders, Fences, and Walls: State of Insecurity?* Farnham, England: Ashgate.

———. 2019. "Border Walls and the Illusion of Deterrence." In *Open Borders: In Defense of Free Movement*, edited by Reece Jones, 156–68. Athens: University of Georgia Press.

Van Houtum, Henk, and Ton van Naerssen. 2002. *Bordering, Ordering and Othering.* Amsterdam: Royal Dutch Geographic Society.

Vaughan-Williams, Nick. 2006. "Towards a Problematisation of the Problematisations That Reduce Northern Ireland to a 'Problem.'" *Critical Review of International Social and Political Philosophy* 9 (4): 513–26.

Venkatesh, S. A. 2000. *American Project.* Cambridge, MA: Harvard University Press.

Viggiani, Elizabeth. 2006. "Public Forms of Memorialisation to the 'Victims of the Northern Irish Troubles' in the City of Belfast." MA thesis, Queen's University of Belfast.

Virilio, Paul. 1997. "The Overexposed City." In *Rethinking Architecture: A Reader in Cultural Theory*, edited by Neil Leach, 381–89. London: Routledge.

Visiongain. 2013. *Global Border Security Market, 2013–2023: UAVs, UGVs, and Perimeter Surveillance Systems.* London: Visiongain.

Vithoulkas, Dionysis. 2013. "Policeman and Two Albanians Dead in Armed Confrontation" [in Greek]. *To Vima*, August 8. http://www.tovima.gr/society/article/?aid=546771.

Vogt, Wendy. 2013. "Crossing Mexico: Structural Violence and the Commodification of Undocumented Central American Migrants." *American Ethnologist* 40 (4): 764–80.

Wacquant, Loïc. 2001. "Deadly Symbiosis: When Ghetto and Prison Meet and Mesh." *Punishment and Society* 3 (1): 96–134.

Wagley, C. 1968. "On the Concept of Social Race in the Americas." In Wagley, *The Latin American Tradition.* New York: Columbia University Press.

Wainwright, Richard. 2010. "Borders and Barriers: The Belfast Peace Lines." Richard Wainwright Photography, October 14. http://www.richwainwright.com/blog/foreign-assignments/borders-and-barriers-the-belfast-peace-lines.

Waldron, Arthur. 1990. *The Great Wall of China: From History to Myth.* Cambridge: Cambridge University Press.

Walia, Harsha. 2013. *Undoing Border Imperialism*. Oakland, CA: AK Press.

Washington Post. 2015. "Full Text: Donald Trump Announces Presidential Bid." June 16.

Weber, David J. 1992. *The Spanish Frontier in North America*. New Haven, CT: Yale University Press.

Weber, Leanne, and Sharon Pickering. 2011. *Globalization and Borders: Death at the Global Frontier*. Lanham, MD: Palgrave Macmillan.

Weizman, Eyal. 2007. *Hollow Land: Israel's Architecture of Occupation*. New York: Verso.

West-Pavlov, Russell. 2011. "Haunted Europe: Virilio and Sangatte." In *Hexagonal Variations: Diversity, Plurality, and Reinvention in Contemporary France*, edited by Jo McCormack, Murray Pratt, and Alistair Rolls, 321–36. Amsterdam: Rodopi.

Whyte, James. 1990. *Interpreting Northern Ireland*. Oxford: Clarendon.

Williams Castro, F. 2013. "Afro-Colombians and the Cosmopolitan City: New Negotiations of Race and Space in Bogotá, Colombia." *Latin American Perspectives* 40 (2): 105–17.

Williams, Eric. 1945. "Race Relations in Puerto Rico and the Virgin Islands." *Foreign Affairs* (January).

———. 1970. *From Columbus to Castro*. New York: Vintage.

Willis, Henry H., et al. 2010. *Measuring the Effectiveness of Border Security between Ports-of-Entry*. Santa Monica, CA: RAND Corporation.

Wilson, Steve Harmon. 2002. *The Rise of Judicial Management in the U.S. District Court, Southern District, Texas, 1955–2000*. Athens: University of Georgia Press.

Wilson, W. J. 1987. *The Truly Disadvantaged: The Inner City, the Underclass and Public Policy*. Chicago: University of Chicago Press.

Wilson-Doenges, G. 2000. "An Exploration of Sense of Community and Fear of Crime in Gated Communities." *Environment and Behavior* 32 (5): 597–611.

Winichakul, Thongchai. 1994. *Siam Mapped: A History of the Geo-Body of a Nation*. Honolulu: University of Hawai'i Press.

Wolfe, Michael. 2009. *Walled Towns and the Shaping of France: From Medieval to the Early Modern Era*. New York: Palgrave Macmillan.

Wolfe, Patrick. 2006. "Settler Colonialism and the Elimination of the Native." *Journal of Genocide Research* 8 (4): 387–409.

Young, Iris M. 1990. *Justice and the Politics of Difference*. Princeton, NJ: Princeton University Press.

Participants in the School for Advanced Research Advanced Seminar "A World of Walls: Why Are We Building New Barriers to Divide Us?" cochaired by Randall H. McGuire and Laura McAtackney, April 17–21, 2016. *Left to right*: Dimitris C. Papadopoulos, Amahl Bishara, Zaire Dinzey-Flores, Randall H. McGuire, Anna McWilliams, Laura McAtackney, Reece Jones, Michael Dear, Miguel Díaz-Barriga, and Margaret E. Dorsey. Photograph by Garret Vreeland. © School for Advanced Research.

AMAHL BISHARA
Department of Anthropology, Tufts University

MICHAEL DEAR
College of Environmental Design, University of California, Berkeley

MIGUEL DÍAZ-BARRIGA
Department of Sociology and Anthropology, University of Richmond

ZAIRE DINZEY-FLORES
Department of Latino and Caribbean Studies, Rutgers University

MARGARET E. DORSEY
Department of Sociology and Anthropology, University of Richmond

REECE JONES
Department of Geography and Environment, University of Hawai'i, Manoa

LAURA MCATACKNEY
Department of Archaeology and Heritage Studies, Aarhus University

RANDALL H. MCGUIRE
Department of Anthropology, Binghamton University

ANNA MCWILLIAMS
School of Historical and Contemporary Studies, Södertörn University

DIMITRIS C. PAPADOPOULOS
Institute for Intercultural and Anthropological Studies,
Western Michigan University

Page numbers in *italic* text
indicate illustrations.

Univision News, 170
Ur, 27, 29
urban planning, 50, 66, 71, 75
US Border Patrol (USBP), 22, 159, 161, 163,
    164, 165–67, 171, 172, 174, 180, 184, 188,
    189–92, 205, 206, 207
US-Canada Border, 165–66
US Census, 55–56, 60n1
US Civil War, 159
US Coast Guard, 161
US Court of Appeals, 175–76
US Department of Homeland Security,
    5, 155, 161–63, 164, 165, 167, 172, 181–83,
    185–86, 187–89, 193nn5–6, 193n8, 206
US Forest Service, 165
US House of Representatives, 162,
    163–64, 170
US Immigration and Customs Enforce-
    ment (ICE), 161, 162, 164, 166, 172, 174,
    186–87
US-México Border, 2, 5, 8, 9, 16, 17,
    18, 19, 22, 27, 94, 155–76, 179–94,
    196, 205–6, 207, 214; apprehensions,
    164–65; Border-Industrial Complex,
    165–67, 174–75, 207–8, 214–15; Border
    Industrialization Program, 160; border
    lands, 152, 155–56, 168–76; boundary
    monuments, *158, 163*, 202; checkpoints,
    180–83, 188, 190, 192, 193n2, 194n11;
    Constitution Free Zone, 180, 192;
    deaths on, 160, 166, 175–76, 190, 205–6,
    207; deportations, 164, 166–67; deten-
    tion centers, 166–67, 174; enforcement
    with consequences, 161; environment,
    105, 172, 205, 208; future, 11, 22, 169,
    172, 174, 211; history, 157–61; Operation
    Gate Keeper, 161, 205; Operation Hold
    the Line, 205; prevention through
    deterrence, 162, 164; Secure Border
    Initiative, 161, 162–65, 174; Secure
    Communities Program, 166–67; third
    nation, 168–76; tunnels under, 119, 207;
    walls and fences, 159–60, *161, 163, 163*,

170, 171, 175–76, 179–80, 181, 188–92,
    205–6, 207–8. *See also* México
US National Guard, 165
US Senate, 167
Utah, 155
Uzbekistan, 8

Vallet, Elisabeth, 197
Venice, Italy, 32
Vermont, 165
victims, 14, 68, 76, 80, 83, 139, 175
Victoria Guadalupe, 157
Vietnam War, 27, 160, 179
Villa, Poncho, 159
violence, 51, 53, 59, 67, 68, 70, 74, 76, 83,
    85, 86, 88, 90, 94–96, 97, 103, 106, 134,
    143, 148, 150; gendered, 105
Viollet-le-Duc, Eugéne, 39
Visigoths, 25
voids (also inertias, death strips and
    buffer zones), 1, 4, 27, 66, 113, 118, 124,
    125, 131, 137, 147–48

walls: city, 27–31, 37–39, 50; aesthetics, 52,
    58, 113, 117, 119, 192; change, 6, 12, 13, 16,
    26, 36, 38, 42, 51, 66, 73, 75, 96, 97, 103,
    118, 124, 129, 151–52, 203, 208, 212, 214,
    216, 217, 220; control, 52, 58; definition,
    3–5; defense, 47, 131; domestic, 47,
    60, 96, 101; division, 63, 66, 106, 112,
    114, 116, 128–29, 131, 134, 135, 145, 148;
    efficacy, 2, 5, 15–16, 22, 23, 24, 26–28,
    30, 31, 35, 36, 42, 162–63, 172, 190–91,
    198, 203, 204–9, 212, 214, 218; fall down,
    27, 37–42, 43, 107, 113, 117–19, 127, 129,
    172, 204, 207, 214, 217, 219, 220; global
    phenomena, 1–26, 27–43, 195–209,
    211–20; as heritage, 2, 21, 26, 38–40,
    76–77, 126, 127, 216; inconvenience of,
    17, 26, 28, 37, 38, 41, 42, 43, 206–7; local,
    2, 8, 19, 25, 27–34, 212–13; long, 27,
    34–37, 40, 42; maintenance, 3, 4, 22, 23,
    27, 127, 146, 148, 153; militarized,